HELPING PROFESSIONS WITH INDIGENOUS PEOPLES

The Bedouin-Arab Case

Alean Al-Krenawi
John R. Graham

University Press of America,® Inc.
Lanham · Boulder · New York · Toronto · Plymouth, UK

Copyright © 2009 by
University Press of America,® Inc.
4501 Forbes Boulevard
Suite 200
Lanham, Maryland 20706
UPA Acquisitions Department (301) 459-3366

Estover Road
Plymouth PL6 7PY
United Kingdom

All rights reserved
Printed in the United States of America
British Library Cataloging in Publication Information Available

Library of Congress Control Number: 2008936609
ISBN-13: 978-0-7618-4407-5 (paperback : alk. paper)
ISBN-10: 0-7618-4407-4 (paperback : alk. paper)
eISBN-13: 978-0-7618-4408-2
eISBN-10: 0-7618-4408-2

∞™ The paper used in this publication meets the minimum
requirements of American National Standard for Information
Sciences—Permanence of Paper for Printed Library Materials,
ANSI Z39.48—1984

DEDICATION

*The book is lovingly dedicated to our families:
To Monawar, Liali and Muhammad Al-Krenawi; to Susan Graham and
Tasha; and to the memory of Nick Morgan and of Theep Al-Krenawi*

Contents

Acknowledgements	vii
Chapter 1: Localization of helping professionals practice, education, and research	1
Chapter 2: The Bedouin-Arab	21
Chapter 3: Individual, group, and family interventions in Bedouin-Arab society: Case vignettes	45
Chapter 4: Polygamous family intervention: Case vignettes	73
Chapter 5: Helping professions in the context of blood vengeance	101
Chapter 6: Traditional mediation and conflict resolution: Collaboration with social workers at the level of the community	115
Chapter 7: Case studies in cultural and religious healing practices	139
Chapter 8: Conclusion	169
References	175
Index	205

ACKNOWLEDGEMENTS

Special thanks go to the communities and professionals with whom we have worked, and who are too numerous to mention. We are grateful to the Adenauer Foundation (Germany and Israel) and the Social Sciences and Humanities Research Council (Canada) for invaluable funding that helped to facilitate data collection. Thank you to Cathryn Bradshaw, Jenine Hamonic, Katelyn Harker, Sarah Meagher-Bromley, Michael Shier, Eyalet Sanderovich, Alexandra Sears, Sigal Shellav, Oren Steinitz, and Jennifer Trew, who provided timely and helpful research assistance. Some of the content of this book is based on research published in a variety of academic journals; we are grateful to the following journals for allowing reproduction, in part, from the following sources:

Al-Krenawi, A. & Graham, J.R. (2006). A comparison of family functioning, life, and marital satisfaction, and mental health of women in polygamous and monogamous marriages. *International Journal of Social Psychiatry* 52(1), 5-17.

Al-Krenawi, A. & Graham, J.R. (2004). Somatization among Bedouin-Arab women: Differentiated by marital status. *Journal of Divorce and Marriage,* 42(1/2), 131-144.

Al-Krenawi, A., Graham, J. R., Dean, Y. Z., & Eltaiba, N. (2004). Cross national study of attitudes towards seeking professional help: Jordan, UAE, and Arab in Israel. *International Journal of Social Psychiatry,* 50(1), 92-104.

Al-Krenawi, A., Graham, J.R., & Fakher-Aldin, M. (2003).Telephone counselling: A comparison of Arab and Jewish Israeli usage. *International Social Work,* 48(4), 495-509.

Al-Krenawi, A., Graham, J.R., & Slonim-Nevo, V. (2002). Mental health aspects of Arab adolescents of polygamous/monogamous families. *Journal of Social Psychology,* 142(4), 446-460.

Al-Krenawi, A., Graham, J.R., & Izzeldin, A. (2001). The psychosocial impact of polygamous marriages on Palestinian women. *Women and Health, 34*(1), 1-16.

Al-Krenawi, A., & Graham, J.R. (2001). The cultural mediator: Bridging the gap between a non-Western community and professional social work practice. *British Journal of Social Work, 31*(4), 665-686.

Al-Krenawi, A., Graham, J.R., Ophir, M., & Kandah, J. (2001). The utilization of mental health services in Israel and Jordan. *International Journal of Social Psychiatry 47*(3), 42-54.

Al-Krenawi, A., Graham, J.R., & Kandah, J. (2000). Gendered utilization differences of mental health services in Jordan. *Community Mental Health Journal, 36*(5), 501-511.

Al-Krenawi, A., & Graham, J.R. (2000). Islamic theology and prayer: Relevance for social work practice. *International Social Work, 43*(3), 289-304.

Al-Krenawi, A., & Graham, J.R. (2000). Culturally sensitive social work practice with Arab clients in mental health settings. *Health and Social Work, 25*(1), 9-22.

Al-Krenawi, A. (2000). Bedouin-Arab clients' use of proverbs in the therapeutic setting. *International Journal for the Advancement of Counselling, 22*(2), 91-102.

Al-Krenawi, A., & Graham, J.R. (1999). The story of Bedouin-Arab women in a polygamous marriage. *Women's Studies International Forum, 22*(5), 497-509.

Al-Krenawi, A., & Graham, J.R. (1999). Social work practice and female genital mutilation. *Social Development Issues, 20*(1), 29-36.

Al-Krenawi, A., & Graham, J.R. (1999). Gender and biomedical/traditional mental health utilization among the Bedouin-Arabs of the Negev. *Culture, Medicine, and Psychiatry, 23*(2), 219-243.

Al-Krenawi, A., & Graham, J.R. (1999). Conflict resolution through a traditional ritual among the Bedouin-Arabs of the Negev. *Ethnology: An International Journal of Cultural and Social Anthropology, 38*(2), 163-174.

Al-Krenawi, A., & Graham, J.R. (1999). Social work and Koranic mental healers. *International Social Work, 42*(1), 53-65.

Al-Krenawi, A., & Graham, J.R. (1999). Social work intervention with Bedouin-Arab children in the context of blood vengeance. *Child Welfare, 78*(2), 283-296.

Al-Krenawi, A., & Graham, J.R. (1998). Divorce among Muslim Arab women in Israel. *Journal of Divorce and Remarriage, 29*(3/4), 103-119.

Al-Krenawi, A. (1998). Family therapy with a multiparental/multispousal family. *Family Process, 37*(1), 65-81.

Al-Krenawi, A. (1998). Reconciling western treatment and traditional healing: A social worker walks with the wind. *Reflections, 4*(3), 6-21.

Al-Krenawi, A., & Graham, J.R. (1997). Nebi-Musa: A therapeutic community for drug addiction in a Muslim context. *Transcultural Psychiatry, 34*(3), 377-398.

Al-Krenawi, A., Graham, J.R. & Al-Krenawi, S. (1997). Social work practice with polygamous families. *Child and Adolescent Social Work Journal, 14*(6), 444-458.

Al-Krenawi, A., & Graham, J.R. (1997). Social work and blood vengeance: The Bedouin-Arab case. *British Journal of Social Work, 27*(3), 515-528.

Al-Krenawi, A., & Graham, J.R. (1997). Spirit possession and exorcism: The integration of modern and traditional mental health care systems in the treatment of a Bedouin patient. *Clinical Social Work Journal, 25*(2), 211-222.

Graham, J.R., & Al-Krenawi, A. (1996). A comparison study of traditional helpers in a late nineteenth century Canadian (Christian) society and in a late twentieth century Bedouin (Muslim) society in the Negev, Israel. *Journal of Multicultural Social Work, 4*(2), 31-45.

Al-Krenawi, A., Graham, J.R., & Maoz, B. (1996). The healing significance of the Negev's Bedouin Dervish. *Social Science and Medicine, 43*(1), 13-21.

Al-Krenawi, A., & Graham, J.R. (1996). Tackling mental illness: Roles for old and new disciplines. *World Health Forum, 17*(3), 246-48.

Al-Krenawi, A., & Graham, J.R. (1996). Social work and traditional healing rituals among the Bedouin of the Negev, Israel. *International Social Work, 39*(2), 177-88.

Al-Krenawi, A. (1996). Group work with Bedouin widows of the Negev in a medical clinic. *Affilia: Journal of Women and Social Work, 11*(2), 303-318.

Chapter 1

LOCALIZATION OF HELPING PROFESSIONALS PRACTICE, EDUCATION, AND RESEARCH

Traveling north through Israel from its southern-most point, one reflects on the region's immense diversity. Eilat is a coastal tourist haven. From its port Egypt is clearly visible to the west. The town of Akaba is to the east, with an immense Jordanian flag proudly displayed, port-side. And if one were to travel the hundreds of miles down the Red Sea as it empties into the Indian Ocean, the west coast encompassing Egypt would give way to Eritrea and Somalia. The east coast, meanwhile, is the Arabian Peninsula, jutting into a massive terrain of desert and oil, with the present day Kingdom of Saudi Arabia eventually giving way to Yemen, and east of the latter, Oman. Both sides of the Red Sea represent a geography that is grand, and a populace that is predominantly Arab and Muslim.

Eilat, almost consciously, turns its back to this context. There is the sea; but few tourists visiting Eilat venture much beyond immediate visibility of the town. The water is safe, but to most who visit Eilat, the coastal authority is foreign. This distinction is legal, but beneath this are culture, politics, and, underlying all: history.

Many, on the other hand, make the long trip up Israel's interior, through a barren and uncompromising terrain that is desert. Whether one travels along the Egyptian-Israeli border, or through the centre of the gradually expanding Israeli northward territory, one is immediately taken by the silence of the wind, and the few people or visible animals. Traveling the Israeli interior, through the gradually expanding Jordanian Valley there are hills on both sides; to the east is Israel, to the west is Jordan. If your car cuts into the winding hills prior to the Dead Sea and the Jordan River, a probable destination is Beer-Sheva. Abraham is important to the People of the Book. Christians and Jews believe Beer-Sheva to be the site of Abraham's covenant to God; literally translated, the city is a Well of Oath. But for centuries, it was a collection of wells where shepherds watered their flocks.

For thousands of years, the Bedouin-Arab have roamed the vast swath of territory along the northern coast of Africa through to and beyond the Arabian Peninsula. A nomadic and ancient people, the Bedouin-Arab have lived through foreign occupations since before Islam became an established religion, and since the period of the Crusades. In recent times, the Ottoman Empire gave way to European suzerainty during World War I. By then, the city of Beer-Sheva had become a colonial administrative centre, and to this day, the core of the city has visible evidence of an Ottoman, Arab, and Muslim past. Outside of the city there are settlement towns, industrial towns, and commuter towns, each of variable economic and cultural background, and each emerging since the 1948 creation of the state of Israel. There are Bedouin-Arab villages too. Clustered along the desert, sometimes one or two tents, sometimes several, these sporadic and nomadic patterns of habitation go back millennia. Within the past 30 years, the Bedouin-Arab have been forced to create permanent modes of habitation. Across the immense desert there are "recognized" villages: those that have the official sanction of the Israeli state. Sectored off in quadrants that represent extended family and tribe, these villages can number several thousand, and have permanent houses and minimal standards of plumbing, road, and other infrastructures. Given the contested nature of the region, there are also "unrecognized" villages: shanty towns that Israeli authorities could bulldoze in a moment's notice; towns of temporary appearance that often lack electricity, paved roads, or running water.

The two authors have been working together in this region for over 15 years, and have published some 40 journal articles and numerous book chapters on myriad aspects of social service delivery among the Bedouin-Arab. Alean Al-Krenawi is a Bedouin-Arab by birth, and was born, raised, and continues to live in his home community of Rahat, Israel. With advanced training in social work from the Hebrew University (MSW) and the University of Toronto (PhD), much of Alean's career has been a longstanding effort at trying to reconcile his social work training within Western-based universities with his own lived experiences as a practising professional and community member of a Bedouin-Arab city. He and the second author, John Graham, a white Christian, born and raised in central Canada, met as doctoral students in Toronto. Both former psychiatric social workers, with similar intellectual dispositions, they have worked together closely since, developing culturally appropriate means of helping Bedouin-Arab communities.

That work has been part of a larger wave of research, world-wide. Indeed, the beginning of the 21st century marked 30 years of a movement towards increased awareness of a need for, and development of, culturally, appropriate localized responses to social problems. Here, we need some common definitions to provide clarity to the following chapters. Much of what we write about deals with social welfare; by this, we mean the policies and practices within a democratic system designed to promote access, and compensate for lack of access, to the socioeconomic necessities of life. In some societies public structures co-exist with private and civil society social welfare structures. In others, such as the Bedouin-Arab, culturally-imbedded private structures have always prevailed. The emergence of professional responses to somatic, psychological, and interpersonal issues–that cadre of helping professions that emerged in the nineteenth and early twentieth century West–have been part of the inexorable onslaught of modernization, touching the lives of Bedouin-Arab, as it has the lives of those hundreds of peoples who belong to Indigenous communities throughout Australia, Asia, Africa, and North, and South America. And so a second term—helping professional—is germane; this broad category includes such professional traditions as social work, counselling, education, nursing, occupational therapy, psychology, and psychiatry. The two authors are professors of social work, and much of what they say in this chapter in particular focuses on social work theory—but never exclusively, and always with a view to understanding the implications beyond social work in its limited sense and to social welfare and the helping professions. The Bedouin-Arab experience of modernization, and the helping professions that have been part of that process, has radically transformed its traditional social welfare structures. Our book provides case study insight into how Bedouin-Arab communities in the Negev, Israel, have negotiated and experienced these changes.

In the social work and other professions, helping theory and methods originated in Europe, North America, and other parts of the world known as the Global North. These theories and methods have historically been aloof to these concerns within such societies as the Bedouin-Arab, particularly regarding the latter's culture and religion, family structure and group orientation, and cultural and religious strategies for dealing with psychosocial problems. The literature has made some strides in making its myriad epistemologies less culturally oppressive, but much remains to be done. In our many years' work in the field, much we have observed as ethnographers suggests that people on the ground do not ignore the historic presence of the helping professions, nor the considerable refinements and sophistication they can represent. Rather, there appears to be some sort of negotiation—it is always continuous, always fluid, its boundaries always negotiated—between cultural practices and helping professional practice. Distinctions between the Bedouin-Arab community, helping professional, and social welfare structures are fluid, and are continuously re-negotiated in any interaction. Many Bedouin-Arab take on formal, professional roles that interest scholars such as us, who write about innovations in helping professional theory and practice. These qualifications are essential: we have seen, time and again, attempts by social welfare practitioners, structures, and Bedouin-Arab communities to integrate paradigms, which the helping professional carries out in practice methods and which could lead to the ongoing emergence of a newer social work epistemology, better anchored to the needs and realities of the Bedouin-Arab world.

LOCALIZING HELPING PROFESSIONS

Post-colonial scholarship in the fine arts, humanities and social sciences, like their post-colonial counterparts in the arts, are a vital foundation for thinking about human injustice. Edward Said's *Orientalism* (1978) provides provocative insight into how colonial and post-colonizing societies hold troubling prejudices towards those societies that fell under the colonial rubric. A vast literature examines the continuing legacy of Orientalist assumptions. The entire intellectual system that emerged in Global North scholarship can be seen to have also systematically prevented non-European subjects from occupying positions as fully human subjects (Spivak, 1999). The degree of change required for full inclusion is profound, if indeed it is possible. Scholars have argued for the renewal of pedagogical traditions that honour the voices of indigenous peoples (Archibald, 2007), among others whose voices have been overlooked, seen to have been unimportant, or (as is often the case) both. Many have critiqued post-secondary academic institutions, and the worldviews that they represent, as being non-inclusive of indigenous peoples (Kuokkanen, 2007). These tenets are prevalent across the globe generally, and in the Middle East particularly, where colonial boundaries carved up societies into arbitrary units of statehood. Like much of the world, post-colonial identity in the Middle East therefore emerges out of a legacy of force and subsumation to a more powerful actor (Ismael, 2001; Ismael & Ismael, 2004).

The broader state of helping professional practice and theory, therefore, is in this fundamental instance a tainted product of colonial and post-colonial processes. But hope exists. Over the past 35 years, there emerged an imperative to localize helping profession theory and practice—or make relevant to those local communities in which it occurred. This call originated, in the first instance, in scholarship regarding the Global South. However, it has expanded to encompass the current state of diversity in helping professional theories along any intersection of identity, including but not restricted to race, ethnicity, gender, socioeconomic class, sexual orientation (Bradshaw & Graham, 2007). Social work researchers committed to localizing helping professions began to conclude what practitioners on the ground had probably understood for some time: the professions' mass export to colonial and post-colonial societies during the interwar period and after World War II was entirely, and problematically, grounded in the cultural assumptions of the Global North—where disciplines like social work first emerged (Al-Krenawi & Graham, 2003; Ho, Ping, Lai, & Chan, 2001; Midgley, 1981). Examples of Northern assumptions include Maslow's hierarchy of needs, with self-actualization as its pinnacle; Mahler's notion of separation, individualism and autonomy; and Erickson's ideas on the importance of autonomy in the development of individuals. These and other currents of helping professional theory are strongly grounded to Northern, individualistic cultures, and may have limited applicability to many communities in the Global South that are more collectivist in orientation (Al-Krenawi & Graham, 2003). More recently, cultural biases in theory and practice have been challenged in the Global North, by proponents of anti-oppressive and multicultural practice working in increasingly diverse cultural contexts themselves (Al-Krenawi & Graham, 2003; Mullaly, 2002). In social work, psychology, and other helping professions, scholars are increasingly calling into question universal standards and definitions of professional theories and methods (Gray, 2005; Ho, Ping, Lai, & Chan, 2001). Some have called for an "indigenization" or "localization" of social work theory and practice—that it be reinvented, in theory and methods, in and for the culture in which it is applied (Asamoath, Healey, & Mayadas, 1997; Drower, 2000; Park, 1999). Numerous scholars, in fact, insist upon a profession that is, variously, African (Osei, 1996; Schiele, 1996, 1997; Swigonski, 1996; Walton & Abo-El-Nasr, 1988), Indian (Nagpaul, 1993; 1996a, b), or other.

The helping professions emerged in the Global North, and it is the North that remains the major locus of the professions' research and scholarship. But an important qualification bears emphasis: the North has been far from impermeable to influences from the Global South. In our own time, take, for example, Ibn-Sina's contribution to medicine or Al-Gazali's contributions to spirituality (Davidson, 1992; Frank, 1994). Indeed, the development of professions in the North owes much to the revival of science and mathematics in Europe during the Middle Ages and upon the influence of their custodians, Islamic scholars in India, Persia, and other parts of the world (Graham, 2006). Helping professions today can nonetheless be characterized as having strongly Northern assumptions, which are increasingly questioned within the Arab world's schools of social work, among its practitioners, and in its scholarship (Al-Krenawi & Graham, 2003).

One of the Arab world's leading social work scholars, Ibrahim Ragab, distinguishes between three types of social work practice in the Global South. His thinking is highly applicable to helping professions writ large. The first of his stages would be a traditional way of doing social work, which is to erroneously apply Northern assumptions, values, and techniques to societies that are manifestly different from the Global North (Ragab, 1990). This approach has happened historically, and continues to occur; indeed throughout the Global South many helping professional faculties translate English language scholarship into their local languages, and/or rely on untranslated English language scholarship. Much of that epistemology is from, and oriented to, the Global North. A second approach is "indigenizing" professional practice. This is the most common concept for rendering professions appropriate to the communities in which they work. The degree to which helping professional knowledge and practices are shifted from their Northern routes, to divergent cultures in the South, varies among proponents. This approach is often used in cross-cultural helping professions in North America and other regions in light of increasing cultural diversity in the general populace. But Ragab is critical of indigenization; it "approaches the situation from the wrong side of the issue—i.e. that of the imported models and how they should be more or less adjusted" (1990, p. 43). Indigenization may foster unhelpful, stereotypical assumptions about local communities that obscure and neglect more than they explain or illuminate. "Main proponents of this approach," Ragab writes, "are normally United Nations officials faced with difficulties with certain international cooperation programs; or Western professionals fidgeting over stalled foreign assistance programs or over troubles with the education of foreign students" (1990, p. 43). Some professionals from the Global South "have been brought into this same approach, thus suffering a double jeopardy" of uncritical acceptance of a community's proscriptions for intervention "created by uncritical acceptance of models developed by these same countries to begin with" (Ragab, 1990, p. 43). Thus, this kind of approach may actually serve to perpetuate the oppression that non-dominant cultural or indigenous groups face, and may serve to obscure the fact that this oppression exists.

A third, and in his (and our) view, more desirable approach is the "authenticization" of helping professional theory and practice. By this, Ragab refers to the Arabic word *Ta'seel*, meaning to go back to the roots to seek direction, to restore originality, or to become genuine. Here, he seeks authentic, locally grounded determinants of practice. We think the sorts of principles of intervention we derived for our book are in this latter-most tradition. Practitioners should not be "antagonistic to open-minded learning from others" (Ragab, 1990, p. 44); there may be entirely useful assumptions, methods, and theory that could be usefully applied from conventional helping professional practice. "We do not interpret" this approach "in xenophobic terms" (Ragab, 1990, p. 44). Helping professions in the Global South "will not benefit from self-imposed isolationism, but neither will [they] benefit from the superficial emulation of alien models" (Ragab, 1990, p. 44). Practitioners, in our view, are the conduit through which professional knowledge is appropriately applied to the communities in which they work; and this very process of application, in turn, is part of a broader epistemological enterprise that is knowledge generation. Members of any helping profession—their practitioners, students, and scholars—are custodians of their profession's knowledge base. Each research study, each intervention, each publication, contributes further to the development of that knowledge base. It is never static, never linear; it evolves over time, and its members take responsibility to play a role in that enterprise in a way that maximizes communities' social justice and authentic cultural expression. Helping professionals allow a dialogue between local cultures and professional intervention; in this process, new knowledge is being continuously created. The local (community) and global (social work) co-exist and coalesce towards a new dynamic that is unique. The principles of professional intervention with cultural mediators, polygamous family structures, and traditional healers are all examples, from our book, that are part of this enterprise.

Chapter one captures the thinking of some psychologists, along similar lines. Applying Ragab's terminology to previous psychological theory, there are three ways to knowledge development (Hwang, 2005, p. 7). The first, the traditional, imposes Western assumptions upon the world in an absolute manner, assuming that knowledge is etic, or an interpretation from outside a cultural group's perspective (Al-Krenawi & Graham, 2003). This is how helping professions were exported, from the Global North (of which the West is a part) to the Global South. An indigenous approach, in contrast, is situated to community and its presumptions are relativist, and its methodology is emic, or through the perspective of a cultural community. A final stage—defined as universal by some psychologists but as *Ta'seel* or authenticization by Ragab, assumes a knowledge base that is derived, and philosophical assumptions that are universal. This allows for one community to learn from another, for innovative knowledge transfer to occur across diverse communities. The silos and narrow points of reference that had been part of the Western stage persist in the indigenous stage; only in the third and final stage are they transcended in a way that makes the richest knowledge development possible.

But how, precisely, might helping professionals carry out this *Ta'seel* role in their every day lives? What are the strategies, skills, and techniques that lead to successful, culturally grounded intervention? What are some specific case examples that shed insight into the reciprocal relationship between helping professional epistemology and community traditions and structures? What roles might helping professionals take on, to these ends? Our book is intended as an initial foray, using one community as a means of exploring these questions in greater depth. Based on ethnographic case studies and empirical research in the region, we have found a variety of strategies that communities and helping professionals are utilizing for a more culturally responsive delivery of services among the Bedouin-Arab of the Negev. The remainder of this chapter analyses the literature on how to make social work locally relevant (localizing it); social work is in this analysis a useful proxy for understanding the experiences of helping professions writ large, and principles in this analysis could be extrapolated to social work's allied helping professions. Chapter two places the Bedouin-Arab of the Negev in their historical, social, political, and cultural contexts; here the experiences of this ancient community provide comprehensive background for the chapters in this book. Chapter three provides case study insight into helping professional practice with individuals, families, and groups. One case example provides compelling insight into how traditional healing structures might be used in alliance with professional intervention—and might ultimately improve the quality of intervention. Another case example analyses the intricacies of how professional and cultural canons (codes of conduct defining behavior in interpersonal interactions) may clash through the prism of gender, and how practitioners may effectively resolve these clashes. The final case involves group intervention with several widowed women. That case, like the others, highlights the significance of group identity as well as cultural and religious traditions as meaningful to client systems. These cases, as with others in the book, provide unique insight into how helping professional practice needs to be very significantly adapted to its cultural context; without thoughtful action grounded in community structures and cross-cultural sensitivity, intervention would be unsuccessful.

Chapter four presents empirical and ethnographic evidence on the social significance of women and children members of polygamy, and provides case study insight into culturally grounded helping professional intervention. Chapter five, likewise, covers the culturally grounded experience of blood vengeance. It discusses the social and psychological significance of blood vengeance to community members, and arising principles of helping intervention that should arise. Apart from our own work, no research has been undertaken on how helping professionals might intervene in the contexts of blood vengeance or polygamous family formation. Case vignettes in chapter six provide insight into collaborative work with indigenous mediators, and structures of conflict resolution. Chapter seven gives insight into the profound significance of a variety of traditional healing systems in Bedouin-Arab culture, and into how helping professionals might usefully collaborate with these systems. Chapter eight concludes with further thoughts on the future of helping professional practice, globalization, localization, and indigenous communities such as the Bedouin-Arab. We are entirely aware that there are disciplinary implications beyond social work, particularly in the social sciences and humanities that examine the geopolitics of the Middle East, and their intersections with social welfare delivery systems in the Arab world (Cf Abdelrahman, 2004; Challand, 2008). Our book concerns itself with a finite scope. Future research, beyond the limits of space in the present book, might consider in greater depth the connections between social welfare practices amongst Bedouin and other Arab communities, to these broader cultural, economic, political, and social machinations. Political and economic structures, likewise, are beyond the purview of our analysis.

LOCALIZING SOCIAL WORK

The two authors have written extensively on social work but have also published in journals representing such disciplines as anthropology, area studies, health studies, history, psychiatry, psychology, social policy, sociology, and women's studies. We have been deeply influenced by these intellectual traditions as well. The remainder of this chapter is intended to illuminate a phenomenon that is not limited only to social work, which is the effort to render professional helping theory and methods more culturally responsive to the communities in which they occur. But limits of space and the need for clarity have required us to restrict the following comments to social work. At the same time, we emphasize the analytical points raised in the remaining paragraphs will have significant relevance to other helping professions; future research beyond the scope of the present book could profitably explore these connections.

When referring to culture, we mean the totality of ideas, beliefs, values, knowledge, and way of life of a group of people who share a certain historical, religious, racial, linguistic, ethnic, or social background (Henry, Tator, Mattis, & Rees, 1995, p. 326, cited in Al-Krenawi & Graham, 2003, p. 10). The anthropologist Clifford Geertz explains six facets that are essential to culture: 1) culture is historically and socially constructed; 2) people construe themselves using concepts and other symbolic structures that are available; 3) people develop a theory of mind (i.e. a theory of how the mind works) to understand others; 4) people have beliefs about the world, and they act on those beliefs; 5) people engage in meaningful actions; and 6) culture is subjective and involves the mind and imagination (Anderson, 1991; Kashima, 2005, p. 20).

10 Localization of helping professionals practice, education, and research

Localization of social work, as defined for this analysis, is considered to be the pattern of social work education, practice, research, and/or social service delivery that is adopted or adapted from one culture to another due to differing social or religious attitudes that impact the definition of local social problems and their solutions (Walton & Abo-El-Nasr, 1988). The term is sometimes used synonymously with indigenization; but the latter term is problematic for at least two reasons. The first, as we have discussed, is Ragab's excellent reservations with the term; he argues that indigenization suggests that models of helping imported from the Global North are still appropriate if they are adjusted to suit the perceived local realities, which only obscures and neglects those realities. The second: it could be confused with being applicable only to indigenous peoples, which is not the concept's intention. The term localizing social work is preferred, as it denotes locally appropriate forms of services that could apply to indigenous and non-indigenous contexts (Al-Krenawi & Graham, 2003, 2006c, 2007; Graham, 2006).

The analysis presented here is based on 513 abstracts located in the *Social Work Plus* electronic database in a 2004 search, which were identified by their relation to issues of the localization of social work with indigenous native peoples or ethnic minority groups from countries such as Canada, the United States, Australia, New Zealand, India, Mexico, Ghana, Burma, Algeria, and Nigeria (For further work on this analysis, see Bradshaw & Graham, 2007.). The concepts of localization, indigenization, and authenticization are all captured in this search. Although this literature represents but a fraction of all that is published by social workers on the topic, it provides some basis from which to garner a sense of what issues are being addressed in this area. A content analysis, a research tool used to determine the presence of specific concepts within texts (Berelson, 1952; Krippendorff, 1980; Neuendorf, 2001; Weber, 1990), was used to categorize themes. Content analysis enables the perusal of large volumes of data in a systematic fashion that allows us to discover and describe the focus of the identified literature. Our content analysis yielded five major themes: (1) issues leading to the development of localized social work (practice, research, and/or education); (2) how root problems, such as colonization and cumulative trauma, impact social problems and their potential solutions; (3) defining clinical social work problems and approaches to solutions; (4) social work research; and (5) localization of social work education. These themes became the primary coding categories for the 513 abstracts, and the basis of the following discussion.

Factors Driving the Localization Movement

Localization of social work practice, research, and education has emerged in an attempt to limit the influence of Western social work models, and to promote the development of alternative models that are more responsive to and appropriate for the local culture or with minority cultural groups. Factors identified in the literature that have impacted the movement to localize social work include the lack of sensitivity to non-Western values and the general ineffectiveness of Western treatment approaches; a growing awareness of the multicultural and global context in which we live and work; and an increased appreciation of the influence of cultural identity on self-esteem and identity formation combined with changes in some government policy that supports aboriginal and minority rights.

One factor that lends weight to the push for localized social work practice has been the general ineffectiveness of non-localized, Western-based treatment approaches with many non-Western populations. Examples cited in the literature cross many cultures—American Indians, Maori in New Zealand, African Americans, and Indians from India, to name just a few. A great majority of the literature focused on native and minority cultures in North America and other Western countries, and their social, economic, and health problems; much is known for these populations about addiction rates, suicide rates, rates of family violence or child abuse/neglect, for example. On the whole, the literature points out that Western solutions have been used or imported to deal with these problems, and they have been found inadequate in addressing these social, economic, and health issues. The result has been a tendency to perpetuate a repetitive cycle of ineffective services, and blame/stereotype clients as recalcitrant. The movement to understand cultural differences and how they can impact effective treatment to obtain positive results has gained support among social work practitioners working with cultural groups. For example, one New Zealand study found that 86% of addictions treatment respondents advocated adjusting their clinical practice when working with Maori clients to include referral to specialist Maori groups and/or including family in the treatment process (Robertson et al., 2001). Some authors go even further and purport that social work theory and practice have much to learn from indigenous peoples and other cultural groups when it comes to the helping process, especially in the areas of relational and holistic practices. They suggest that Western practice could be enhanced with the adoption of a more relational and holistic approach to treatment.

Other factors driving the localization movement are the global economic forces and liberal ideology that push social welfare structures towards greater privatization and market-based models (Midgley, 2001). In an era where international trade may be elevated above human rights (Bronson & Lamarche, 2001), social workers, like their counterparts throughout the helping professions, are called upon to take a more conscious social justice stance that is in keeping with the ethical values and traditions of their chosen profession. This has sensitized many to the need to make practice and education more inclusive and respectful of differences. Identity politics—and the appreciation of the intersection of multiple levels of identity—is key to any concept of diversity. Age, age cohort status, creed, culture, gender, geography, language, range of (dis)ability, religion, sexual orientation, socioeconomic class: these, among other parameters, are in a constant state of flux, ever-moving targets of constantly evolving identity.

Along these lines, there has also been an increased recognition in the social work literature of cultural identity, as it intersects with all other positionalities, and their cumulative impact on self-concept and group-concept. The literature is beginning to reflect an understanding that cultural identity can serve as a protective factor for wellness and healing and provide strength to individuals within a cultural group. For example, cultural traditions amongst North American indigenous peoples are well recognized as means of maintaining cultural identity (Weaver, 2001), and increasingly too for bolstering of wellness and healing within native communities (Bodeker & Kronenberg, 2002). In some Western countries, changes in government policy have played some role in focusing on cultural identity for indigenous peoples. For instance, government policy in Canada and the United States has extended tribal self-determination (e.g., child welfare, family preservation) in response to native peoples demanding more control over social services at the community level. This adds credence to the drive for a greater localization of social work.

The overarching case for the localization of social work practice, research, and education is that social work has failed to respond appropriately to the major social problems confronting indigenous peoples and other ethnic groups. More and more, social work is being called upon to ensure that the profession fits into the social, economic, and practice environments in which it operates. Next we will address some of the impacts of the root issue that has influenced the call for localization.

Colonization of Indigenous Peoples

The goal of localizing social work is to create meaningful cultural exchange in the process of helping, rather than to maintain the current form of knowledge-colonialism that effectively disempowers the people caring professionals seek to help. It is based on the rationale that cultures differ in how they define social problems and the mechanisms for their solution, and in the institutional context of social services (Walton & Abo-El-Nasr, 1988).

A small portion of the literature (approximately 14% of the abstracts) that we analysed refers to colonization—and identifies such impacts as oppression, poverty, isolation, and hopelessness as associated with Western colonization patterns and practices. A number of scholars proffer the following arguments. Many social problems such as addictions, child welfare concerns, delinquency, suicide, family violence, and numerous health and mental health problems are seen as embedded within the context of colonization. These problems are exacerbated by the imposition of an alien colonial culture leading to the breakdown of traditional values, institutions, and cultural identity. There are widespread problems in many indigenous communities: poverty, a lack of adequate social and economic infrastructures, and often poor systems of governance. It is within these contexts that indigenous peoples are exerting pressure on the social work community and other helping professions to move towards a more localized model of practice (i.e., how problems are perceived and the way in which solutions are implemented), research, and education.

Further impacts of the traumas imposed by colonization practices may include changes in parenting behaviours and placing children at risk for alcohol and other substance abuse. Poverty is frequently the result of oppression, and indigenous peoples have a long and tragic history of oppression with its incumbent links to economic deprivation, dispossession, and the breaking down of culture and the community. These factors all have impacted and continue to impact the social, physical, mental, and spiritual well-being of the people who were colonized.

Helping Professional Practice—A Localized Lens

There is a great deal of literature on the incidence and prevalence of social problems within indigenous and ethnic minority groups. In our review of the existing literature, we assessed that 382 of the 513 abstracts (almost 75%) addressed issues of social and health problems amongst indigenous peoples and minority cultural groups (See also Bradshaw & Graham, 2007). The problems frequently studied include violence against women and children, child abuse and neglect, addictions (drugs, alcohol, gambling), delinquency and criminal behaviour, health and mental health problems, unemployment, and suicide. Investigations often compared incidence or prevalence of such issues in the majority versus the minority communities, and find the minority or indigenous community wanting. Some studies have highlighted the chronicity, and the comorbidity (indicating the presence of two concurrent conditions) or multimorbidity (referring to the presence of three or more conditions at the same time) within minority groups or indigenous peoples of these social and health problems that makes intervention complex. Often, there is no attempt to understand how or why chronicity and multimorbidity are such a significant problem within these communities, although a couple of authors from North American native communities have categorized the cumulative historical trauma resulting from colonization as the ongoing malaise behind the many manifestations of problems that plague Native Americans.

Many indigenous and ethnic minorities experience significant barriers to social services and interventions designed for dominant Western cultures. The closing decades of the 20th century witnessed a growing movement to understand and include customary values, beliefs and practices in the development of culturally congruous programs. One strong manifestation of this approach in the literature was to understand cultural differences that can impact social work practice including how problems are perceived, what family and typical social support networks are, who provides care, how families make decisions, what family members expect of each other, what cultural values are important to family members, if and under what conditions families are willing to accept services from outside the family, and what concerns families may have about service providers.

Approximately 43% of the abstracts reviewed called for greater cultural sensitivity and more appropriate social work practice when working with indigenous peoples and other ethnic groups. There is a small, but important, segment of the literature that recognizes the unique contribution that traditional help and healing mechanisms, perspectives and rituals could have in shaping social work theory and practice, and social policy. Some authors have attempted to place traditional ways of helping and healing within the context of well known Western theoretical traditions (e.g., Saleebey's strengths perspective, Kohut's self-object theory, and Jungian psychology), and propose that these can provide a new lens for viewing how we practice social work. Other authors emphasize the role of shamanistic traditions and rituals, which call attention to the role and dimensions of spirits and can be powerful resources in the helping and healing process for individuals and for community health and well-being. Still others have raised the issue that cultural traditions have been eroded over time through colonization or dominance of Western customs, and traditional ways of thinking and doing have been lost.

There has been some effort invested into developing guidelines and principles for social work practice, assessment, and intervention that promote culturally appropriate and effective resolutions of social problems and problematic institutions. One vein of the literature in this area focuses on taking into account and utilizing ethnocultural factors as a means of promoting prevention and recovery interventions. Another segment of the literature suggests the incorporation of specific traditional practices or rituals (e.g., Circle of Courage, O'dham Himdag, ho'oponopono) as a vehicle to provide appropriate and effective treatment services. And a third focus recognizes the relational and holistic worldview (integration of spirit, mind, and body) held by many non-Western cultures are more mainstream than extreme, and understands how these connections to extended family and community can be used to further health and healing. This recognition that indigenous cultures hold a wealth of social and cultural resources that can facilitate healing, resilience, and well-being means that the goals and processes of a culturally-based approach should/can be defined within the ethnocultural context of the client or community.

For many indigenous societies the advancement of a holistic community development approach is sought as a means of addressing social and health problems. Of the 513 abstracts reviewed, 54 or almost 11% addressed the issue of community solutions rather than only focusing at the level of the individual.

Localized Helping Professional Research

Of the 513 abstracts reviewed, 87 or approximately 17% of the literature were research oriented. Criteria for inclusion in this category were abstracts that specifically dealt with social work research; that is, they either concentrated on the nature of social work research within a localized context or contained a research study that addressed issues of indigenization (i.e., methodology, results, and need for further research). A small portion of these articles stressed that most research conducted on indigenous peoples and their communities has been characterized by aboriginal scholars as exploitive in terms of motives, methodology, and findings. For example, few studies focused on themes identified as of particular interest to indigenous communities, such as best practices in developing strong communities; reconnecting with cultural heritage (e.g., language and traditions); indigenous governance; and cultural identity as promoting resilience and wellness (McNaughton & Rock, 2002).

This call for more sensitive research practice in social work is gaining prominence within some disciplines and within the agencies that fund the most promising studies. The major Canadian funder of research within the social science and humanities communities, for example, indicates that a paradigm shift is beginning to take place in regards to research vis-à-vis Canadian indigenous peoples from research *on* First Nations peoples to research *with* Aboriginal communities as full partners. This paradigm shift would see research better respecting indigenous knowledge and ways of knowing (e.g., role of oral traditions, role of Elders). Several strategies have been identified in the literature as important in promoting this shift: building strategic partnerships; organizing research with indigenous communities so their priorities are reflected in the research; using indigenous community members as cultural brokers; and developing a significant cadre of indigenous scholars.

LOCALIZATION OF SOCIAL WORK EDUCATION

The social work profession is heavily imbued with Western culture and ways of knowing. Many countries have relied on Western social work educators for the design of their social work curriculum. In order to function within a multicultural world, social workers need training that provides them with the knowledge, values, and skills necessary to engage in meaningful and appropriate social work research and practice. The challenge put forth by a number of authors is how to create viable, relevant, and effective social work education that in the West responds to our multicultural reality, and in developing countries meets the real conditions faced by social workers in that locale.

This sentiment was expressed in many of the 47 abstracts (9% of the abstracts reviewed) that specifically pertained to the need to localize social work education (i.e., undergraduate, graduate, distance and rural education, continuing education). The literature supports the need for social work students to develop both conceptual and practical skills that would allow them to understand the historical situation of indigenous peoples and other ethnic groups in order to carry out a critical analysis of policy and improve practice skills. This knowledge and perspective would permit social workers to identify and/or develop strategies that more appropriately addresses the needs of their clients and communities.

Enhancing cultural awareness and developing cultural competence were frequent themes in the literature on localized social work education. As one author wrote: "the need for indigenous elements of social work education in terms of philosophy, approaches, principles, theories, and study materials cannot be overemphasized because working with people, studying social problems, and administering social welfare programs call for indigenous orientation and skills" (Nagpaul, 1993, p. 217). This cultural awareness is required to meet the needs of a diverse student population in many Western countries and the even more diverse client populations they will serve. This is the Western understanding of the need for localization. The questions that are raised in the literature around localization of social work curriculum centre around what content should be taught, where it can be integrated within the established social work curriculum, and how to overcome the challenge of lack of class time to implement such curriculum changes. There is a scarcity of information that addresses answers to these questions.

In non-Western countries, localization of social work education stresses the design and implementation of a curriculum that is more congruent with the social context in which social work operates rather than the wholesale reliance on Western literature and educational models. The lack of localized curriculum materials proposed in the literature remains problematic.

Another issue that received limited attention in the literature on the subject of localized education was the impact on aboriginal social work students of the need to negotiate their own cultural identity alongside a professional identity that is predominately Western oriented. In a similar vein, several authors highlighted that many social work programs pay some attention to helping students develop cultural competence for their work with clients, but little is known about the degree to which social work education respects the cultural norms and values of students from diverse populations. There was a limited, but encouraging, interest in collaboration between social work educators in Western countries and those in developing countries in the development of curriculum, fieldwork, teaching materials, and research opportunities.

CONCLUSION

Much of the analysis in the remainder of this book is based on English language social work scholarship; future research could profitably consider innovations in the social work field in other languages. English language traditions and literatures, as we subsequently point out, have been important to the Arab world's development of social work. Such diverse and loosely defined social groupings as "Arab", "Bedouin-Arab", "Muslim", "Northern", "Southern", or "Western" are fraught with dangers of reductionism, simplification, and essentialism. Their advantage, on the other hand, is the possibility of considering broad patterns at this early stage in the literature's evolution. And so the generalizations that we present are intended as nothing more than a beginning point. One scholar describes such enterprises as "signposts for future research rather than as definitive conclusions", useful for further reflection and application in more precise and defined geographic, historical, national, and other contexts (Salem, 1997, p. 11).

Insofar as generalizations may occur, the following chapters provide evidence that helping professional epistemology, a largely Northern conception, is nonetheless beginning to create space for other perspectives, including the Bedouin-Arab communities we study, where social work, as we argue, has been a product of colonialism (Al-Krenawi & Graham, 2003). Historically, many aspects of the helping professions have fit poorly with Bedouin-Arab cultures and social structures. Polygamy and blood vengeance are excellent examples of culturally embedded practices for which social work theory and methods had, until recently, little to say. As we also argue, there are other important areas where social work in the Arab world has been enhanced: conflict resolution, collaboration with religion and with traditional healing, and strategies for working with families. Ultimately, our book provides evidence that one may integrate social service theory and methods as they are presently conceptualized in the Bedouin-Arab communities we study, with principles derived from local cultural and religious practices. This process may lead to a more locally responsive, culturally appropriate model of professional intervention.

A final point bears emphasis. As many scholars have described the situation, a new generation of Palestinian youth living within Israel in the wake of the Second Intifada (2000-), is asserting its rights in a context of being denied access to land, essential social services, and educational and employment opportunities (Rabinowitz & Abu-Baker, 2005). This 'Stand Tall Generation', as it has come to be known, will continue to influence helping service structures and mandates. Questions of service accessibility, availability, quality, and intentions are coming to the fore. For the present time, an important question needs to be raised about the intention of helping professional service structures among Arab peoples in Israel, and, for the purposes of this book, Bedouin-Arab communities of the Negev, as described in subsequent chapters. To what extent do they reinforce inherent inequalities between a minority and Jewish majority within Israel? To what extent do they elicit social development, social change, and rights and opportunities that are equal to those of the Israeli majority? The Stand Tall Generation has become more aware of the collective identities and rights of Palestinians living in Israel, and seeks education as a vehicle to social justice and to the community's improvement. Studying at the postsecondary level, with great savvy towards modern technical communications such as the internet, this generation is highly open to influences outside their culture. But it simultaneously commits to values and norms that are its own. Living in multiple contemporaneous worlds, and in particular the dual worlds of Israeli society and Palestinian cultures, this generation is increasingly well organized and vociferous. Indeed, the interaction between forces outside and within is an essential theme in understanding the experiences of Palestinians within Israel, and has every bearing on the analysis that occurs in subsequent chapters on helping professional services with the Bedouin-Arab of the Negev.

Chapter 2

THE BEDOUIN-ARAB

INTRODUCTION

In North America and around the world, indigenous peoples, referring to "people who either live, or have lived within the past several centuries, in non-state societies, although these indigenous societies may well have existed within the boundaries of state societies," have experienced "a resurgence of indigenous consciousness, political mobilization, and cultural renewal" (Hall & Nagel, 2000, p. 1295). Communities in Africa, Australia, Central and South America, the Middle East, North America, Southeast Asia, and other parts of the world are making claims related to land entitlement and control of political rights and economic resources, with success that is often in marked contrast with their lower economic, military, and political power (Hall & Nagel, 2000; Nagel, 1996; Wilmer, 1993). The Bedouin-Arab are one of the thousands of indigenous communities world-wide, and have cultural characteristics and historical experiences that make them unique.

"Bedouin" is the general name for all Arabic-speaking tribes in the Middle East and North Africa that originate from the Arabian Peninsula (*Jazirat-Al-Arab*). An anthropologist describes the Bedouin-Arab as follows:

> nomadic Arabs who live by rearing sheep and camels in the deserts of the Middle East.... The word "Bedouin" is the Western version of the Arabic word *badawiyin* which means "inhabitants of the desert," the *Badia*. Strictly speaking, the term "Bedouin" should only be applied to the noble camel herding tribes, but again it has been used as a general term in English to cover all nomadic Arabs (Kay, 1978: p. 7).

Although some writers refer to non-Arab Bedouin in such regions as Persia and central Asia (Asher, 1986, 1996 as cited in Cole, 2003), our analysis focuses exclusively on the Bedouin of Arab origin. These Bedouin are an indigenous people who have resided in Arab countries along the north of Africa, from Morocco to Egypt, and extending into the Arabian Peninsula from Israel, Jordan, and Syria to Saudi Arabia. Here they have lived since before the establishment of Islam or Christianity.

In describing any cultural community, it is necessary not to essentialize – to assume that their thoughts or behaviour are derivative of the categories used to describe them. It is likewise important to appreciate the significant differences that exist within and between communities, as well as the potential for change among people and groups over time. Moreover, anthropologists have recently called into question the term "Bedouin," given the enormous economic and cultural changes that these communities have experienced. As one scholar remarks, the term "Bedouin" now "refers less to a "way of life" than to an "identity." The way of life was grounded in ecology and economy, the identity in heritage and culture" (Cole, 2003, p. 3). For purposes of the present book, the term Bedouin-Arab will be used to describe any group or community that self-identifies as such.

While all societies, like all people, are in a constant state of transition, the Bedouin-Arab have experienced particularly extensive changes over the past century. A historically nomadic people, many have abandoned the tents and camels of traditional life for the houses and economies of cities and towns. In the past, the herding of sheep, goats, camels, and occasionally cattle, horses, and donkey was a major source of livelihood. Today, numerous livelihoods prevail, many of them non-pastoral. Traditionally, Bedouin-Arab could be identified by the particular dialects that distinguished them from other Arab communities. Yet, this shared identity should not be used to infer a unified, racial, ethnic, or national group with a homogenous style of life. Bedouin-Arab Elders have nonetheless identified certain cultural markers, including tattoos, hairstyles, clothing, headdresses, veils, and distinctive poetry and folklore (Al-Hamamdeh, 2004; Cole, 2003, p. 3).

Physical geography is another important part of this narrative. The Bedouin-Arab have historically lived and traveled extensively in a nomadic fashion in the desert. The environment can be very harsh, livelihoods may be subsistent, and as anyone who has ever traveled extensively in a desert will confirm, people perish if they lose contact with their fellow travelers. Historically, groups who traveled across deserts could be subject to attack by rival tribes. Not surprisingly, group identity and cohesion would be accorded importance: these could make the difference, literally, between life and death (Al-Fuaal, 1983; Al-Hamamdeh, 2004; Mahjoob, 1973, 1977; Saber, 1989). A well-known Muslim Arab historian and sociologist, Ibn-Khaldun, identifies several further Arab cultural constructs that are the basis of Arab culture, tradition, and folklore. The first of these is tribal cohesion—*Asabiyya*. Another is *Nasab* (kinship ties), based upon both blood and symbiotic ties within the family, extended family (*hamula*), and tribe. From early childhood, as folktales point out, great importance could be attached to *Furussiyya*, a term emphasizing courage, gallantry, power, fierceness, and resistance both in battle and in any relations that could involve conflict or negotiation—particularly regarding different *hamula* or tribes. There are likewise many Bedouin-Arab folk traditions that emphasize the legendary practice of hospitality—*Karam*. Yet another value that has emerged is that of simplicity; there are many Bedouin-Arab stories that portray such ideals as naturalness, austerity and the dignified control over desire in public situations (Al-Hamamdeh, 2004; Barakat, 1993; Dhaouadi, 1990). The Bedouin-Arab nomadic traditions have ascribed high social value to animals they herd—particularly camels, but in some tribes sheep or goats—as indicators of wealth (Saber, 1989).

Tribal identity continues to be an important cultural marker. When Bedouin-Arab individuals who do not know each other meet, they may ask about the other's lineage, clan, or tribe. By contrast, a North American may be as likely to inquire into the other's occupation, while residents of Cairo are usually interested in knowing what part of the city the other resides in, which is an important identifier of place (Cole, 2003, p. 5). Tribal status has become more important with sedenterization. Tribal names, more so than lineage names, are increasingly used as last names. Bedouin-Arab identity, as one anthropologist notes, may cut across tribal boundaries that may have divided people more in the past than they do now (Cole, 2003, p. 5).

BEDOUIN-ARAB SOCIAL ORGANIZATION

Historically, Bedouin-Arab society in the Middle East would be divided into units of different sizes based upon kinship and matrilineal descent. A confederation (*qabilah*) or nation is the largest unit and includes a group of tribes collected together in a union. In actuality, this is only an informal association of tribes that offered a feeling of unison and a sense of belonging to one polity, as each tribe traditionally had its own settlement area. The next division is that of tribe—*ashira*, a union of families (*a-ial*) that remain together, wandering, shepherding, and working the land on a communal basis. Next is the *hamula*, a patrilineal kinship structure of several generations that extends to a wide network of blood relations in the extended family (parents, siblings, their spouses and children). The *hamula* is a major concept across the Arab world (Al-Haj, 1989; Barakat, 1993); it is the central family unit in Arab society, and the family itself is the locus of blood bonds, internal commitment, and responsibilities to the collective. Finally, for purposes of this book, there is the modern construction of a nuclear family (the married couple and children). In traditional Bedouin-Arab structures, fathers have been considered to lead families while the *hamula* and tribes have been directed by forums of male elders who ultimately defer to the patrilineal head, described variously as the *mukhtar*, or *sheikh*. The patrilineal heads may act as mediators in instances of internal family disputes, and have been considered the family's principal ambassador to outsiders (Al-Krenawi, Graham, & Al-Krenawi, 1997).

SOCIETY IN TRANSITION

Like many indigenous peoples, the process of modernization has been transformative among several Bedouin-Arab communities, and in numerous instances, governments have encouraged the processes of permanent settlement and integration in economies that are historically external to the Bedouin-Arab. Traditional economies based on herding animals and nomadism may give way to participation in industrial capitalism. Tents may give way to houses; communities that were once nomadic may settle in close proximity to non-tribal communities. Televisions, radios, cars, and other modern technologies have brought the modern world closer to many Bedouin-Arab. Boys and girls in modernizing communities may receive higher levels of education than their forbearers. Modern health care, social service, and educational services interact with daily community functions. Traditional norms and values within the tribe may be transformed accordingly. Some Bedouin-Arab continue to be nomadic and own livestock, but herding may be increasingly done by hired shepherds or select family members rather than entire households as before. Tradition and consumption remain important to the maintenance of livestock, but markets may be increasingly important. The twentieth century creation of political states within the Arab world and the modernization of society and the economy have been highly transformative. As one anthropologist puts it:

> Bedouin-Arab are today citizens of states, carry national identity cards, vote where voting is allowed, and are no longer differentiated administratively from other citizens or nationals as previously occurred in some cases. Younger generations of Bedouin-Arab, both settled and from among those on the range, are increasingly literate with growing proportions completing secondary school and going on to universities. Occupationally, most Bedouin on the range have small-to moderate-scale enterprises (Cole, 2003, p. 20).

A 1965 Desert Social Development Conference held in Marsa Matruh, Egypt, was among the first to grapple with the Bedouin-Arab's emerging transition from nomadic to settled ways of life (Al-Fuaal, 1983). The conference was careful to distinguish between two kinds of settlement: that which is initiated by the Bedouin-Arab, and that which is imposed upon them by a government. In either instance, assimilation into mainstream society tended to occur, and was lauded. The question was not so much whether assimilation should occur, but whether it should be coercive or a collective choice of the Bedouin-Arab. Other indigenous communities, such as the Aboriginal peoples of Canada, were subject to similar calls for assimilation into the mainstream (Graham, Swift, & Delaney, 2003). In these and other instances, the prevailing theories in social development of the time tended to laud all societies' transition from traditional subsistence to full cultural, economic, political, and social integration into modern modes of economic growth, consumption, trade, and political participation. The conference, completely in keeping with this outlook, criticized traditional Bedouin-Arab ways of life. Their assumptions were as follows:

1. The Bedouin-Arab life is an obstacle to primary, secondary, and post-secondary education.
2. Because Bedouin-Arab prefer tribal to national loyalty, governments encounter problems with Bedouin-Arab communities in agreeing to and implementing state laws.
3. The Bedouin-Arab life is out of step with the goals of modern industrial capitalism and political and social development.
4. The Bedouin-Arab life has a negative impact on the national economy because Bedouin-Arabs play a minor role in the national economy.
5. The Bedouin-Arab life is often at the subsistence level and affords few educational or economic opportunities. The Bedouin-Arab would be better off settling and changing their lifestyle.

These assumptions would be echoed in social development circles throughout the Arab world. The present case study of the Bedouin-Arab of the Negev illustrates these assumptions at work.

Bedouin-Arab of the Negev

The Bedouin-Arab have lived in the Negev—the desert region in the southern part of present day Israel—for millennia. The Negev—a Hebrew word for "dry land"—comprises 58% of the territory of the State of Israel's pre-1967 borders, but only 10% of the population resides there (Cwikel, Lev-Wiesel, & Al-Krenawi, 2003). The region is characterized by both a sparse population distribution and by physical and psychological distance from the population centers of Israel.

The first Bedouin-Arab tribes are said to have moved into the region from the Arabian Peninsula at the beginning of the "Arab Rule" of the region in the seventh century CE. This process was accelerated during the period of Ottoman Rule (1517-1917), and by the turn of the twentieth century, the entire Negev was under the control of Bedouin-Arab tribes. Most of the lands remained *mawat*—(Arabic for dead land): land that is primarily pastoral and that belongs to the collectivity rather than (as Ottoman rulers might have preferred) being registered to individuals or tribes (Ginguld, Perevolotsky, & Ungar, 1997, p. 571). The period of the British Mandate (1917-1947) brought few changes to the region. The Negev Bedouin-Arabs lived as seasonal nomadic shepherds roaming the dry desert, accompanied by the introduction of spontaneous sedenterization among some tribes. Beer-Sheva, a city in the northern part of the Negev, remained an administration center (Al-Aref, 1934; Maddrell, 1998; Falah, 1989).

In 1921, The British Mandate Government gave landholders two months to register *mawat* land, after which the land would be classified as state land. There were several problems with this system. First, the British registration system proceeded from north to south, and some private properties and Bedouin-Arab settlements in the Negev were not registered or marked on the map. Secondly, due to a number of factors, many Bedouin-Arab did not register their lands: a) a tradition of not cooperating with foreign government authorities, b) a lack of information and knowledge about the registration system, c) fear of taxation and military conscription based on registration records, and d) indifference toward administrative processes (Yiftachel, 2003). Like other indigenous peoples, the Bedouin-Arab continued to use their traditional means of demarcating boundaries, and did not use the Western system of land registration and ownership.

Following the establishment of Israel in 1948, 80-90% of the Negev's Bedouin-Arabs were expelled from the region to Jordan, the Sinai, or other parts of the Middle East. Only 11,000-18,000 out of 60,000—100,000 remained in the Negev (Hasson and Swirski, 2006; Almi, Dloomi and Sawalha, 2006). The impact of 1948 was profound (Falah, 1989; Maddrell, 1998). Of the 95 tribes living in the region before the war, only 19 remained (Marx, 1974). Those who stayed were moved to an area (*Siag*, Hebrew for confinement) that was assigned for Bedouin-Arab resettlement, centered around Beer-Sheva. The Bedouin-Arab were subject to martial law, and movement in and out of the Siag was strictly controlled until the early 1970s. Between 1948 and the 1970s, most of the Negev – formerly belonging to the Bedouin-Arab – was appropriated by the government of Israel and was settled by Jews who lived as farmers or who worked in a growing number of settlement towns (Ginguld, Perevolotsky, & Ungar, 1997).

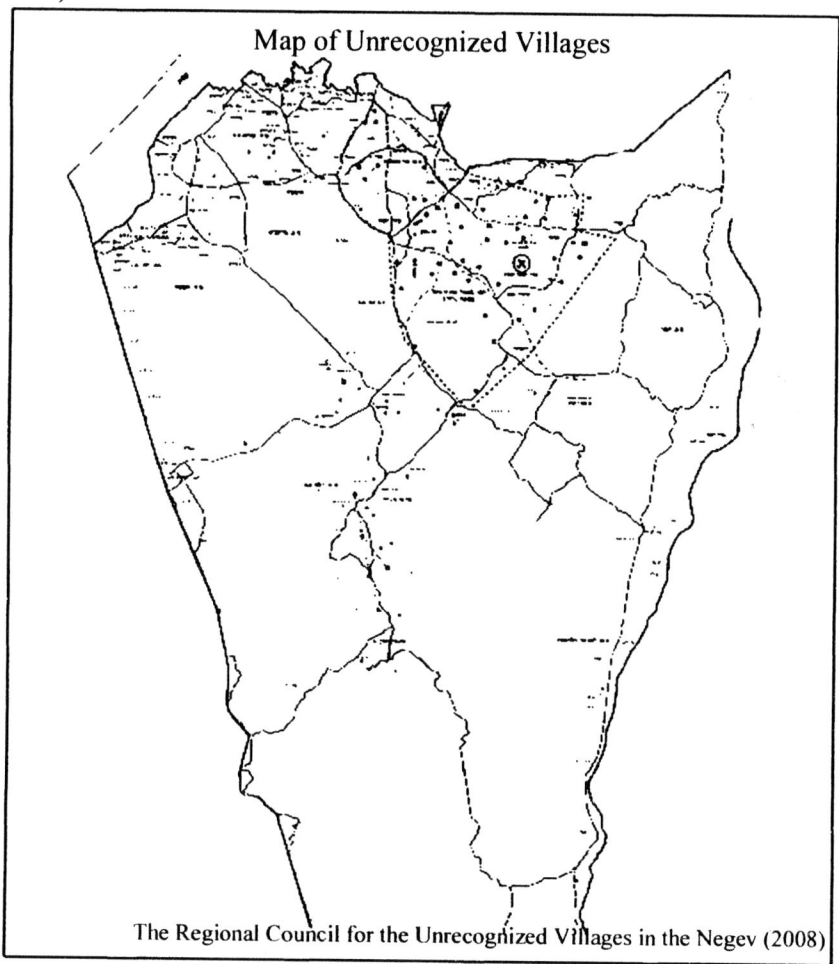

The Regional Council for the Unrecognized Villages in the Negev (2008)

A series of legal procedures declared uncultivated land *(mawta)* and all property of refugees "absentee property." Israel's Land Acquisition Law (1953) proclaimed as state property all land that that was not being cultivated or resided on as of April 1, 1952; because the Bedouin-Arab had been transferred to the *siag* region prior to this date, they lost their lands even when possessing proof of ownership (Yiftachel, 2004). Thus the Bedouin-Arab lands became "empty" and open for Jewish settlement. Indeed, the current legal construction of the Bedouin-Arab as "trespassers" on their own lands is a consequence of legislation and legal practices that presuppose that the lands were empty. Moreover, because the land was administered by worldwide Jewish organizations for the Jewish state, nationalized land meant exclusive Jewish access.

Because the relationship between the new state and the Bedouin-Arabs was not clear, an area was allocated to the Bedouin-Arab, and a military appointed for it, extending from Dimona and Arad to the Kibbutzim Shoval and Mishmar HaNegev. The Bedouin-Arab were allowed to migrate to seasonal grazing sites in the region, but patterns of grazing, particularly the movement, duration, and type of livestock, were increasingly restricted by government regulation. This radically affected the main source of their economy, and was a major factor leading to the gradual process of sedenterization. In addition to the traditional tents, the Bedouin-Arab started to establish tents that were wood-framed, well-fastened, and covered with thick cloth. Next, the Bedouin-Arab started to build tin huts and even houses made of stones. After some years, spontaneous and unplanned villages came into existence. No streets were planned, and no areas were allocated for public institutions. Many of these villages continue to be unrecognized by the Israeli authorities.

Life can be difficult in these villages: there may be no electricity, no running water, and no sewage systems. Garbage may accumulate near houses, and sewage may flow close by. Villages can be very crowded and may lack basic health and medical services. Transportation to schools is not always available, and children may have to walk long distances. Nevertheless, many Bedouin-Arabs prefer to go on living in these villages. Most would like the government to recognize these villages and offer basic services. Some political authorities worry that recognizing these villages is tantamount to rewarding those who—in the eyes of the Israeli state—violated laws and built unlicensed houses. Moreover, the narrow roads and the villages' lack of accord with urban planning, the argument goes, makes it difficult to plan, pave roads, and install other infrastructure according to established standards.

The Bedouin-Arab have submitted over 3,200 legal claims for the disputed land, but to date, 95% of these claims have not been settled (Almi, Dloomi and Sawalha, 2006; Yiftachel, 2004). Many Bedouin-Arab who moved to the recognized townships continue to hold claims. However, the Israeli government effectively withholds services as a tool of coercion to those who refuse to relinquish a presence on their land. Bedouin-Arab who move to the townships are forced to choose between receiving a house and access to basic infrastructure (namely water and electricity), and retaining any presence on previously held lands. Because of this precondition, most of the Bedouin-Arab who moved to these towns were landless farmers who had lived under the protection of other tribes for generations.

The Israeli state construed Bedouin-Arab settlement on a large area in the Beer-Sheva sub-district as spontaneous, unplanned, and an obstacle to governmental plans for the region's economic development and Jewish-dominated demography. The government has wanted residents of these unrecognized villages to move to those enjoying official state recognition. Here has been a crucible of power, identity difference, politics, and resistance. Successive governments have attempted to champion the movement of Bedouin-Arab to recognized villages, and have gradually, and usually reluctantly, agreed to recognize sporadic unrecognized villages as recognized. But disagreements have persisted regarding levels of compensation, where to move and—among many Bedouin-Arab—why a move should be proposed, given their historic claims to land tenure. Moreover, integration within recognized villages may be impeded by competing tribal status. Additionally, some Bedouin-Arab in unrecognized villages fear that recognized villages may be antagonistic to traditional Bedouin-Arab culture, which is based on a close association with the land (Shamir, 1996). These reservations are not without cause. Settlement has been associated with changes in tribal life, particularly the reduction of Sheikh and paternal power and the increase of individual over historic group orientation. Women's status has likewise changed, with growing numbers of women seeking employment outside the home and younger women seeking high school and post-secondary education. However, as proponents of settlement point out, these phenomena, particularly women's education, have also occurred among communities in unrecognized villages.

Further elaboration on the development of Bedouin-Arab towns and villages bear comment. Beginning in 1966, the Israeli government actively sought the establishment of planned Bedouin-Arab villages, and for the next ten years, the government established seven recognized Bedouin-Arab villages and towns: Tel-Sheva, Rahat, Ksaifa, Hura, Arara, Laqia, and Segev Shalom—all in the areas of Beer-Sheva and Arad. Tel-Sheva was the first Bedouin-Arab village established according to decisions of the government. This was a modest and problem-fraught beginning, mainly because Bedouin-Arab communities were not involved in the town's planning. Planners did not understand that the Bedouin-Arab attribute special importance to tribal relations and did not plan separate neighborhoods for different tribes. Moreover, houses were not built to the scale with which the Bedouin-Arab were accustomed; they felt crowded, with insufficient numbers of rooms for large families and no separate receiving rooms for men and women in accordance with cultural customs.

These mistakes were avoided in planning Rahat, now the country's largest Bedouin-Arab town, when it was established in 1972. This town was clustered into distinct zones according to tribal status. Community members were given the chance to build their own houses and to plan them according to their needs and financial capacities. Each sector has its own schools and shops and the downtown core had common institutions such as the town hall, banks, and the town market.

In Rahat there is a municipality, while the rest of the villages are operated by local councils. In all of the villages but Arara, the area of the village or town is less than 10,000 acres. Rahat and Tel-Sheva, the oldest, are very crowded: 3.77 and 2.26 people per acre respectively. In other villages, the situation is better: 0.58 and 0.87 people per acre in Ksaifa and Arara. In addition, there are 46 unrecognized villages according to the Regional Council of the Unrecognized Villages. These villages are not included in the statistics of the Central Bureau of Statistics as they are not licensed by the authorities.

The number of Bedouin-Arab in the Beer-Sheva district increased from 85,700 in 1995 to over 160,000 in 2004. A little over 50% of this total live in the region's seven recognized villages: a population that increased from 47,500 to 82,700—approximately 74%—in this same period. The Bedouin-Arab community in the Negev has a large proportion of youth. The percentage of children up to 4 years old is 25%, compared to 10.3% in the general population. The percentage of elderly among the Bedouin-Arabs is 1.3% compared to 9.8% in the general population. Over 50% of the population of recognized localities is under the age of 17(Statistical Yearbook of the Negev Bedouin, 2004, p. 185), while in Rahat, 62% of the population is under the age of 18.

Impact of Modernization on Indigenous Peoples

Often, the impetus for change to a state society involved some form of colonization: the application of 'modern' techniques, methods, ideas and understandings to all aspects of life. The Bedouin-Arab, like many other indigenous societies world-wide, have been subject to modernization. What occurs is first and foremost economic, entailing changes in lifestyle (for example nomadic to sedentary), agricultural practices, and participation in labour and commodity markets. The implications cover all aspects of life, and in every person and community experiencing it, modernization causes a constant re-negotiation and redefining of cultural values. The sorts of grand patterns that scholars tend to look for are true. But modernization—one of these patterns— is best understood as an ideal type: an abstraction that captures some of reality, in its broadest sweep, but never all of it in its nuanced details. Individual lives move within these grand terms, but the pace of change may be more subtle: incremental, subject to myriad gradations and shifts, and potentially inside or outside the abstraction at any point in time. The following pages need to be understood in these respects.

Traditional methods of obtaining food, livelihood, social structure, governance, and healing may be discouraged or unrecognized by the dominant colonizing paradigm. The implications can be profound; as Kunitz (2000) states, "wherever there is evidence in the contemporary world, indigenous people who have been incorporated into the state have lower life expectancy, lower income, and worse health than non-indigenous inhabitants of the same state" (p. 1531).The imposition of foreign understandings and ways of life may affect cultural identity, mental health and overall well-being of indigenous people Godoy et al. (2005). When one culture has been oppressed (which occurs when the values of one culture are seen as better than the values of another), the people of that culture feel the effects of that oppression in ways which affect their mental health, and thus perceived identity and overall-well being (Williams, Yu, Jackson & Anderson, 1997).

The Bedouin-Arab of the Negev are disadvantaged citizens in Israel (Dloomy, Almi, & Sawalha, 2006). They are dispossessed of much of their traditional lands. Many, particularly those living in (unrecognized) villages that are not officially sanctioned by the Israeli state,, struggle to receive basic services such as "running water, electricity, garbage collection, proper education, and social services", and are "living under the continuous threat of home demolition, crop destruction and displacement" (Dloomy, Almi, & Sawalha, 2006, p. 4).

But the world over, the Middle East included, indigenous people have experienced "a resurgence of indigenous consciousness, political mobilization, and cultural renewal," (Hall & Nagel, 2000, p. 1295) and this often occurs in response to the harmful effects of colonization. Indigenous communities in all parts of the world: Africa, Australia, North, Central, and South America, the Middle East and Southeast Asia are claiming entitlement to land and control over political rights and economic resources, often with a measure of success (Hall & Nagel, 2000; Nagel, 1996; Wilmer, 1993). In the Negev, the Bedouin-Arab continue to claim land and political and economic self-determination from the Israeli government (Dloomy, Almi, & Sawalha, 2006). Yet social development, including the administration and delivery of social welfare services for indigenous peoples, has had mixed success (Bending, 1997; Neutze, 2000).

Economy

The Bedouin-Arab have always relied on several sources of livelihood. Traditional means centered around raising animals in semi-nomadic contexts;

searching for water for their herds of sheep, goats, and camels part of the year while remaining stationary for the rest of the year to pursue agriculture—mainly rain-fed cereal crops. Indeed, British Mandate data notes that the Bedouin-Arab planted over 1 million dunam of wheat in the Negev in 1947 (Maddrel, 1998). Other activities, now a distant historical recollection, included caravan escort, protection-fees paid by farmers on the desert frontier, raiding on other Bedouin-Arab tribes/clans, and smuggling (Ginguld et al, 1997, p. 58). Many of today's Bedouin-Arab, particularly those living on the periphery of established villages or in unrecognized villages, continue to herd animals (Abu-Rabia, 1999). But most are trying to integrate into the mainstream Israeli economy. To that end, the government was never particularly committed to training the Bedouin-Arab or providing the necessary capital infrastructures that would lead to integration into the factories, farms, and other machinations of the economy. Most attempting to seek work within this mainstream have encountered discrimination and barriers—in relation to culture, capital, class, and training. Two anthropologists summarize the situation: "the Bedouin of the Middle East contribute their share to their countries' national economy. As pastoralists they generally earn a higher income than as peasant cultivators." Unfortunately, certain governments in the region, including the government of Israel, have sought "to settle them [the Bedouin-Arab] and to decimate their herds, causing losses to the national economy and potentially reducing the Bedouin to unemployment, poverty and despair." According to these observers, some major problems are caused by the fact that "governments often do not appreciate the Bedouin's economic contribution and do not recognize their rights to land." Deeply problematic, these dynamics in turn "cause high rates of unemployment among men and even higher ones among women" (Gardner & Marx, 2000, p. 21).

For women, the consequences of this economic modernization have often been mixed—at best. While Western perspectives may dictate that gender equality is the ideal, traditional Bedouin-Arab cultural perspectives exist within a completely different context, and women's traditional roles – though not equal – may be valued by the whole community. Modernization has changed the gendered roles of the Bedouin-Arab, and these constructions are constantly evolving. And so the following comments on traditional conceptions of gender need to be understood in these highly fluid terms. Traditional conceptions of gender hold women, responsible for rearing animals, utilizing the by-products for home use and consumption, and caring for family members. A woman would often pass down to subsequent generations the skills of embroidery and rug making: important sources of additional familial income. She could be a valued member of society due to her active participation in all phases of home life, and her status could be commensurate to her input. In the modern economic system, many women have not had the same economic opportunities, particularly in relation to workplace participation outside of the home. Women's status has been significantly affected, and although the effects are largely adverse, this is not always the case. Settlement and wage labour have increased sexual segregation but have also increased many women's access to other women. As men have had to go outside the home to earn a living and are away from the home most of the day, women have devised a close network of relations. These networks are utilized for information on good marriage prospects for children, mutual support, friendship, and solidarity, as well as good relations within the extended family, tribe and community.

Unemployment rates among the Bedouin-Arab of the Negev are among the highest in Israel, estimated at more than 55% of the adult labour force: 34% of men and 80% of women are unemployed (Hasson and Swirski, 2006). A variety of factors may be associated with the higher rates of unemployment among women: lower aggregate educational achievement, traditional cultural proscriptions against working outside the home, and prohibitions on traveling outside of their immediate communities. Among men, the rate of self-employment is low (approximately 8% of workers) and most Bedouin-Arab, who are employed (57%), work in the city of Beer-Sheva (Abu-Saad & Lithwick, 2001). In Rahat, one of the country's most prosperous Bedouin-Arab towns, close to 20% of the male population is unemployed and registered at the government's National Insurance Institute.

Family

The following paragraphs analyze gender differences in traditional Bedouin-Arab society. Modernization is profoundly important to our narrative. Social structures are being modified rapidly by virtue of exposure to mainstream Israeli society, to modern economic systems, and to education and cultural influences. Family structures of course change over time and place. At the same time, there are several comments that bear emphasis in relation to traditional notions of family and related constructions. Age and gender have been important factors in determining external and internal boundaries. While a teenage boy may easily socialize with peers outside of the home, many females in a traditional context may not be allowed as many freedoms. Within the family itself, a mother or grandmother may act as a mediating influence upon social roles. For example, either may strongly dissuade a teenage daughter from wearing certain clothing or these women may help form family coalitions in order to mobilize family pressure. But family dynamics are intricate, and leverage points are essential. The same daughter, for example, may enlist a mother or grandmother to mediate between her and her father in order to convince the father to agree to an activity the daughter wants to undertake. The mother may be traditionally perceived as the emotional hub of her nuclear family, responsible for nurturing her husband and children. While wielding tremendous emotional power and often acting as the relational and communication link between father and children, she may often have, in traditional contexts, little expressed and explicit public power and authority and may defer to her husband, his parents, and the elders in the husband's extended family. Also in a traditional context, women's social status may be strongly contingent upon being married and rearing children, especially boys. Sons contribute to a woman's social status and to her economic well-being throughout her life. Thus, the presence of boys and expectations for future good fortune, for some, are inextricably linked. According to traditional cultural values, having few sons or an inability to have sons is always the fault of the mother rather than the father. In the case of traditional divorce, the husband is entitled to custody of all of the children, irrespective of their ages. As a result, many women may endure undesirable marital situations rather than be separated from their children. A divorced woman in a traditional context also knows that she may only marry again as a second, third, or fourth wife, or as the wife of an old man.

The family is considered to be sacred to Bedouin-Arab life and is the locus of decision-making for major life events (e.g., who to marry, where to live, choice of groom, what career to pursue). Health and psychosocial problems may be collectively articulated and resolved within the family structure. To the outsider, roles within families and between family members and their environment may appear rigid and inflexible: a family may appear to put up a "defense mechanism" and may initially view outsiders with suspicion and as an intrusion. Although family structures, like other social relations in Bedouin-Arab society, may be authoritative and hierarchical, helping professional concepts may be misapplied. Take the notion of closed and open families: if practitioners/researchers proceed with unchecked biases, they could wrongfully infer a family as "closed," meaning that a family has strict regulations limiting transactions with the external environmental, incoming and outgoing objects, information, and ideas. In point of fact, however, Bedouin-Arab families may be far more "open" (i.e., more accepting of external influences) than considered. Two examples of this are the acceptance of primary, secondary, and higher education for children (occasionally regardless of gender), as well as the recognized value of outside personnel such as social workers.

In this same traditional context, a Bedouin-Arab man is often the dominant figure, and the women and younger men in his family are in some instances expected to obey him unquestionably. A family's honour depends, to a great extent, on the modest behaviour and chastity of the women in his family. This notion of "women's honour" (*Ard*) is deeply rooted to Islam and Bedouin-Arab culture and has resulted in traditions of secluding women and of vigorously defending their honour at all times. A man of honour is a person who no one has dared to disgrace by compromising the honour of his wife or daughters, meaning that this man, his fathers, and his grandfathers have been strong enough to prevent others from stealing their property or raping the women that belong to their tribe. Bedouin-Arabs believe that it is possible to wipe away every stain of dishonour or shame, but that of *'ard* is never wiped clean (Abu-Lughod, 1985a; Arad, 1984; Dodd, 1973; Ginat, 1987; Peristiany, 1974). Language is a useful way of further understanding these concepts. The Bedouin-Arab use the word *harim* (literally translated as the women's part of the house) to name women; while another term used to identify women is *mahram* (literally, "the women's section of the tent"). All of these words are derivatives of the Arabic word *haram*, namely, forbidden.

Historically, the Bedouin-Arab woman experiences three different stages in her life. From the age of 10 up until she is married, a Bedouin-Arab girl would often not be allowed to have social relations outside her family's home. Once she is married, the woman's relations would extend to her husband's family. When she grows old and is post-menopausal (i.e., when she cannot give birth and is no longer considered to be "dangerous") she would gradually become more autonomous and would be able to receive guests when her husband and sons were away (Al-Krenawi, 1996; Mass & Al-Krenawi, 1994). Women would commonly be taught these principles throughout childhood and would be expected to adhere to them as they grow up (Ben-David, 1981; Lewando-Hundt, 1984; Al-Krenawi, Maoz, & Riecher, 1994). Despite the highly differentiated sex roles, Bedouin-Arab women may utilize their power in a variety of ways: to gain access to and transfer information, and as they mature, they might use their role within the family as "power" over their children. Women tend to have limited access to some economic resources. Power may be based in and exercised from the domestic sphere, but it can be used to influence events and persons beyond the immediate circle.

The status of some Bedouin-Arab women has improved in the Negev. Some are now able to enlarge the circle of their social relations by taking part in activities outside of their homes, such as dealing with family health problems and taking their children to clinics. Women tend to go to these clinics early, and while waiting they have the opportunity to communicate with others (Al-Krenawi, 1996; Mass & Al-Krenawi, 1994). For the most part, however, women are often still restricted by their traditional roles.

As for an individual's psychosocial development, strongly paternalistic and authoritarian family structures in some Bedouin-Arab communities have been described as emphasizing conformity, rather than independent thought and creativity. From early childhood, the individual learns that knowledge and wisdom are passed on by the old to the young, and not vice versa. This viewpoint is expressed in numerous fables and sayings, such as "Wisdom is found among adults," or "Anyone who is a day older than you in age is a year older than you in understanding" (Al-Krenawi & Graham, 1999a). Thus, conformity, rather than independent thought and creativity, may commonly predominate.

Marriage

Marriage in traditional Bedouin-Arab society is based upon an agreement between two families, not just between the married couple. As a result of the marriage process, there are many factors involved in choosing a partner, such as the status of the girl's family, particularly the wealth and social status of a girl's father and brothers. Bedouin-Arab Muslims are in some instances encouraged to marry and have children as early as possible. The couple may know each other prior to marriage, but cannot be together without a chaperone prior to their marriage. There is usually no period of dating or courtship, as in the Western tradition, nor is "love" seen as a prerequisite for marriage. In fact, as Denny (1988) states: "romantic love is regarded as a feeble basis for something as important as marriage. The Muslim view is that love should grow after marriage but at the outset the most important basis for marriage is made of commitment, honour, mutual respect and friendship" (p. 301). Courtship, engagement, and the marriage process vary among Bedouin-Arabs in the Middle East. In some areas cultural mediators are used to go between the two families, while in other places, the groom's family may independently ask the girl's parents for their daughter's hand in marriage.

The dowry would be common to most courtships leading to marriage (in Arabic the *"mahr"* or *"Siag"*). This involves creating an agreement about the sum of money that the groom's parents will pay to the bride's family. The sum varies from family to family and is based upon hierarchy in the blood relationship. The agreed amount (*mahr*) is stipulated in the marriage contract and is given directly to the bride's family at the time of the marriage. It should be noted that mediators also take part in the process of determining the amount of the *mahr*. Women do, however, often have a great deal to say about the marriage of others and often initiate marriage proceedings and prepare the groundwork for the formal arrangement between the two families. However, the woman's intervention in such a process is frequently done behind the scenes.

Types of Marriages in Bedouin-Arab Society

Most of the marriage systems in the Middle East are endogamous. Women may be considered to represent the family's purity, its lineage and tribe, and as symbols of honour, women are protected and guarded by men. Retaining women within the group would be a major way to maintain this traditional notion of protection. As a result, traditional marriages may be arranged for girls by parents or parent-substitutes; prior consultation may be limited, and in some cases marriage may be against her objections. One type of marriage is the Exchange Marriage ("*Badal*"), which occurs when two men are married to each other's sisters. Inter-familial, intra-*hamula* marriages may occur when a man is persuaded to marry a woman from his extended family. This may occur if someone from another tribe wants to marry a woman of the tribe but is considered by the extended family to be unsuitable or of lower status. The family members might then try to find a man from within the extended family or the tribe to marry the woman instead. By accepting such a marriage, the family member solves the family's problem. Another type of marriage is "*Attia*," often involving the marriage of cousins, which may involve male family members determining which children will marry whom when the latter are still children.

Even though males in traditional Bedouin-Arab society may have a commitment to marry their female relatives, whether or not they love them, they may seek to marry another wife. The main goal of this polygamous relationship would be to keep both women within the extended family and tribe, preserving dignity and family honour. In instances of more than one wife, multiple households may co-exist within common or separate physical structures. The significance of polygamist marriage structures for professional helping theory and practice are considerable, and are the subject of a subsequent chapter.

Parent Child and Sibling Relations

In traditional Bedouin-Arab families, the father's primary role is to carry out familial leadership and decision making. In contrast, the traditional mother's role is to educate, nurture, rear, and care for the children. Children are required to show respect for parents and relatives through obedience and submission, and to meet the expectations of parents, the extended family, and the wider community. It should be noted that in the Bedouin-Arab family unit, as is common in other Arab communities, the child's relatives may take an active part in their education and rearing.

Different gender constructions typify traditional societies. Boys may be expected to be strong, brave, intelligent, obedient, submissive, and respectful towards parents and relatives and caring towards all family members. Girls in this traditional context and representing the family's honour, would often be obedient, submissive, helpful to her mother, and would behave always in a way that protects family honour. Girls may be allowed to show feelings (e.g., by crying) and emotions (e.g., fear), while boys may not.

As is common in traditional Arab society, generally, and in traditional Bedouin-Arab families, age and gender—rather than ascribed or earned qualifications—tend to influence the type of relations that occur between brothers and sisters. The older brother may be more dominant than his younger brothers and sisters, and boys in general often have more power in the family than their sisters. The older brother may be expected to take care of his younger brothers and sisters throughout their life span, not just when they are young, and boys may be expected to care for their sisters in the family. The older brother may also be important as a role model for his younger siblings, and when his father is away, the elder son would often be expected to take the role of family patriarch. Gender socialization tends to be segregated to each sex.

Self in Relation to Group

The concept of the unindividuated self (the psychological autonomy and individuation that many Western psychosocial theories describe) bears only limited relevance to the common pattern of psychosocial development in traditionally collectivist Bedouin-Arabic cultures. The Bedouin-Arab's identity in this traditional context is often strongly derived from the family; self-concept is enmeshed in the family concept, and an individual's needs, attitudes, and values stem from those of the family. Thus, if a family member contradicts social norms, the entire family may be shamed, whereas if a family member is successful in professional or remunerative terms, it is to the credit of the entire family. As the typical concept of self in Bedouin-Arab communities is vastly different from that of a Northern context, the implications for professionals in the helping fields are considerable.

Emotions in traditional Bedouin-Arab society may not be outwardly expressed by adults. For example, family members may avoid expressing negative emotions such as anger or jealousy. Other emotions may be expressed through acting out behaviours away from the attention of others or through body language. Communication styles may be restrained, impersonal, and formal rather than overt, personal, and expressive. The implications for helping professional practice are profound, as future chapters elaborate.

While growing up in a Bedouin-Arab family, one of the dilemmas individuals may invariably experience is the choice between conformity versus self-serving objectives. This dynamic is especially present in, but is not restricted to, those in adolescence and early adulthood. When individuals adopt the conformist choice, they may accept support provided by the family and social environment in exchange for realizing a more pronounced expression of individuality. If individuals make a self-serving choice, they assert the right of self-expression and personal decision, but social support provided by the family and traditional community may be reduced. From early childhood, traditional social norms of Bedouin-Arab society may condition the individual towards choices that are seen as conforming to family and community norms. Pragmatism is often valued over idealism, and life activity may be focused on the present time. Furthermore, unlike Western notions of being the master of one's own fate, the Bedouin-Arab belief is that one is not in ultimate control. Individuals are always an integral part of the larger encompassing universe that has authority over them.

HELPING PROFESSIONAL SERVICES

Those Bedouin-Arab villages that are officially recognized by the Israeli state have social service infrastructures that nonetheless tend to receive less funding than those within mainstream Israeli communities. Some recognized villages have social services, but community access to services and community expectations can vary. A 2004 survey of 376 Bedouin-Arab women in various communities in the Negev revealed an association between levels of education and awareness of health, mental health, and social services. Availability of and accessibility to these helping professional services is higher in recognized villages, where the service providers are situated, than in unrecognized villages where they are not. Not surprisingly, the survey revealed that women in recognized villages tended also to be more aware of, and utilized helping professional services more frequently than, their counterparts in unrecognized villages. The survey also revealed that women whose economic status was higher tended to utilize services less, and that satisfaction and economic status are positively correlated.

Mental health services require particular attention. A very small proportion of the 376 sample utilize these services, and most expressed dissatisfaction. These services are associated with particularly high levels of stigma, and their underutilization is confirmed by research in other parts of the Arab world, where mental health services tend to be associated with stigma and tend to be underutilized. What, then, do the Bedouin-Arab look for when they seek helping professional services? Instrumental assistance and concrete advice tend to be among service users' major expectations. Subsequent chapters in this book will examine specific strategies that have been used in the field in order to make helping professional services less culturally oppressive and more accessible and meaningful to users.

There are several basic health and sanitation problems in unrecognized localities. There is no waste management infrastructure and as a result, waste accumulates outside of the residents dwellings. No organized garbage collection results in disease-carrying pests, such as mosquitoes, flies, wasps, dogs, snakes, rodents, and cockroaches. Many residents choose to burn their solid waste and because they burn organic and inorganic wastes together, a range of potent toxic chemicals are released into the air – causing an elevated proportion of respiratory diseases in these villages (Almi, 2003). Unrecognized villages also lack sewage systems, and consequently residents have resorted to cesspits a short distance from their homes. Unrecognized villages are not connected to clean water supplies. Many residents suffer from dehydration or stomach infections from unclean water. Water must be obtained from storage containers, which they must refill at points at some distance from their residence. Others absorb the cost for independent water connections (Almi, 2003). Unrecognized villages are not connected to the national electricity grid. Residents often purchase generators at their own cost, which are operated in the evenings. Many homes do not have refrigerators or most types of electric devices (Almi, 2003). There are also environmental and health problems caused by industry. Several unrecognized Bedouin-Arab villages are located in close proximity to Ramat Hovav, Israel's major chemical industry center, and the toxic waste from this facility has caused major health problems for this population, including cancer and birth defects. In 2002 the Israeli authorities began aerially spraying pesticides on Bedouin-Arab crops located on what they claimed as illegally cultivated land (Almi, 2003). These health and sanitation problems common to Bedouin-Arab villages call for increased helping professional services pertaining to these specific needs: particularly public health services.

Laws and Courts

Over the centuries, Bedouin-Arabs in traditional, nomadic contexts would not have had police, courts, written laws, and other instruments of social control that exist in contemporary modern life. They created, as useful proxy, traditions that are still practiced to the present time: even in a modern country like Israel, the legal system and the traditional means of conflict resolution co-exist. Traditional Bedouin-Arab conflict resolution includes traditional judges who bear verdicts based on community norms and precedents. Complainants bring their own witnesses and evidence, and swear an oath of truth to Allah. There are also elaborate systems of informal community mediation, conducted by tribal leaders, which will be discussed in a subsequent chapter.

The Educational System of the Bedouin-Arab Society in the Negev

The creation of Israel in 1948 had profound implications for educational delivery among Bedouin-Arab of the Negev. Since 1948, most Bedouin-Arab who remained in the Negev attended schools in close geographic proximity to their communities. A 1960 study indicated that 8 out of 9 schools that Bedouin-Arab children attended were built near the encampments of tribal sheikhs. These sheikhs headed committees to raise funds for and to administer the construction of the buildings. The number of Bedouin-Arab students increased commensurate with population growth; in 1950/51 there were 360 students, 100% of whom were boys. These numbers increased to 556 in 1960/61, 2,659 in 1970, 10,356 in 1980, and 35,125 in 1997/98; while the percentage of boys gradually dropped to 91% in 1960, 77% in 1970, 67% in 1980, to 54% in 1997/98 (Abu-Rabia, 1999).

More recent years have seen the growth of post-secondary educational attainment. Between 1998 and 2003, the number of Bedouin-Arab students at the region's major post-secondary institution, Ben Gurion University (BGU) tripled, from 108 to 345. Comparable increases have occurred among female students, leading to the point of near parity with men by 2003. Currently 58% of the Bedouin-Arab students enrolled at BGU are studying for their BA degree, 12% for a Masters level degree, and only 2% for a doctoral level degree.

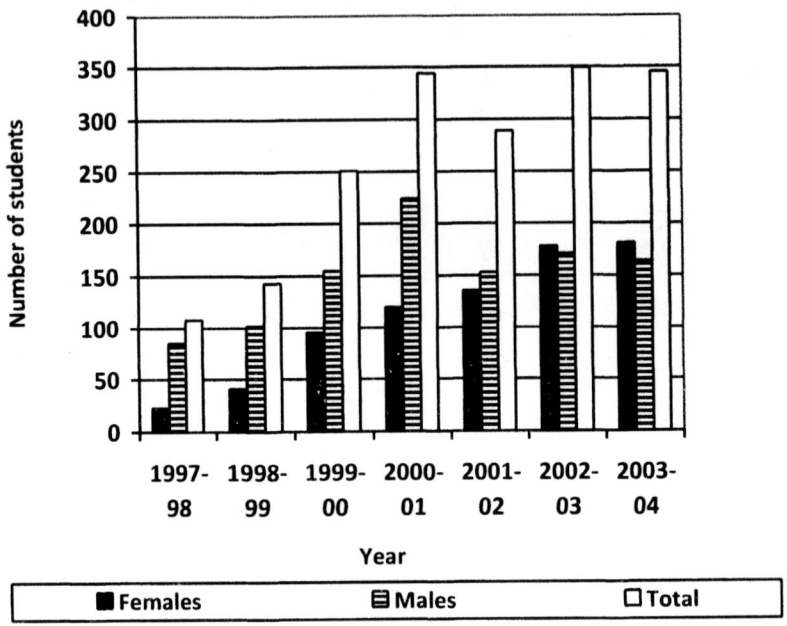

Bedouin students enrollment in degree programs, 1997-2004

Taking secondary and post-secondary graduation as a whole, while the proportion of Bedouin-Arab women in school has increased, a greater proportion of men continue to graduate from high school and to attend higher education than women; in 1997/98, 39% of the Negev's Bedouin-Arab graduating grade 12 were female, and 62 male students as opposed to 10 females were enrolled at BGU between 1995 and 1999. However, in 2003-04, there were 424 Bedouin-Arab students at BGU, and 51% were female. These numbers ought to be looked at critically; women tend less than men to study outside the Negev region; and these numbers capture all university enrolment—from educational certificates, to preparatory programs, through to the PhD; thus, even though, overall, 51% of students are women, it is likely that most of those enrolled in the highest educational programs are still male. Further, drop-out rates continue to be significant within the community. The Negev Bedouin-Arab have the highest primary and secondary dropout rate in the country (37%) and the lowest scores on high school matriculation examinations (Ministry of Education and Culture 2004).

Questions of educational quality have been raised within the past 10 years. In a survey of the Bedouin-Arab educational system in the Negev conducted by Abu-Rabia, Al-Bador, and El-Atawna (1996), it was found that schools in the Bedouin-Arab sector are below the acceptable standards of schools in Israel, and the situation was found to be markedly worse in the unrecognized villages. The schools in these villages consisted of shacks or huts without electricity or established water sources; many were wanting of the most basic supplies as well as books, laboratories, libraries etc. Many unrecognized villages lack educational institutions altogether, and the distance from these communities to local schools in recognized villages has prevented students from attending school on a regular basis. A lack of teachers and educational personnel in Bedouin-Arab society is an additional matter that post-secondary institutions such as BGU have attempted to address through recruitment and retention of Bedouin-Arab students.

CONCLUSION

Bedouin-Arab society has undergone some dramatic changes during the last century that have impacted all areas of social and personal life. Traditionally nomadic, more and more Bedouin live in an urban, sedentary society where modern norms and traditional ways intersect. Cultural awareness and sensitivity on the part of helping professional personnel can help to create positive alliances and ameliorate some of the negative effects of these social changes. Chapter three will discuss several case studies that highlight how culturally competent approaches can occur.

Chapter 3

INDIVIDUAL, GROUP, AND FAMILY INTERVENTIONS IN BEDOUIN-ARAB SOCIETY: CASE VIGNETTES

INTRODUCTION

This chapter examines three case vignettes, each of which illustrates individual and family interventions among Bedouin-Arab communities in the Negev. The case studies integrate modern professional helping principles with Bedouin-Arab cultures, including traditional healing systems. The first case is of a man (M.) who is initially misdiagnosed by the modern helping system and after collaboration with the traditional healing system, is provided help that improves his situation. We then look more closely at a clinical intervention involving the intricacies of how professional and cultural canons may clash through the prism of gender, and how practitioners may effectively resolve these clashes. The final case involves group intervention with several widowed women. That case, like the others, highlights the significance of group identity as well as cultural and religious traditions as meaningful to client systems.

CASE ONE

The first case begins by describing a male Bedouin-Arab psychiatric patient who was initially misdiagnosed and treated as a paranoid schizophrenic. The modern mental health care system correctly understood the "form" of the patient's symptoms: auditory and visual hallucinations. It did not however appreciate their "content," or cultural significance. The patient had unresolved anger toward his family which manifested in an angry exchange with his mother. This exchange created guilt and the belief that the patient had sinned against God and was possessed by demons. A psychiatric social worker was able to reconcile the patient with his mother and to incorporate a traditional Bedouin-Arab healer, the Dervish, to exorcise the patient. The patient was cured by the Dervish, re-diagnosed as a neurotic by the modern system, and continued successfully with both systems for several months in follow-up treatment before being discharged. The case study provides excellent insight into the integration of biomedical helping systems (both primary and psychiatric health care) with such cultural systems as traditional healing.

The patient, M., is a thirty-one year old male, married, without children, and a life-long resident of the Negev. Although uneducated, he is articulate and intelligent. His family has no reported history of psychiatric illness. M. is the youngest of six children (three brothers and three sisters, himself included), all of whom are married. His father is deceased. His mother, age sixty, is healthy. All children live near their mother in one of the Bedouin-Arab settlements in the Negev, Israel. M. and his wife live with M.'s mother.

M. described what appeared to be a dysfunctional family background. His father used to hit his mother; this angered him and his brothers, who usually sided with the mother, but they did not dare intervene. M.'s relationship with his father was one of ambivalence. Though the father was a difficult person, and sometimes even cruel, M. felt that his father was also good to him because he was the youngest in the family. The relationship between the brothers was cooperative and cohesive. They all felt that their mother was the most important person in the family, even though she was quiet and attended to her activities without attracting attention to herself.

M. described himself as disciplined and as a conformist—that is, he always did what his parents expected of him. M. was a shepherd from an early age. He stated that he often had to face difficult and frightening situations (e.g. sleeping alone in the fields). As a youngster, though, he was not allowed to express his fears, non-emotive strength being a gendered expectation within Bedouin-Arab culture. Prior to coming to the mental health clinic, the patient was never physically or mentally ill.

When M. reached the age of twenty, his father died of a heart attack. This was very hard on M. even though he felt ambivalent towards his father. After his father's death, the family sold their sheep and moved to another Bedouin-Arab settlement. The brothers moved out on their own and M. continued to live with his mother in their new home. M. felt that it was his responsibility to continue living in his father's home. As he noted, his relationship with his mother had always been very good, and he tended to identify himself as a favoured child.

From the time he was fifteen years old, M. wanted to marry a girl (a distant family member) whom he loved, but her parents disapproved since they had promised that she would marry another distant cousin. This issue created arguments between M. and the entire family, but he ultimately relented, and a year later he was matched-up by one of his brothers to another member of the tribe and married this woman the following year.

Since M. and his mother moved to a Bedouin-Arab village, 13 years ago, he had worked at any job that he could find, and continued to do so after he was married. His employment record was sporadic, with frequent bouts of unemployment, absences from work, multiple jobs, and poor job performance. His wife is described as loyal, quiet, and devoted; there appears to be little discord between M. and his wife.

The same cannot be said of M's relationship with his mother. His choices of work, his approach to work, and his small wages caused frequent arguments between M. and his mother. M.'s wife consciously did not involve herself in these disagreements. However, on one occasion, the mother's anger towards her son was displaced to the son's wife. This made M. quite angry towards his mother, so much so that he almost hit her. A few weeks after this incident, M.'s mood started to deteriorate; he became withdrawn, uncommunicative, and lacked energy, and his tribal status consequently decreased. Thus it appeared as though this one incident—the mother's displacement of anger towards M.'s wife—was the catalyst that tapped into M.'s longstanding anger towards his mother and family.

The Modern Referral

As a result of the changes in his behaviour, M. was referred by his family physician to the psychiatric ward of Soroka Hospital, the region's major health care facility. In the hospital, he was examined by a psychiatrist. M. described hallucinations of terrifying characters who were trying to hurt him. M. made little sense while trying to describe his situation, and he appeared to be in a disoriented, confused state. His physical examination and tests were within the normal range. There were no signs of alcohol or drug abuse.

The Modern Diagnosis and Treatment

The psychiatrist diagnosed M. as a paranoid schizophrenic. He was treated with anti-psychotic medication (Haldol, up to 30 mg per day) and remained under observation. The medicine helped to calm him but did nothing to eradicate his auditory and visual hallucinations; although they were less frequent, they still disturbed him and prevented him from functioning normally at home and at work.

M.'s situation attracted the attention of a Bedouin-Arab psychiatric social worker employed at the hospital. The social worker took M. on as a client, and had six sessions with M., as discussed below in condensed format from the social worker's case notes.

Session 1

I try to find out what the hallucinatory images that disturb M. are, and why those images are making fun of him. M. does not know the images or their names but he is familiar with them since they have appeared sporadically for the past six months. M. feels that they want to hurt him for not listening to them. He states: "they push me and try to force me to do what they want and if I don't comply, they shout at me and threaten me." M. starts to cry. M. continues to describe those "people" that are after him, and while doing this M. becomes restless and starts to walk around the room, agitated; apparently, the "people" have appeared in the room. He describes them as bearded and dressed in white. They don't look like ordinary people: "you cannot see them." I try to find out from M. why those "people-images" have been following him for such a long time. M. does not answer, but wants his medication and to go home. We stop but agree to meet again.

Session 2

At this meeting M. explains that these "people-images," which he describes as "demons" or *Jinn* (a spirit, vaguely feared, but not always malevolent, (Watt, 1970, p. 153), therefore distinguished from other cultural concepts of a still more pernicious possession by the devil), look like the elders of his Bedouin-Arab tribe. They shout at him and he insists that he wants to get rid of them. He states: "Sometimes they are funny and make me happy, and at other times they pressure me to do things. They force me to do things that are embarrassing, but they also prevent me from committing suicide." At the end of the session, M. admits for the first time that malevolent spirits were after him. He refuses to expand upon this comment.

Session 3

M. arrives on time at the meeting, smiling. This time he is willing to continue to discuss the "demon images." They appear to be small and amusing, but M. is afraid to laugh at them. He states that the "demon-images" chose to reside in his mind because he committed bad things. M. admits that once, before he became sick, he was out of control and cursed his mother and almost hit her. He states that he did not like to think of it because it hurt him.

It seems that M. sees the "demon images" as a punishment (an explanation a local *Dervish* had provided to M.'s brother):

Therapist: "Why did you not go to the *Dervish*?"

M: "Maybe because I ran wild at home and the family physician referred me to the mental health clinic."

We continue to discuss his relationship with his mother.

M. tells me that he loves his mother very much and because of her, he started to pray every Friday (the day in which Muslims worship communally). "The demons are trying to interrupt my prayer, but I try to concentrate on my prayers." At this point, I broach with M. the possibility of learning how to control the demons instead of them controlling him. I attempt a paradoxical cognitive maneuver, suggesting that in this session and in future sessions, he should call them when he is depressed in order for them to entertain him, rather than to make him feel oppressed. In this way, a repeated pattern involving the patient's shame-filled painful feelings may start to be broken.

Likewise, it should be remembered that the client had an obviously difficult relationship with his mother. I decide to introduce her gradually into the social work intervention; she first joins the therapy session via imaging therapy. I ask M. to close his eyes and to try to hear his mother's voice. At this point he starts to cry, to scream, and to hurt himself. While in his trance, his mother tells him that she loves him, and that she prays for him.

Session 4

This time M. arrives sharply dressed, shaved, and in a good mood. He tells me that his mother pampered him and blessed him, and he promised to listen to her, and to stay close to her. At the same time, M. presents guilty feelings and regret. It appears that M. is very child-like, enmeshed with his mother—Oedipal ties—in stages of developing independence and individualization—ties that never broke. In order to break these childlike feelings of guilt and regret towards his mother, I suggest that he work with the theory of directed imagination and role play. I ask him to imagine his mother sitting in a chair in front of him having a conversation with her. M. kisses his mother's feet (a common act of Bedouin-Arab respect for a parent), and he demonstrates a lot of emotions. M. says that since he hurt his mother, he is now punished by God, and he has asked for forgiveness because he loves and respects her. He appears to wait for punishment from his mother. He believes that if he antagonizes her, he also antagonizes God.

M. requests that his mother should help him, forgive him, pamper him, and pray for him in order that God will forgive him, and finally that the demons that have ruined his life will disappear. I suggest that we change roles, that M. should sit on the chair and play his mother's role. He takes on his mother's role, and shows a lot of anger towards M: "are you not ashamed, don't you have a conscious?" M. starts to cry and to pray to God to help him.

Session 5

As a result of those four meetings, I decide to organize a meeting between M., his mother, his brothers, and myself (since major familial decisions are made by men, the sisters were not included). M. and the mother agree to this arrangement. I arrive at their home for the fifth meeting. I am the go-between for M. and his mother. At the beginning, I converse with the mother while M. sits quietly, looking ashamed. Then he asks his mother for forgiveness for his behaviour. He declares his guilt and that his illness is his punishment. M. cries, kisses his mother's feet, and they embrace. Afterwards, the brothers and M.'s wife arrive and in their presence, he again shows remorse and regret and promises to respect his mother. The brothers show sympathy towards their brother. After we drink coffee, the mother suggests that they go see the *Dervish*, in order to open a new chapter in their life. I agree to go with them. The mother has a conversation with the *Dervish*, and arranges a meeting. She returns home, and summons everyone to the *Dervish*'s home. M. is happy to see that his mother is concerned about him.

Session 6: Meeting with a Traditional Healer

The *Dervish* greets each person as they enter his home. He gets the group to sit in a circle, lights incense, and begins the session with several prayers. These are followed by a period of deep silence. The *Dervish* then asks M. to join him in the centre of the circle, lying down on the floor. Several more prayers are said, and M. is encouraged to relax and if he felt like sleeping, to sleep.

Once M. appears to have fallen asleep, the *Dervish* creates a dramatic scene—he tries to speak to the demons, a language that no one could understand, following the *Dervish* tradition of *Tazeem* (dialogue with the spirits) in which the *Dervish* overpowers the evil spirits, and which is comparable to the Western notion of an exorcism (Sharp, 1994). The evil spirits appear resistant to this intervention, and so the *Dervish* prepares more incense, a fire, plays a drum, and starts to sing holy songs. The demons still refuse to leave M.'s body. Following the *Dervish* tradition of *Hashar Al-Jinn*, the *Dervish* puts M. on a mattress and starts to hit him with a stick while calling out "Allah Allah." M. is struck repeatedly on the foot, the site where evil spirits are thought to leave the body. M. does not appear to feel the pain because he is in a trance. Suddenly M. cries out a strange sound—this is the cry of the demons that the *Dervish* insisted should leave his body. As this is going on, the *Dervish* has a brief conversation with the demons, invoking them out of M.'s body. M. starts to shake while they leave his body.

The treatment lasts an hour and a half. Afterwards, M. is in shock but then recovers and appears to be in good spirits. The voices and the images have disappeared; it appears as though there was resolution of the patient's anger. The *Dervish* explains that the demons had entered M.'s body because he had done a bad deed. M.'s mother insists that M. should be under observation by the *Dervish* and the social worker, and both agree. The *Dervish* tells M. to continue at home with the incense as a healing process, to continue prayers, and asks him to come back. The *Dervish* also recommends a ritual to visit a saint's tomb, a site where, according to Islamic culture, healing and rejuvenation can take place (El-Islam, 1982; Eliade, 1987).

Aftercare

That month, M. continued as an out-patient with the clinic, reducing appointments to biweekly. It should be noted that the chief psychiatrist assessed M., and concluded that the initial diagnosis had been incorrect: the patient was a neurotic, and the medications that had been prescribed were inapplicable to the patient's case. M. continued with the *Dervish* on a weekly basis for two months, and subsequently returned to his normal routine and activities; thereafter, his interactions with the *Dervish* were occasional, as M. saw fit. Following the chief psychiatrist's assessment, M. had two follow-up appointments, one month and three months later, as well as a final session with the social worker. Thereafter, his visits to the mental health clinic came to an end.

Case Analysis

In the above case, the psychiatrist appears to have made an error in diagnosing M. as a paranoid schizophrenic and in treating him with antipsychotic medication. M.'s problem, it turned out, was embedded in his familial and tribal relationships. M., the youngest in his family, was always very close to his mother and emotionally dependent upon her. His relationship with his father, in contrast, had been ambivalent, given the latter's cruelties. M. was always one to give up, to compromise, and to eschew aggressive behaviour. Yet when he fell in love with a girl, he was presented with a situation requiring the ability to confront his family, particularly his father, and to advocate to the wider tribe for what he felt was right. This presented an awkward series of dilemmas. He had hoped that his mother would understand his position and ultimately advocate on his behalf, but she did neither. M. himself lacked the skills to push successfully for his own position and never broached the matter with his family's principal decision maker, his father; the one person whose tribal status might have provided sufficient leverage to change M.'s plight. The end result of losing his beloved, of not effectively preventing this loss, and of agreeing to marry a different woman, was the source of unresolved and unarticulated anger.

This anger surfaced during a stressful period of unemployment and economic difficulties. It erupted with an intensity that was out of character for M., inconsistent (as will be seen) with what he believed to be cultural norms regarding respect for his mother, and possibly in excess of the anger he felt from his current job difficulties. M. felt guilty for his anger and expected, like a child, to receive some form of punishment. However, his mother chose to ignore the incident, and thus it remained unresolved. This lack of resolution was made all the more significant, psychologically, because of M.'s long-standing unresolved anger over his marriage towards his tribe, his family, and his father in particular. Moreover, the latter was readily conjured up in light of M.'s near-violent encounter with his mother.

In this context, M. developed a psychiatric condition requiring treatment, and he exhibited symptoms that were embedded within a culturally constructed narrative (Dean, 1993; Gaines, 1992; Gergen, 1985). The social worker successfully struck a therapeutic alliance with M., and, using cognitive restructuring and role playing, allowed M. to begin to understand the significance of the "demon images" and begin to resolve his guilty feelings towards his mother. The fifth session, deliberately moved to the patient's home, allowed the patient to finally address the precipitating problem and enabled a venting of feelings, allowing reconciliation to take place.

However, had the therapy ended there, it would have been incomplete. M.'s angry, aggressive behaviour towards his mother must be understood on religious grounds. Muslims perceive respecting one's mother as a matter of particular importance, and see lack of respect as a grave sin. As the Prophet Muhammad commented on parental respect: "First your mother, second your mother, and third your mother, and then your father" (Jamal, 1974; Najati, 1993). According to Islam, paying honour to parents is thought to bring about prosperity, success, health, and happiness (Abou El Azayem & Hedayat-Diba, 1994; El-Islam, 1982):

> God said: "Serve no other gods besides Allah, lest you be despised, forsaken. Your Lord has enjoined you to worship none but Him, and to show kindness to your parents. If either or both of them attain old age with you, show them no sign of impatience, nor rebuke them; but speak to them kind words. Treat them with humility and tenderness and say: 'Lord, be merciful to them. They nursed me when I was an infant.'" (Koran, Suruh Al-Isra, v. 22-23)

In hurting his mother, M. was convinced that he had sinned against God, and God had punished him for his sins by allowing the "demon images" to control M.'s mind. This insistence upon an external locus of control is entirely consistent with the Bedouin–Arab mind-set, which perceives diseases as originating from both natural and, as in M.'s case, supernatural forces (Al-Krenawi et al., 1994; Young, 1976). Since the causes of his problems were supernatural, only someone with special supernatural powers, such as the *Dervish*, could possibly free the ill man from the demons.

This case provides several lessons. It shows that modern and traditional therapeutic models can both be used successfully, in parallel. They have the potential to be mutually complementary (Chung & Lin, 1994; Edwards, 1986; Meketon, 1982; Schwartz, 1985). True, there may be stark epistemological differences between modern and traditional systems; yet there are ways of achieving coexistence and of having one model enrich the other (Garrison, 1977; Heilman & Witztum, 1994; Ruiz & Langrod, 1976; Wessels, 1985). As the social worker demonstrated, it is possible, and clinically beneficial, for a modern practitioner to be involved with both systems—and to be a broker between them. This case demonstrates how important it is to know the patient, their background, and specifically their ethnic, religious, and cultural roots (Bilu & Witztum, 1993; Comaz-Diaz & Griffith, 1988; Ibrahim, 1985). This does not require that a professional be a cultural expert; becoming aware of cross-cultural beliefs and understandings is incremental—a life-long process that we all undertake. However, being skilled at methods of inquiry is essential. It is important to discern the patient's world view and thereby appreciate how the symptoms' forms, the hallucinations, were inextricably linked with their content (i.e., possession by the demons). Had this knowledge not been at the forefront of treatment, one wonders how—or moreover whether—the patient could have been successfully helped.

The next section provides an excellent illustration of one particularly salient professional issue that emerges when practitioners work with patients of the opposite sex. Although this issue is not restricted to practice with Bedouin-Arab patients, it illustrates the importance of understanding the cultural background of a patient and utilizing this understanding to create a positive and productive helping alliance. This example highlights the intricacies of opposite sex helping professional encounters in Bedouin-Arab society: in this case, a male clinician and female client. The effects of the conflict on the transference relationship are examined through a case presentation of a female patient, whose behaviour during therapy, the clinician had perceived to become seductive. Rules of conduct acceptable in both the professional realm and Bedouin-Arab society (e.g., maintaining a suitable distance between client and therapist) are proposed as an avenue toward resolution.

CASE TWO: ENCOUNTERS IN THERAPY

Patriarchy, a family or society in which authority is vested in males, through whom descent and inheritance are traced, can be an important aspect of Bedouin-Arab life. Bedouin-Arab women of all ages are permitted to meet men professionally in connection with health issues, and a doctor or other professional in the Bedouin-Arab settlement may refer a female client to a social

Individual, group, and family interventions in Bebouin-Arab society

worker or other mental health professional in a general health clinic for counselling. There is no restriction on therapeutic sessions with male Bedouin-Arab therapists, so long as the setting meets the requirements of the professional canon: privacy, predetermined duration, and supportive listening by the professional to the client's expression of feelings.

Halima was referred to a social worker by a clinic doctor. She had a variety of physical complaints, primarily focused around an inability to stand or walk. She described feelings of paralysis, although physical examination revealed no biological explanations for her paralysis. Halima, a divorced woman of 30 with no children, was the youngest daughter in a family of five, and had no formal education. . Her father, her stepmother, and a married brother lived in the same village, while a married sister lived outside the village.

Until the age of 15, Halima had lived in a supportive environment. The relationship between her parents was good, as was their relationship with her. Her mother was the most emotionally significant figure in Halima's childhood; she listened to Halima, supported her, and tried to back her up, even though her husband threatened to send his wife back to her family when she tried to voice an opinion in family decisions. Halima fulfilled her family's expectations and lived well.

When she was 15 years old, her father, with no explanation, gave Halima to a man of 60. She was summoned to a tent where the old man fell on her and raped her. She claimed not to have known what was happening and to have lost consciousness during the sexual act. In the morning she ran in a panic back to her father's tent and refused, despite much pressure, to return to her husband's home. At this juncture, her parents became proactive and threatening where they had previously been supportive. A year later she got a divorce, thus breaching her father's promise. This increased not only her father's disapproval, but also that of her brother and sister who taunted and belittled her.

A few years later, her mother died. Her father married a woman who was apparently mentally disturbed and who forced Halima to leave her father's house. She went to live with an uncle, her father's brother, who sometimes gave her small sums of money as charity. A few men from her tribe asked to marry her, but she refused. It was at this point that Halima began to develop physical symptoms. Her paralysis, perhaps, legitimized her dependent and debilitated status and her unsuitability for marriage.

At their first meeting, the therapist assigned to the case assured Halima of confidentiality and suggested that together they might find a way to rebuild her life. During the first few meetings, she was very withdrawn, her clothes were dirty, and she covered her face with her headveil. She did not look at the therapist, spoke very little, and answered questions only after they were repeated several times, and then only briefly. To encourage trust, the therapist set short-term goals to help her organize her life and met with her twice weekly. By arranging income maintenance and medical insurance for her, he helped her gain economic control of her life. At this point, meetings were reduced to once a week.

Halima's behaviour began to change. Her dress became neat and clean and she was more relaxed during meetings. She described her traumatic marriage in minute detail, unfolding the following sequence of events: an unforeseen marriage with no preparation and without a ceremony was consummated by a violent sexual act; as a result of this traumatic event, her trust in her father and in her family was shattered, as was her trust in men in general. Her self-esteem was badly damaged and she felt that she had become an object to be given as part of a bargain. After she left her husband, she had no emotional or financial support. All of these events led to a deep sense of loneliness and alienation.

The helping process involved much support and attentiveness by the therapist, and it provided legitimacy for her venting and expressing her anger and desperation. Gradually, she began to remove her black scarf (traditionally worn over the white scarf when going out of the house) from her head, to sit comfortably on her chair, and to look directly and often at the therapist. Later she shook hands at the beginning and end of the meeting. She gradually ignored the fact that she did not even have the white scarf that women must wear at all times on her head. This kind of behaviour is considered seductive in Bedouin-Arab social life, and it developed further, with Halima kissing the therapist's hand on entering the room while putting her other hand on his shoulder. She also brought him a valuable gold ring and, when he explained that he was not allowed to receive gifts, she merely exchanged it for a pen. This put the therapist in a difficult position: if any of these actions were seen, they would be viewed as invitations to a sexual relationship. The therapist, too, felt that seductiveness, rather than appreciation for his professional work, was the true nature of these acts.

Conflict with the Professional Canon

Violation of Social Taboo

Fifteen years of research experience and myriad conversations with practitioners and clients of social services, lead us to infer several things. Many women come to therapy following traumatic sexual experiences with men. Women who have experienced sexual violence often lose trust in everyone around them, including themselves. The harm to one's self identity is significant – one's sense of trust is a very basic necessity of development as a human being. Those that have experienced trauma typically develop social isolation, often as a defense mechanism, and, as in Halima's case, have few social supports (Herman, 1992). The support provided by the therapist is a welcome and necessary step to recovery from such an event. However, in such a patriarchal society where a woman's social status is dependent on her relationship with a man, and where women are viewed as sexual objects, Halima's initial understanding of this relationship was—to some extent invariably—a sexual one.

This situation may be not only embarrassing to the female client because she has been misled, it may also be dangerous for her. This is because there is a possibility of Halima losing the one relationship which has contributed to her healing, and also if recognized by the wider society, it could be interpreted as a violation of the social taboo against sexual relations between an unmarried couple. In traditional societies, rumours may spread quickly, and such a rumour could do enormous harm, not only to Halima, but also to the professional involved and to the profession as a whole in the Bedouin-Arab community; families would refuse to allow female clients to come for treatment.

The whole idea of therapeutic work by men with Bedouin-Arab women was thus called into question: should it be discontinued because it encouraged seduction? Should it be restructured so as to limit discussion to concrete issues only?

As a member of the Bedouin-Arab society, the male therapist understood the violation of the social canon inherent in these situations. His encounters with women stood on the thin line between modern and traditional societies: women were permitted to visit the clinic on the understanding that they went for medical treatment of physical symptoms. This permission did not encompass treatment based on close emotional ties between client and therapist. Thus the therapist felt that the professional relationship that had evolved was socially taboo. Possible explanations for this behavior are presented below. These are provided from the view of the therapist, which are then contrasted with an alternative Western psychoanalytic theory. Although other explanations are possible, they are not discussed as they were not considered in the original case.

Halima's case was representative of many of this therapist's professional encounters with women. He understood the centrality of sexual seduction in those interactions as stemming from the Bedouin-Arab social preoccupation with the danger of women's seductive powers, a preoccupation that viewed women as sex objects. The therapist indicated that this perception of women had been the central theme in Halima's trauma. As a member of the Bedouin-Arab society, the therapist saw it as part of his professional mission to change this perception. However, the avoidance of such encounters would reaffirm Bedouin-Arab social perceptions and would thus betray this mission. Avoidance, in effect, prevents both parties from properly defining the therapist/patient relationship, and as such encourages an understanding of the relationship to be guided by the perceived context. The therapist felt a professional obligation to help women receive support and understanding from a man in such a way that the helping process would not be transformed into a seductive situation.

Activities based on a canonical code are made with the tacit understanding that the rules apply to all participants. However, the perception of the therapeutic situation by the female clients may not have been the same as was intended by the therapist. Rather than regarding it as a situation in which their views and feelings were treated as significant, they may have seen it as one in which they were to offer themselves as sexual objects. Obviously, this reaction was not solely a response to the situation within the cultural context (as subjective considerations must be factored in). However the main concern here is that there is a conflict between the therapist's and patient's conduct expectations within the therapy setting. While there is overlap in either world view, and none are static; the therapist's expectations derive largely from a Western culture, while the patient's derive from largely the Bedouin-Arab culture. The process of treatment involves continuous, reciprocal dialogue between these world views such that new and shared knowledge is constantly being constructed. But this process may also generate potential misunderstandings about the therapist/patient relationship. The patriarchal system which supports the view of women as sex objects appears to both contribute to these misunderstandings, as well as contribute to the actions by men that had traumatised the women and brought them to therapy.

Role of Transference

Because the rules of professional behaviour are derived from authority rather than practical situations, the mental health professional's code of behaviour can be said to constitute a canon. While both the preset time framework and the privacy of the meetings can be explained in terms of their efficiency and confidentiality respectively, the rule of neutrality on the part of the therapist is based on a specific theoretical approach and is not, in fact, accepted by professionals who are influenced by other theoretical approaches. This is, indeed, a hallmark of a canon.

Sigmund Freud, acknowledged sexual seduction as a theme in therapy very early in his career (Breuer & Freud, 1895/1955). He often treated women who had undergone sexual trauma and sought a solution for the behaviour of a patient who perceived her relationship with him as seductive. Freud saw the use of a neutral stance as a way of discouraging such perceptions and creating a safe atmosphere for the patient, allowing for the transference of her feelings and images of a past trauma to the present relationship with the therapist. The therapist's neutrality would serve as a screen onto which the trauma was projected and could be dealt with "here and now" within the therapeutic relationship. With time, however, the relationship between the trauma and the theme of seduction became blurred, and Freud believed that the theme came to be related to the sexual fantasies of the patient (Masson, 1984).

The therapist's professional code of behaviour is designed to facilitate a transference relationship. Regular meetings of a fixed duration foster feelings of constancy and safety, while privacy encourages exclusivity and trust. These elements are necessary to such relationships. Their use in the therapeutic situation is designed to encourage primary relationships in order to elicit a patient's desires, fears, longing for images, and experiences from the past. The therapist's neutral position is designed to block the development of interpersonal relationships and to allow the patient to delve deep into their feelings and images from the past. The contribution of this concept to clinical intervention processes has been discussed by Perlman (1979) and Sterba (1948), and understanding how it applies can help to shed light on a client's method and degree of cooperation, need for excessive attention, and unrealistic expectations.

The concept of transference remains controversial, however, in terms of the degree to which it represents an exclusively intrapersonal phenomenon (i.e., a distortion of reality, internal to the patient, created by the patient's projection of feelings about a significant figure from his or her past) and the degree to which it represents an interpersonal phenomenon (i.e., one that develops within the therapist-client relationship itself, as this also involves experiences, desires, and images from the client's past) (Racker, 1968; Sandler, Dare, & Holder, 1979). This controversy was reflected in the Bedouin-Arab therapist's dilemma in his meetings with Halima and other female clients.

From this perspective, we might have made the inference that Halima's seductive behaviour was attributed to intrapersonal rather than interpersonal dynamics. In psychoanalytic terms, she experienced a sexual trauma and developed a neurotic symptom—paralysis—in reaction to it. Aside from the fact that this is a typical reaction to those suffering from post-traumatic stress disorder, in cultures which do not allow for the expression of feelings, somatic complaints are typical reactions to emotional trauma. Thus, her experience of being sexually attacked prevented her from marrying and involving herself in social relationships. This appears to be in sharp contrast to her seductive behaviour in her therapy sessions. Freud would have believed that Halima's case thus fulfilled the criteria for hysteria (Freud, 1905/1953), a condition that would explain her seductive behaviour toward the therapist as transference, an expression of intrapersonal dynamics. This explanation, however, is devoid of cultural context and may be too oversimplified and overgeneralized a concept to accurately describe the rationale behind a specific woman's behaviors in this setting.

Within the Bedouin-Arab sociocultural context, the neutral-supportive position taken by the therapist provided the scenario for Halima's behaviour because that position was an inherent violation of the social canon, as was the entire set of rules derived from the professional canon. However, the therapist, unaware that behaviors prescribed by this canon would be so incompatible with the cultural dynamics, had not realised that seduction would be an expected theme in therapist-client relationships. He assumed that the issue was specific to his own therapeutic situation and did not discuss it with anyone because of his embarrassment and fear. In all of his meetings with female clients, he struggled with the stress of the situation by "expelling Satan from the meeting," in this way paradoxically confirming the presence of Satan, and as such confirming an assumption that may not have been the only, or correct, reason.

The therapist was thus trapped in the clash between the professional canon and the social context of the Bedouin-Arab. Just as Halima's behaviour could not be understood merely as a distortion stemming from her transference relationship, so the therapist's response could not be explained merely in terms of counter transference. The therapist's understanding of the polarisation between the two canonical systems did not ultimately constitute a distortion of perception.

Mediating the Conflict

The polarisation of professional and social canons forced a choice between the two, and the Bedouin-Arab therapist ultimately chose to follow the professional code. Although he recognised that his choice violated the social canon, it affirmed his membership in a professional group and may have helped him to cope with the feeling of isolation arising from his wish to change basic attitudes in his society. When the origins of the professional canon and the central role of transference in the therapeutic relationship were clarified, he could perceive his relationship with female clients in a new light and understand that the theme of seduction was not unique to therapy with Bedouin-Arab women. By coincidence, events in his community then gave the therapist an opportunity to put his new understanding to use.

A young Bedouin-Arab woman living in the village was referred to the hospital by a male social worker in protective services after she had attempted to commit suicide by swallowing Paracetamol. She had been forced to return to her parents' home after the attempt, despite her fear of returning. She was 17 years old, belonged to a large tribe of which her father was a respected member, and had been forced by her father to marry her cousin about a year prior to her hospitalisation.

The therapist began his treatment of the girl with a home visit. He learned that she had had a romantic affair with a boy from another tribe after her marriage. He had been seen jumping from a window of her home, and members of her husband's family had caught and beaten the boy quite badly before he escaped. Her husband's family then drove her back to her father's house, and her husband immediately divorced her. This all seemed to fulfill the Bedouin-Arab proverb: *Kher Al-Hurma Iajozhi washarhi Lahalhi* ("a woman's parents get her troubles, while her husband profits from her"). She attempted suicide because she was convinced that her parents would kill her.

The protection service worker's first step was to seek police protection for the girl against her parents. Although her family members all signed a police warrant agreeing to their imprisonment if they harmed her, she was constantly threatened. Her brothers beat, tortured, and planned to kill her. The worker therefore arranged for her removal to a shelter far from her home town. After consulting the tribal leaders, who were afraid that the story would spread and bring dishonour to the family and the tribe, the girl's father took charge of her safety, brought her back to his home, and agreed to allow twice-weekly visits by the protection services worker.

The therapeutic relationship developed well, and the girl was able to express her anger towards her family and Bedouin-Arab society. During these visits, the worker learned that most of the tribe treated her with contempt and that she was afraid to leave her father's house.

After things had calmed down, her father gathered the leaders of the tribe together to ask if anyone from the tribe would be willing to marry his daughter. When it became clear than no one would, her father declared that the social worker could decide what was to be done with her. This started a rumour that the worker would marry her, and when the women of the tribe asked the girl if she wanted to marry him, she answered in the affirmative. The worker's supposed marriage proposal became the talk of the town, and a meeting of the town council was called to discuss the matter. There was public talk that the worker was to be fired for violating the ethical code.

The worker sought advice. He had never proposed marriage and viewed such behaviour as a violation of the professional code. He was debating whether to get his own tribe involved in order to protect his honour, but accepted an offer of mediation from the social worker who had been Halima's therapist. The mediator met with the members of the council and reported the protection worker's version of events, giving a brief explanation of transference relationships. He was able to convince the council that the girl's reaction was to be expected in the treatment situation and that her responses were characteristic of the therapeutic process. The fact that the deputy head and the members of the council were of the mediator's tribe was no doubt helpful in persuading them that the rules of professional activity should not be dictated by a political body. After the mediator talked to all members of the council, the subject was dropped from further discussion.

This demonstration that mediation was possible between the Bedouin-Arab social system and the professional system inspired the mediating therapist to further explore ways of bridging the gap between the professional and social canons.

Proposed Rules of Conduct for Therapy

In light of the transference process, the therapist saw that, in a society in which "Satan is invited" to every encounter between a man and a woman, the therapist's supportive and attentive position could not be neutral. Since the very encounter created a situation that endangered both the therapist and the female client, the professional canon needed a stance that would actively dispel "Satan's presence" and allow professional encounters to be based on safety and trust in the context of the social canon. After discussions with elders in his society—Sheikhs, religious leaders, and *Dervishes* (traditional healers)—the therapist developed a proposal for a set of behavioural rules. This proposal was set up in stages, with each stage leading to the next.

Stage 1: When a Bedouin-Arab woman comes for professional help, maintaining a suitable distance between client and therapist should be facilitated by avoidance of physical contact (including hand-shakes), the choice of an unprovocative sitting position by the therapist with a table set between the client and the therapist, and avoidance of frequent eye-contact with the client.

Stage 2: Once the client has provided information about her personal background and problems with her family and environment, her situation is assessed and the necessary intervention decided. At this stage, she is categorised in accordance with the social canon as a young woman (single or married), an older woman (at the age of menopause), or an old woman.

Stage 3: The professional suggests that the client think about the therapeutic relationship as that of a sister (*aocti*) and brother. This up-front clarification of the relationship reflects the social work principle of transparency, or being open, frank and candid. Thereafter, a few meetings will be suggested to discuss their difficulties. If there is any hint of courtship behaviour by the client, she will be asked whether this is appropriate behaviour for a brother and sister. To the older woman client, the relationship is clarified as that of aunt (*khalati*) and nephew, whom aunts are not permitted to think of sexually. With old women, the relationship is described as that of grandmother (*jaddah*) and grandson. Although society is not strict about meetings between men and women of this age, consistency and the use of the social codes are important.

In the Bedouin-Arab social canon, these relationships permit men and women to spend time together. By basing the therapeutic relationship on this canon, the ever-present theme of seduction in such encounters may be avoided, and the neutrality required for a professional relationship may be achieved. At the same time, the primary relationships—brother, nephew, grandchild—clarified in the proposal allow for the evolution of transference. The proposal therefore offers a solution by bridging the gap between the professional canon and the social canon.

It is too soon to report on the results of applying the proposed mediating code in therapy. However, the explication and clarification of the conflict between the professional and social canons was greeted with considerable relief by other Bedouin-Arab therapists, as was the proposal itself.

From the process described here, the significance of the authoritative element in the professional canon becomes evident. Social workers, like others in the helping professions, often underestimate the meaning that they themselves attribute to their relationships with their clients because they consider adherence to the professional canon to be the hallmark of professionalism. In ignoring their own attributions, they are likely to be ineffective in their work with clients. This is illustrated by the reaction of a female Bedouin-Arab social worker to the mediator-therapist's proposed bridging code.

The wife of one of the female social worker's clients had died suddenly and the young man had started consultations with the social worker in an attempt to rebuild his life. The meetings became quite frequent, almost every other day, and the client developed the habit of staring at the therapist, began to sit in provocative positions, and started to talk about issues irrelevant to his difficulties. The therapist realised that her client was fantasizing about intimate relations with her. She was distressed and told him: "I am a married woman and I am pregnant. I understand you and your desires but I cannot respond to you." The client's behaviour changed immediately; their meetings grew less frequent, he may have been suppressing his feelings, and he related only to concrete issues.

The worker felt uneasy, realising that she had set limits not only on the relationship but also on the help that he could get from her. Her distress was increased because she could not share her problem with colleagues who were not Bedouin-Arabs and who therefore, she believed, did not have to deal with the theme of seduction. A meeting with the therapist concerned with the cases described above was her first opportunity to discuss the matter and was her introduction to the fact that the theme of seduction was a constant in professional encounters, not only between men and women in Bedouin-Arab society but in all patriarchal cultures.

She felt that using the proposed set of rules for therapist-client encounters in therapy may have prevented the therapeutic situation from becoming a courtship. Alternatively, an understanding of the basis of transference would have enabled her to interpret the situation within the helping relationship, thus avoiding the disruption that occurred. She added that when she was single, she had been unduly rigid with her male clients because of the element of seduction—such behaviour was not in character for her and it had made her uncomfortable. This, she felt, had impaired her professionalism. To protect her family's honour she had tried to avoid working with male clients.

Final Comments

The need to adapt the professional canon to the social context within which it is applied is evident from this discussion of the violation of the social canon inherent in professional mental health encounters between women and men in Bedouin-Arab society. Because Bedouin-Arab mental health workers learn their profession outside of their social milieu, they acquire a code of behaviour that is very different from that which is dictated by their traditional social canon. The therapist who was involved, either directly or as a consultant, in the cases described here looked for a solution to the conflict rather than avoiding the complicated, even dangerous, relationships with his women clients. He felt a sense of mission to change the status of women in his society and was therefore not content to abide by a social canon that viewed these women as sexual objects. In preserving rather than denying the conflict between professional and social canons and by examining the foundations of both, he was able to work out a possible solution stemming from the social canons of his own culture that would be acceptable under both codes of behaviour.

The situational reality that develops in the therapeutic milieu should not be attributed solely to distorted perceptions. The impact of the social-cultural context on that reality must also be taken into account since the situation arises from the interaction between objective and subjective reality, as well as between knowledge and values (Hamilton, 1951). The therapist operates at the interface between subjective internal reality, expressed in the evolution of the helping relationship, and objective external reality, expressed in the sociocultural perception of reality.

The particular set of rules adopted for use in the Bedouin-Arab social and therapeutic context must be tested over time to see whether it does, in fact, facilitate professional mental health therapy in Bedouin-Arab society. It seems probable that similar adaptations would be useful in other cultural contexts where societal and professional canons are in conflict.

CASE THREE: INTERVENTION IN A GROUP CONTEXT

The final case analyzes helping professional intervention in a group setting with Bedouin-Arab widows. It provides excellent insight into the application of culturally grounded principles of practice, and demonstrates processes that can lead to effective group intervention within the Bedouin-Arab community. In Israel, Bedouin-Arab widows who have settled in villages often have few resources to sustain their well-being. The book's co-author, a Bedouin-Arab clinical social worker, set up a culturally sensitive widows' support group in a medical clinic to help these women deal with material and personal hardships. Through sharing, mutual support, and mutual helping, the goal of the support group was to empower women to deal with their grief, isolation, economic difficulties, problems with children, and negative societal attitudes. The remaining narrative is in his voice.

Among the cases that I treated were widows who suffered from economic and personal problems, physical illness (somatization), and a lack of information about their rights in the community. Other psychosocial symptoms included insomnia, loss of appetite, and bad dreams (in which their husbands wanted the women to join them: that is, to die).

In forming the therapy group, I selected candidates from tribes that had recently moved to Rahat and who had become widows before they settled in the village. In individual interviews, I determined that they could give and understand oral instructions, did not know the other potential candidates, and had not been in a therapy group before. When offered the chance to participate in a group, the women were not sure what that meant, but they agreed in principle to the framework. In the first meeting, the group decided to hold 15 weekly 2-hour sessions in the clinic and agreed that they should not bring friends to the group and that they would not convey anything that was said in the meetings to persons outside of the group. For this meeting, I provided the refreshments; in subsequent meetings the members took turns doing so.

The group consisted of 12 women aged 25-40, all of Bedouin-Arab origin, who were born in Israel. Five of the women had been widows for 3 years, four for 2 years, two for 1 year, and one for 8 months. Three had been second wives, two had been first wives to husbands who also married second wives, and seven had been the only wives of their husbands. Ten had been widowed as a result of their husbands' illnesses, and two as a result of automobile accidents. Ten of the women had received no schooling and two had finished elementary school. None were employed outside of the home. The number of children ranged from 0 to 10 per widow. As a result of the death of their breadwinner-husbands, all of the families were treated as welfare cases.

As this was the first Bedouin-Arab therapy group that I had conducted, I had several concerns. How well would the group members communicate about their own and each other's weaknesses? Would they fully reveal themselves? How would I deal with the fact that they were all women and that I was the only man in the group? I was particularly anxious to find a culturally appropriate approach that would enable the group members to trust me as a man and as a social worker. Toward this end, I decided to call the women *Yaa Khawati*, which means "my sisters" and to have them call me *Yaa Aki*, which means "my brother." These terms, and what they implied, helped me to build a close relationship with the group members by reducing Bedouin-Arab cultural suspicions about meetings between a male and females and the chance of sexual fantasies (transference) (Al-Bostani, 1988; Mass & Al-Krenawi, 1994). Because the use of the terms *sister* and *brother* approximated a quasi-familial relationship between the group members and me, it made this gender-mixed group, dedicated to the discussion of potentially intimate feelings, more acceptable to Bedouin-Arab society. Also, I suspect that because I referred to the women as my sisters, the members may have looked on me as mature, responsible, serious, and motivated to provide help.

The Group Process

Achieving the Goals of the Group

The first goal of the group therapy sessions was to address the women's material needs. The women said that their children demanded many things that their economic situation prevented them from providing, such as books and money for school trips and other activities. One woman expressed her frustration by saying, "We want help today, but nobody cares for us. Everyone takes care of his own family, and we are punished by God." The women said that their houses were barren: they had no appliances and no furniture. Because of their poverty, they attempted to live a traditional life in their modern houses. They also complained about the many things that they had to pay for, such as municipal taxes, school taxes, and medical insurance, whose reciprocal benefits appeared nebulous and, in many cases, nonexistent.

To help deal with these problems, I invited a delegate from the welfare department of Rahat to attend a meeting to inform the women about their rights to material support from the welfare department. In addition, I explained their rights in the local council, in the National Security Foundation, and in the National Health Service, and their rights to tax discounts. I also told them about school fees and discounts. As a result of this meeting, the women not only applied for and received material support from the welfare department, but they asserted themselves during the process.

The second goal was to address the problems of the widows' children. One issue that arose during the group process was the women's concern about enuresis, or bed-wetting, in their children, which, they complained, made them feel that their lives had become dirty, and they did not know how to deal with it. One woman stated, "The doctor said everything is OK with my child, but I do not know what to do." (There was no medical reason for the enuresis; it was a psychological symptom.) After the group members discussed this problem, they agreed to have me invite a Bedouin-Arab doctor from the clinic to explain how to cope with enuresis. Initially, I gave only fundamental support and information. After these concrete problems were addressed, the widows were ready to let me into their personal and social lives.

Consequently, the third goal was to deal with the women's personal and emotional problems—the loss of their husbands and the implications of that loss on their interpersonal relationships. Sometimes they expressed their difficulties by saying, *Bachtna Asmr*, which means "Our fortune is black." The legitimacy that was given to these problems within the group aroused anger and perhaps helped to free the emotions that follow the loss of someone close.

The widows whose husbands had married second wives found their adjustment to the loss of their spouse to be easier; their efforts focused on their children's needs more than on the loss itself. In contrast, the second wives seemed to be more troubled by the loss and discussed its influence on their personal lives. The difference in the reactions of first and second wives perhaps reflects the type of relationship the women and their husbands had before death. When a Bedouin-Arab man in the Negev takes a second wife, she is usually younger than his first wife; he spends more time with her and often cares more for her than for his first wife (Mass & Al-Krenawi, 1994).

The fourth goal was to help the women deal with their social problems. As the meetings progressed, the group discussed the interference by, and lack of help from, their husbands' families. One woman said, "My husband's family asked my kids, 'How is your mother: does she give you everything?' and 'Where does she go every day?'" Others felt that their husbands' families hated them and that the women in their husbands' families were at fault. As one woman put it, "All of you do not understand the issue: This is not the men [in our husbands' families]; they do what they do because of their wives' influence." In response to their perceptions of their husbands' families, the women expressed anger at them, especially the married women in these families, for the cessation of economic support. One said, "My brothers have many children and they cannot help; I can understand them." Others claimed that economic support was the responsibility of their husband's families, not their own. The women also expressed anger about the transition their society was undergoing from a traditional to a modern ethos; as one woman put it, *Alrheil Had Hiatna* ("the transition broke our lives").

The societal attitudes toward widows were discussed as well. The ideal widow in Bedouin-Arab society continues to mourn for her husband and sacrifices her life to help her sons grow up and become good men in their tribe, thus preserving her husband's name. She also accepts that her daughters should be raised to be traditional Bedouin-Arab women. Therefore, the Bedouin-Arab widow has a limited social life. She must be careful to take good care of her children and to be perceived as doing nothing unless it is for them. She cannot leave her home for long, for if she does, her husband's parents will say that she neglects her children and will demand that she return to her parents' home. Her relationships with other women are also limited. As one woman explained, "They are afraid of us, and they think that we are going to take their husbands."

At the next-to-last meeting, an important issue arose. One woman said: "During my marriage, I never felt free; my husband controlled my life, and he was a very hard man. At least today, I can manage my life and my children's lives as I want." This statement led all the other women to talk about how their husbands controlled them. Some of them, especially the first wives whose husbands had married second wives, told how their husbands had treated them badly.

During the group process, the women gave each other support and became close to each other. If a group member missed a meeting, others told me why she was not there. Before each meeting, the women met at the clinic and shared different issues. They began to contact new widows outside the group and offer them help, and they even referred new widows to my office for help.

Other Issues that Emerged

Religion

All of the group members believed in God (*Allah*). After sessions involving the expression of anger or other painful emotions, they asked for forgiveness from God, in case they had said something unacceptable according to the Islamic religion. When they dealt with death, they tried to convince each other that this was *Hakmat Allah* ("God's judgment") or *Maktoub* ("it is written"). One woman explained that a person has an *Amanat* ("deposit") in this world: "When God wants our *Amanat* to occur, why are we angered? We have to accept God's order." Fate was also a common theme. Another woman said, "This is *Gadernaa*" ("This is our fate"). The belief in fate is a part of Islam. All things that happen to a person, both good and evil, are thought to be the will of God (Wikan, 1988). Therefore, people must accept their fate with strong faith, courage, and great patience.

The Negev Bedouin-Arab use these words and ideas during burial ceremonies and mourning rituals, and therefore I used the same words with the group members. Religion can provide individuals and groups with a sense that life has meaning, which may help them to find consolation in difficult times (O'Dea, 1966). Because it puts human sorrows in a fathomable context, it can help some widows cope with bereavement (Wilkerson, 1987).

Dreams

In discussing dreams in which their dead husbands appeared, the women said that these dreams made them afraid and emotionally upset. They used a traditional interpretation of this kind of dream: the idea that the soul of the dead person wants to attack the dreamer, arousing the fear of death in the dreamer. Members who had experienced this kind of dream told the others how to cope with it. The dreamer has to do *Rahamah*—a memorial ritual discussed at greater length in chapter seven. The purpose of this ritual is to provide support and comfort to the dreamer through discussion with family members and friends.

Remarriage

The rate of remarriage among Bedouin-Arab widows is very low. Eleven of the widows in the group refused to remarry because of the societal expectation that they devote their lives to their children, and they chose to accept their situation as God's will. All of the group members said that their sons would take care of them (*Absalamet Awladna*) and that they would be better off in the future. However, they encouraged the remaining woman, aged 25, who had no children to consider remarrying because she was childless. This woman said that her parents had also encouraged her to remarry after the *Hul* (the year of mourning).

It should be noted that this woman's childlessness was a particularly significant issue. From the Bedouin-Arab cultural perspective, children give a woman social status and respect, and in the future, her status will be strongly linked to the strength of her son's reputations. If the woman in question had a son, the group members would have probably advised her *not* to remarry, given the expectation that she care for the son and devote her life to this task.

Finally, it should be noted that in Bedouin-Arab society of the Negev, there is a great emphasis on advice giving. As one saying has it, during a time of crisis or disease, "Ask one who had personal experience of having had the same problem; do not ask an expert." Consequently, the group members were naturally inclined to consider each other as the best source of mutual support and advice regarding widowhood. It is a small wonder, then, that group therapy was culturally acceptable.

Benefits of the Group Experience

The widows gained the following benefits from involvement in the group:

- the development of new social networks and social support to replace those lost from Bedouin-Arab society as a result of the transition to modern life;

- the provision of material support and information about their rights;
- the strengthening of their self-assurance;
- help in dealing with the loss of their husbands and its implications, including confirming a life-direction for the future;
- validation that their problems were universal in Bedouin-Arab society;
- assistance with particular problems, such as their children's bed wetting and the learning of new social skills; and
- organization of a self-help group that takes care of new widows.

In addition, the clinic gained some secondary benefits from the group: The frequency of the women's solo-visits to the clinic for stress complaints was reduced, the clinic was able to provide preventative treatment, and another source of help for recent widows was established in the community.

This group for widows was an effort to provide new social networks to replace those that were lost because of the social changes in Bedouin-Arab society. Because there has been little professional intervention in traditional Bedouin-Arab society, the Bedouin-Arab are typically unfamiliar with the helping profession. However, as this chapter has illustrated, there are ways to build bridges between Bedouin-Arab norms and the modern profession.

The clinical intervention began by offering instrumental and informational help to the widows and as the professional gained rapport with the women, the helping relationship progressed to offer help with personal problems. The group was conducted in a modern setting, and the context of the group allowed for the integration of both modern and traditional methods. I helped the group members to cope with grief in their own traditional ways. My efforts to avoid a clash between the cultural and professional canons enabled the group to discuss personal issues, which is usually difficult for Arabs to do (Banawi & Stockton, 1993).

Relating to clients in an authentic and respectful manner provides the necessary, if not sufficient, condition for successful, cross-cultural, professional helping efforts. As Siporin's (1985) quote of the famous proverb "He who knows himself, knows others" indicates, in a cross-cultural setting, we social workers need to know both ourselves and others before we can be authentic and effective helping professionals.

CONCLUSION

The preceding three cases provide convincing evidence that there are strategies, currently being utilized, that could be profitably shared with the wider helping professional community. The approaches consciously utilize cultural and religiously grounded techniques in order to promote working alliances between community members and helping professionals. The latter may be members of the Bedouin-Arab community, or not. Either way, as subsequent chapters indicate, helping professionals represent an epistemology that is outside of Bedouin-Arab cultural traditions. The need to be respectful and to adapt professional theory and methods is no more evident than in the next chapter on polygamous family formation. As it points out, strategies need to be different in these contexts, and theory and methods have hitherto been insufficient in responding to cultural and social phenomena that have received little academic attention.

Chapter 4

POLYGAMOUS FAMILY INTERVENTION: CASE VIGNETTES

INTRODUCTION

This chapter briefly introduces the practice of polygamy, and then the significance, based on empirical evidence, of polygamous family structures in relation to marital relationship, life satisfaction, and mental health status. Here we utilize data comparing the mental well-being of Bedouin-Arab women in the same communities of the Negev: some are polygamous marriages, and are compared to monogamous marriages. Following this are two studies that explore the unique case of polygamous families in the Negev. The first provides an in-depth look into a polygamous family including interviews with the wives and observations of the family dynamics. The second considers helping profession practice strategies in light of the implications of polygamy for children and their families. These strategies include comprehending the cultural and personal significance of polygamy to family members, appreciating the significance of polygamy to children's functioning, selecting children as a target system for successful family intervention, and reinforcing the value base of interventions via the cultural canon of Islam. The final section of this chapter addresses the issues brought up throughout the chapter and offers five principles which could form the basis of social work practice with Bedouin-Arab polygamous families.

POLYGAMY

Anthropologists typically define polygamy as "a marital relationship involving multiple spouses" (Kottak, 1978 as cited in Low, 1988, p. 189). It includes three types, only the first of which is of concern to the present chapter: polygyny (one husband is married to two or more wives; hereafter referred to as polygamy), polyandry (one wife is married to two or more husbands) and polygynandry (a group marriage scenario in which two or more wives are simultaneously married to two or more husbands). Of the three forms, the first is the most common world wide (Valsiner, 1989, p. 69).

Attitudes towards polygamy vary across societies from complete acceptance to total condemnation. Even within practicing societies, the social construction of polygamy is heterogeneous, reflecting culturally specific social mores, values, and customs (e.g., Low, 1988; White, 1988a, 1988b). With this in mind, one should proceed cautiously with generic, trans-cultural principles of helping profession intervention. This chapter deliberately analyzes polygamy in one society, providing a beginning point for practitioners and scholars to consider how best to work with polygamous families trans-culturally. It thereby joins a growing body of helping profession research providing strategies for working with non-Western societies and with individuals whose ethno-cultural background is non-Western (e.g., Al-Krenawi & Graham, 1996a; Lum, 1982, 1992; Mass & Al-Krenawi, 1994). While a small body of research examines family therapy with "informal polygamy" (Rivett & Street, 1993), this chapter is the first to consider helping profession intervention in the context of *formal* polygamous marriage. Polygamy is not legal in most Western countries. However, it should be stressed that knowledge of the phenomenon is needed for successful practice among ethno-communities where the practice is, or has been, prevalent.

Polygamous marriage is practiced in the Middle East, Africa, Asia, and Oceania, but it is also known to occur in Europe and North America, among other Western societies (Broude, 1994). It is typically found within social systems where human resources are among the most important. In contrast, "where resources such as land or forms of private property predominate, monogamous nuclear family forms tend to be the rule" (*Macmillan Dictionary of Anthropology*, 1986, p. 228). Many scholars have found that better educated and urban women are less likely to favour polygamy (D'Hondt & Vandewiele, 1980; Ferraro, 1991; Pool, 1972; Ware, 1979). Studies on polygamy in sub-Saharan Africa suggest that women's attitudes toward polygamy may vary both within and between societies (Adams & Mburugu, 1994; Dorjahn, 1988; Kilbride, 1994). There is evidence in some practising societies that polygamy is declining in popularity, particularly among the young (D'Hondt & Vandewiele, 1980; 1986). Sociologists view polygamy "as a reproductive strategy by which men maximize the number of their offspring but minimize investment in each child" (White, 1988a, p. 871). In many cultures, polygamy is a mark of high social, economic, or political status. In some, the right to polygamy is reserved only for certain classes of men.

Polygamous wives may live together, although they most commonly have independent households where each lives with her children (Broude, 1994, pp. 207-208). In some societies, polygamous wives benefit. Co-wives may co-operate in trade and economic affairs. Since their husband tends to be wealthy, the pool of labourers supplied by a larger domestic unit reduces the need for hiring wage labourers (Adams & Mburugu, 1994; Borgerhoff-Mulder, 1992; Dorjahn, 1988).

A senior wife is defined as any married woman "who was followed by another wife in the marriage." A "junior wife" is "the most recent wife joining a marriage" (Chaleby, 1985, p. 57). Many societies accord high status to senior wives: they may have power over the other wives, privileges that the junior wives do not enjoy, and increased influence over the husband. In one society, the senior wife is the manager of the household, overseeing the work and other activities of the remaining wives and the distribution of supplies. In another society, the senior wife arranges and consents to the husband's next marriage (Broude, 1994, pp. 208-209). Among the Bedouin-Arab, in contrast, the senior wife has lower status than the junior wife. Among most practicing societies there is an imperative to treat co-wives equally regarding the provision of economic resources, social support, and attention. Unfortunately, this is not always the case in Bedouin-Arab polygamous arrangements.

Turning to marital quality, research shows that polygamous marriages are more likely to be torn with spousal conflict, tension, and jealousy, than monogamous marriages (Achte & Schakit, 1980; Ware, 1979). Mothers and children in particular are predisposed to psychological problems (Al-Issa, 1990; Eapen et al., 1998). These women are often unhappy, and the addition of new wives can be very distressing and may be perceived as a very traumatic and abusive experience (Hassanoueh-Phillips, 2001). Relationships between co-wives, and the in-laws, may be strained. The children of subfamilies may also be in mutual conflict (Al-Krenawi, Graham, & Al-Krenawi, 1997). Jealousy, competition, and acrimony between co-wives and children in each of the subfamilies are common as well (Al-Krenawi & Graham, 1999b; 2001a). The literature suggests that marital distress is linked with suppressed immune function, cardiovascular arousal, psychosocial distress, and an increase in stress-related hormones (Al-Krenawi, Graham, & Izzeldin, 2001; Brown & Smith, 1992; Gottman, 1994; Gottman & Notarius, 2000; Kiecolt-Glaser et al., 1987). Given that many women in polygamous societies are not employed outside the home, they are economically dependent on others and often feel pressured to marry into a polygamous family and remain in these relationships (Elbedour et al., 2002). A mother's distress can reduce her level of caring, supervision, and involvement in family life, and can lead to withdrawal, depression, and hostility. These risk factors (marital conflict, marital distress, and financial distress) are assumed to mediate and/or moderate the relationship between the polygamous marital structure and children's level of adjustment (Elbedour et al., 2002).

A great amount of research has established that polygamous families experience a higher rate of marital conflict, family violence, and family disruption than do monogamous families (Al-Krenawi, 1998b). Marital troubles, conflict, and distress have a direct effect on children's mental health (Elbedour et al., 2002), which could in turn exacerbate marital tensions, creating a downward spiral of conflict. Amongst children, these events may predict poor social competence, the lack of a sense of security (Davies, Myers, & Cummings, 1996), poor academic achievement (Emery & O'Leary, 1982), behavioural problems and aggression (Cummings, Zahn-Waxler, & Radke-Yarrow, 1984; Rutter, 1975), hostile interactions (Katz & Gottman, 1993), and elevated heart rates (El-Sheikh, 1994). Marital conflict is also likely to disrupt effective parenting and parental involvement (Engfer, 1988), and thus may have lasting effects on parent-child relationships. A negative appraisal of the marital relationship and increased rates of negative behaviour by husbands are related to negative sibling interaction as well as negative mother-child interaction (Krishnakumar & Buehler, 2000; Peterson et al., 1977). Indeed, women in polygamous marriages may repress anger towards their spouse, their life circumstances, and commensurate stress and they may project this anger towards their children, adversely affecting parental relations and communication within the family. Here, in turn, we see that stressful experiences in polygamous families are more likely to be associated with childhood maladjustment (Elbedour et al., 2002). It may also be possible that the children in these families become targeted scapegoats for the family's problems (Crosson-Tower, 1998), or that the older children take on parental roles in order to maintain stability and order in the household (Elbedour et al., 2002).

The following section examines the marital relationship, comparing the mental well-being of women in polygamous marriages to that of women in monogamous marriages. This section is based on surveys conducted in 2003 among the Bedouin-Arabs of the Negev (Al-Krenawi, 2004). The sample included 376 women, 237 of whom were in monogamous marriages and 139 in polygamous marriages. The mean age of sons and daughters was 5.46 (SD = 3.46). The mean age of the women was 36.15 (SD =11.87). All of the participants were asked to complete a questionnaire asking about their current life circumstances. This questionnaire provided scores on four scales: family functioning, marital relationship, psychological functioning, and life satisfaction.

Family Functioning

For family functioning, we used the McMaster Family Assessment Device (FAD) that was developed by Epstein and colleagues (Epstein et al., 1983; Miller et al., 1985). It includes 60 items on seven dimensions of family functioning: problem solving, communication, roles in the family, emotional involvement, behavior control, emotional responses and general functioning. All sub-scales range from 1-4, with higher scores indicating more problems in a family's functioning. Section points discriminating between "clinical" and "normal" families in American populations are available, though there are none for Israeli families. The scale has satisfactory reliability (Cronbach's Alpha = 0.72-0.92), good test-retest reliability ($r = 0.66$) and high validity, as indicated by comparing the scale's scores to other measures of the same matters (Epstein et al., 1983; Miller, Epstein, Bishop, & Keitner, 1985).

For marital relationships, we used the ENRICH questionnaire, whose original details were selected following a comprehensive overview of the literature on marital problems and interpersonal conflicts (Fournier & Olson, 1986, cited in Lavee et al., 1987). The questionnaire, which measures satisfaction with marriage and quality of adjustment to it, is divided into eight parts, each containing ten items. Several studies (Fournier, Olson & Druckman, 1983, cited in Lavee, 1987) found that it has a rather high reliability (Chronbach's Alpha = 0.88-0.89). Other studies indicated a high degree of discriminating validity and concurrent validity.

For life satisfaction, we used the Diener et al. (1985) scale which consists of five items examining life satisfaction. It uses a likert scale from 1 (low) to 7 (higher satisfaction); the scale has high internal reliability (Cronbach's Alpha = 0.87), and good stability examined by test-retest reliability ($r = 0.82$). Diener et al. (1985) tested the validity of the scale by comparing it to existing scales, finding good validity. The internal reliability in the current research was satisfactory (Cronbach's Alpha = 0.80, $N = 375$).

For psychological functioning, we used the Brief Symptom Inventory (BSI), a shortened version of the Hopkins Symptom Checklist (H-SCL-90), used as a screening instrument to measure psychiatric symptomatology (Derogatis & Melisaratos, 1983; Derogatis & Spencer, 1982). It includes 53 items that elicit perceptions of symptoms during the last month. The nine dimensions of the BSI are: somatization, interpersonal sensitivity, obsession-compulsion, depression, anxiety, hostility, phobic anxiety, paranoid ideation, and psychoticism. In addition, the scale provides a General Severity Index (GSI), a Positive Symptom Index (PSDI) and a Positive Symptoms Total (PST).

Table 1. Marital relationship, family functioning and psychological functioning according to type of marriage: Means, SDs and 1-way ANOVA results

		Type of Marriage		
		Monogamous marriage	Polygamous marriage	F df = 1,364
Family functioning	M	2.94	2.49	59.58***
	SD	.52	.56	
Marital relationship	M	2.99	3.94	76.68***
	SD	1.22	0.84	
Psychological functioning (GSI)	M	.80	1.39	57.81***
	SD	.61	.87	
Life satisfaction	M	4.57	3.72	30.62***
	SD	1.38	1.47	

*** $p < .001$

Table 2. Psychological functioning subscales according to type of residence and type of marriage

		Type of Residence			Type of Marriage		
		Recognized	Unrecognized	F	Monogamous marriage	Polygamous marriage	F
Somatization	M	1.02	1.12	.99	.76	1.45	51.61***
	SD	.93	.96		.76	1.08	
Obsession-Compulsion	M	1.03	1.11	.81	.80	1.40	52.27***
	SD	.80	.86		.69	.92	
Interpersonal sensitivity	M	1.13	.95	3.72	.81	1.37	38.31***
	SD	.88	.84		.70	1.02	
Depression	M	.87	.95	.74	.62	1.26	58.10***
	SD	.85	.82		.65	.97	
Anxiety	M	1.15	1.26	1.48	.93	1.50	41.81***
	SD	.86	.85		.74	.96	
Hostility	M	1.01	1.13	1.49	.78	1.40	48.36***
	SD	.87	.90		.73	1.00	
Panic (phobic anxiety)	M	.96	1.11	2.46	.79	1.29	32.56***
	SD	.89	.79		.71	1.00	

Paranoid ideation	M SD	1.20 1.00	1.24 .92	.11	.93 .85	1.56 1.04	40.61***
Psychosis	M SD	.85 .80	.96 .84	1.54	.65 .64	1.21 .96	44.73***
PST	M SD	29.01 14.09	31.54 15.06	2.58	26.60 13.64	35.51 14.21	34.98***
PSDI	M SD	1.75 .63	1.71 .55	0.48	1.59 .52	1.98 .64	39.03***
General severity index (GSI)	M SD	1.03 .75	1.10 .76	0.61	.84 .60	1.42 .85	56.80***

*** $p < .001$

In general, the results of the comparisons between monogamous and polygamous families show that women from monogamous families perceive their lives as better than those of women from polygamous families on all marital, familial and psychological aspects. Family functioning is perceived as higher in monogamous families as compared to polygamous families ($M=2.94$, $SD=.52$ vs. $M=2.49$, $SD=.56$, respectively), and women from monogamous families were found to be more satisfied with their lives than women from polygamous families ($M=4.57$, $SD=1.38$ vs. $M=3.72$, $SD=1.47$, respectively). In addition, as the table shows, women from polygamous families express more psychological symptoms than women from monogamous families ($M=1.39$, $SD=.87$ vs. $M=.80$, $SD=.61$, respectively*)*.

In order to examine the women's psychological functioning, 11 subscales of psychological functioning were computed. These subscales are presented in table 2. Table 2 indicates that no significant difference was found between women from recognized and unrecognized villages, but significant differences were found with respect to all of the subscales of psychological functioning between women from monogamous families and polygamous families, and the findings were significantly worse among women from polygamous families.

Discussion

Women in polygamous marriages, as the data of this survey show, scored significantly higher on all of the psychological dimensions noted in the BSI. These dimensions may be associated with stress common to women in polygamous marriages, be it related to economic issues, relations with children, their husband or in-laws, or other problems. As previous research indicates, somatization may be more prevalent in the non-Western world (Al-Issa 1995; Kirmayer 1986). Thus, higher somatization scores among respondents in the present study may be ethno-racially grounded, and can be associated with Arab peoples' relative inability to express emotional distress (Al-Issa, 1995, p. 21; Al-Krenawi & Graham, 2004). It is common for Arab women to experience somatic complaints. As one scholar indicates in research on Saudi women, "negative feelings, unhappiness, and conflict, both within herself and between her and members of her family, are readily translated into somatic terms since physical symptoms in that culture are safe, morally acceptable, and generally lead to some form of help-seeking" (Racy, 1980, p. 213). Likewise, both depression and anxiety occur frequently within Arab societies (Al-Issa, 1969; Racy, 1980, 1985).

The next section takes a closer look into the experiences of one polygamous family in particular. Observations and interviews with the six wives who share one husband were conducted over a four week period by a female Bedouin-Arab university student. The following section discusses what was found.

CASE VIGNETTE: INSIDE A POLYGAMOUS FAMILY

Six wives, all having the same husband, were interviewed using an open-ended, semi-structured questionnaire. Observation was also conducted. Being a female Bedouin-Arab university student, the data collector was familiar with the culture, had good standing within the community, and was familiar with the family. Given that Bedouin-Arab society is gender segregated, the researcher's gender enabled her to connect with the wives and to further gain their trust. The wives and their husband consented to the interviews. All identifying factors including names, geography, and time periods have been changed, to preserve the anonymity and confidentiality of the parties involved. The order of the wives has been indicated alphabetically: A being the first wife, and F being the sixth. Given the data's sensitive nature, the respondents requested that no recording devices be used. Notes were taken during and immediately after each interview, and post-interview follow-up questions clarified outstanding points.

Family Background

The husband, Ahmad, is 73 years old and now in poor health, with partial paralysis. Retired, he receives social security benefits. By virtue of birth, he is considered one of the dominant people in his tribe. Prior to settling in the village where he currently lives, he, like others in his tribe, had lived on land outside of the village.

His six co-wives range in age from 30 to 67. Between all six wives, there are a total of 60 children, consisting of 26 sons and 34 daughters. The eldest son is 40 years and the youngest is two months old. The youngest wife has five years of education, the next youngest has four years, and the others, like the husband, have no formal education and are illiterate. Each wife lives in a separate house with her children, and each house is in immediate proximity to the others. No wife is employed outside of the home.

Ethnographic Data

Part 1

A large territory within the Bedouin-Arab village now expands to over three acres and looks like an immense back yard behind a stone wall. Inside are the houses of five of Ahmad's six wives. Washing hangs in the separate yards whose borders are not marked but are strictly observed. Children are seen scuffling, others waving sticks, others playing football on the road, and others wandering idly around the property and street. The fourth wife, D., lives in a large two-storey house surrounded by a high stone wall. Ahmad, the husband, initially planned to give each wife a room within the two-storey house, but gradually each woman had a house of her own constructed. Aged 73 and somewhat disoriented because of a stroke, Ahmad spends most of the day in the inner covered court yard next to a pile of smoldering coals and a pot of coffee, brought to him by one of his children. He spends much of his day sleeping or wandering drowsily between his wives' homes, visiting with them and the children.

At night he sleeps with one of his two latest wives, "the little ones," as they are called by his first wife, A. "I gave him up long ago," she said, a flash of stubbornness in her glazed eyes. "My youngest son is 23, and at that age I had already given up on my husband; I knew he wanted another wife. It doesn't matter how I felt, what's important is that he left me. He took five wives after me," she added, still fresh with anger. "He used to spoil the newest one and then throw her over, put her with all the others and look for a new one. I'm fed up. I try to forget as best as I can."

D., the fourth wife, raised a small flock of sheep for many years, sired from two sheep that she received as a wedding present. Saving the pennies from the child allowance and from what her daughters earned from working outside the village, D. received help from her parents, sold all of her gold jewellery, and bought, without her husband's knowledge, a plot of land when it was still possible to lease land cheaply in the Negev. Then, in a moment of strength, after the first three wives had managed, each in her own way, to get a house for themselves, she managed to take over the large house in return for her land. Today, the house is in her name. Aged 48, she is large and temperamental, her face swathed in a white kerchief and glowing with anger and enmity that have not softened with the years.

"Go away, who gave you permission to come into my house?" she roared at the old man who came into the room, with an amused expression. "You're still my wife," he retorted. "I did this, I didn't do that, what does it matter? They're all here, what do they lack?" he added, as if revealing a secret, his eyes flashing. "I gave them children, I built them houses, look, none of them ran away, if it was so bad they'd have run away." "You only bring me trouble," D. threw back at him. "I wish you'd turn into a worm and die. I remember every second of my life, all hate. It's not the life I dreamed of. I dreamt I'd find a boy who'd understand me, live with me and my children, help me to raise them, be a husband for me alone. Today no one helps me. I'm mother and father, I'm fed up, full of illness and always feeling there's something big missing in my life. I only live for my children. I don't want to remember my life; it's just suffering." She then pointed to a framed motto on the wall: "I will suffer until suffering tires of me and until God decides what to do with me and until suffering realizes that I suffer from something worse than suffering." The dream of "a nice house," "children who study," and "a husband of my own" is common to all 6 wives, young and old.

Because of the legal ban on polygamy in Israel, only one wife receives a recognized marriage agreement, while the others are married unofficially according to Israeli civil law, and officially according to Islamic *Shariah* (religious law). As time goes by and the husband takes a fifth wife, a previous wife is unofficially divorced, as Islam allows a maximum of 4 wives. Even after divorce the wives continue to live in the husband's household, and are subject to his authority. They and their children live a subsistence existence, relying on the children's allowance and National Insurance benefits. The pecking order is particularly long in such families, and the price continues to be paid by the children as well. Legally, polygamy does not exist. However, it is impossible to forbid a man from keeping "girlfriends." The results turn up on the doorstep of welfare offices in the villages.

Part 2

Gradually, the six wives assemble in the house of C., the third wife. A. is the first, "the first love," giggled F., the sixth wife, aged 30, tapping C's knees. "I was only 14, I didn't know what love is," muttered A. "My brother loved the man's sister and he forced me to marry him in an exchange marriage. Afterwards I had no choice, so I loved him. It's better to love, isn't it?" she ended defensively, while the others egged her on laughing: "Enough, you can say you loved him, then you were [the] only one," teased wife C. A. sighed and slipped out of the room.

When A. and her husband met, in the early 1950s, the tribe wandered around the Segev Shalom area. Her husband had high status, but had not risen to his current level of tribal authority. "My father married me to him by force," said B., the second wife, aged 53. Her sagging face grew hard in a kind of unexpected arousal. "I didn't know, it wasn't the custom to ask the woman. Suddenly at night I saw a car, they told me they'd come for me. I ran away through the fields, till my father caught me, beat me and threw me into the car. Even now I wish my parents ill," she burst out. "I tore my clothes, I screamed," she continued. "I was 15, the same age as his children, I couldn't look them in the face. I don't like my past: all the time quarrels, curses, he used to beat me half to death. Every night I used to go to sleep and wake up on a pillow that was wet with tears. What a life! I had no life. All the time I ran away and my father brought me back. Even now when I've got 10 children from him, I hate him."

B. was put into a separate tent next to A.'s tent, and for the first nights, Ahmad's relatives guarded her to stop her from running away. A. ignored her. "I didn't look for her or anyone else. Of course I was jealous, anyone would be jealous, but I ignored her. I didn't feel I was married and I didn't hate anyone except him. I hated him with all the hate in the world. Why did he take me? He didn't even love me, no man who loves marries others," she exclaimed in her hurt. "A horrible life," put in F., the youngest, large bodied, her pleasant face flushed. "Another miserable one," muttered B., "She managed very well."

Part 3

Over time, Ahmad learned about "important Jews" said B. He also gained an important position within the tribe, and through contacts with the newly formed state of Israel, he gained many benefits in land leases. Correspondingly, his wealth and status grew. A whole new world of spousal manipulation opened up.

He had already obtained C. by cunning, said one of the women. "Poor thing, she also suffered, all in the same boat," sighed D., who for years had struggled against the most immediate wife she had replaced. C. had no father, and was raised by her mother. One day an old man came to her mother's tent and took C. to visit his wife, a relative of C.'s mother. C., aged 15, did not return from the visit. By chance it emerged that the old man's wife wanted to save her own daughter from the bitter fate of the exchange marriage that her husband was planning. So to distract him from his plan, she kidnapped C. for him. "My mother went to the police, but she couldn't find me. For three years he [the old man] hid me in Kfar Kassem and Kfar Saba. I was weak, small, I knew nothing of life, everything was done by force. I was afraid of every strange man who came near. He shut me in a room and that's it. A black night. It was like rape."

C. grew older and "began to understand things." She got a taxi and returned to her family. Her brothers threatened to take revenge on the old man, and the family required the intervention of an important tribal leader. The man they turned to was Ahmad. He forced the old man to give her up, for a large sum of money, and hid her in B.'s hut (they lived in spontaneous, nomadic settlements, not houses). "We knew he had his eye on her," said B. scornfully. "We saw them spending nights together, talking. I said to him, if you want to marry, divorce me. He wouldn't, he knew that I wouldn't run away because of the children." [Islamic conventions hold that fathers have custody over boys after the age of 7 and girls after the age of 9 (Amar, 1984)] "Poor A. was jealous, always saying to me: look she'll marry him soon. I told her, what do I care about him?" sighed B.

Ahmad was then 40, in his prime. He paid and did not ask for anything. "She's free," he told her mother, "but as soon as she marries her husband she must pay the debt." Her mother realized that no one could pay the debt, so she suggested to her daughter that she marry Ahmad. C. agreed. "I said, OK, he's only got two wives, it doesn't matter, I'll have two children and stay with them, and now I've got 11. That's the whole story, it hurts. I tell my children, don't do what your father did, he fathered children like sheep. That's the story, our lives are ruined."

After C. it was another's turn, D., her cousin, a refugee from Gaza. Her parents forced her to marry Ahmad because they were opposed to her love for a cousin who was destined to marry a different cousin. Economic conditions in Gaza were very poor. D.'s father was unemployed; perhaps he needed money, she didn't know. She wept and cried at the prospect of marrying this man and became sick with a high fever. At knife point, her brother forced her into Ahmad's car. She is still convinced that C. suggested her to Ahmad.

"She knew he was looking for a wife, so she preferred me," recalled D. "I sat in the car and wept. It [the car] was a Peugeot; C. and another woman held me on both sides to stop me from jumping out. There was no wedding, there isn't a wedding for married men. My girl friends made me a party, but it was a funeral not a wedding, everyone wept. He was a respected man in the tribe, and my family owed him. He saved C. and I was the victim. I'll never forget that first night—everything by force. I hit him but he was strong and without mercy. That hurts the most. Until my third daughter I lay with him and covered my eyes, he made me sick. Afterwards I got used to it, but I felt dead."

"God help me," mocked Ahmad, who appeared in the doorway, "but life is good." "God helped you to marry six wives?" challenged D. "They should have put him in prison from the first and stopped him from marrying," she muttered to herself. "He enjoys seeing women suffer. If he wants a girl he's not satisfied until he gets her. Lots of times he said to me, 'I'll make you suffer, I'll destroy you,' and he really did."

For many years, D. could not forgive C. for cooperating with Ahmad and making her marry him. "I begged her, I said to her: I'm in love with my cousin, why must you destroy me? But she didn't listen." C. was embarrassed: "I didn't help." Her angry silence threatened to break any moment. "No woman helps her husband to marry. He asked me to talk to her father, what could I do? I didn't think her father would agree, but he preferred his niece to his own daughter." "Never mind," sighed D., "I'm convinced, that's my fate. We're all in the same boat, none of us could say no."

Part 4

When Ahmad stopped taking C. on shopping and other trips and visited her less, "it was hard for me" she admitted. D. hated the old man, but like her predecessors in the role of youngest wife, she couldn't help enjoying her new situation of power. Every argument turned on jealousy, which had its own existence, removed from the reality of the women's oppression. Each of them was convinced that Ahmad loved her, and secretly she scorned the others.

The wives' relationships also affected the children's quarrels. C.'s children used to beat D.'s little girl, and the two women expressed anger against each other in defense of their children. Once, D. went into her room and found Ahmad with B. In her anger, she began to collect her things to run back to her parents, but Ahmad beat her with a door handle until he drew blood. "B. ran off," D. recalls.

Ahmad was supposed to spend a night with each of them, but he did not always do so. None now wanted him, the wives concurred, but they felt humiliated when he went to one of the others. Even their common suffering did not terminate their jealousy.

The older women needed time for themselves. Twenty years ago, a representative of the National Insurance Institute told them that they were entitled to receive child allowances directly rather than through their husband. B. plucked up her courage and agreed. A. was afraid of angering Ahmad, and even C. and D. were nervous, said B., but in the end followed her. "We're all strong women, not pathetic. Life made us like this," said B.

B. finally threw him out of her house shortly before he married his youngest wife, F., 17 years ago. She slammed the door in his face and locked it. Since then, if he wants to visit her children, he stands in her doorway and shouts to them, but he doesn't dare enter. He still visits the others sometimes. "He comes, he goes, like a stranger, shalom, shalom and that's it," said C. somewhat sadly. "He's not interested in the children, hardly knows their names. Not one of his children has even finished ten years of school, they wander around, some take drugs, others date Jewish women, all because of him. It's sad." C.'s eldest son married a Jewish drug addict and now he's in prison for drug dealing. She wept telling the story. The son's wife uses their children to beg for charity. Last week, C. went to a major city to save her grandchildren from further poverty and deprivation, only to hear from her daughter-in-law that she wouldn't let her children "grow up with Arabs."

"Once you start with problems and suffering, it never ends," wailed E., the fifth wife, aged 37, tall, with an old brown jacket stretched over her body. Her hair was untidy, a charming smile occasionally lit a tired face. E. apparently married Ahmad voluntarily 20 years ago. Her father consented without asking her, but she did not resist. Her father's second wife had treated her badly, forcing her to do heavy manual labour in the fields, she said. Ahmad knew how to combine pouring money into the father's pockets with longing gazes at the daughter. E. believed that he loved her and secretly melted. "I was pretty and that attracted him, not like now, nearly 40 and looking old" she despaired. "I didn't feel anything, without thinking I married him, just to get away from the house and the work."

"She married him to give me problems," joked D. "Love at first sight," teased E., giggling with embarrassment. "He did fall in love with her, she lived opposite us and he used to spy on her from the window with binoculars," D. went on. "He fell in love with every woman he saw," she hastened to explain. "All the women in the world weren't enough for him. We argued the whole time so he did it to spite me. I said to him, get married, what do I care, just give me the house."

E. didn't manage to enjoy her position for long. She didn't love Ahmad, and was too busy consolidating her status. When her oldest son was eight months old, Ahmad brought a new wife, a member of a family from Gaza. One of her family members had killed a member of a different tribe whose members were seeking blood vengeance, or the obligation to kill in retribution for the death of a member of one's family or tribe, against him. As a result, the family name was disgraced. Ahmad was asked to intervene, and went to the family home. When F. served him some watermelon he looked deep into her eyes and embarrassed her. He gave her family the names of twenty men prepared to marry her to save her family from disgrace, and his name was at the top of the list. He showed her warmth and understanding. Her parents opposed her marriage to Ahmad, who already had five wives and a reputation as a wife-beater. But as her distress grew stronger, F. decided to defy her parents in the only way open to her and married Ahmad.

"I escaped from hell but I knew I was going to another hell," said F. "When he came to take me in his car, I sat in the back between D. and one of his daughters, and I looked at his hands on the wheel. What big hands, I thought, how did I agree to marry him? Afterwards I didn't stop trembling the whole night. He went to D. and said to her, 'she's still trembling, what should I do with her?' And she told him, 'Don't touch her.' The second night I continued to tremble, and on the third night he hit me and threw me out. At that moment I stopped trembling and after he did what he did, he let me go to my parents. He didn't want me to run away a virgin."

E. remembers the day that F. appeared as a "black day." "I felt rotten, I was angry, I didn't understand. My little boy was only eight months old and he was getting married? Who would look after me? Why did he marry me if he wanted another?" D. reminded her that "he did it to all of us," and she stopped. "I don't care about the others, I'm speaking about myself," she whispered. "He told me he's getting married and that's it. He said somebody had asked for his hand," she mocked F., and D. quickly replied: "You get yourself into trouble. Words like that breed hate." "It hurts," E. continued, "We're all sitting there and suddenly he caresses one and not another, on purpose, to hurt us. He used to spend twenty days with one of us, then get cross with her and go to another. It's annoying, I'm living with him, aren't I? I can't block him out, he's always there in front of me. Even if I don't love him, even if he takes me by force, I live with him. Suddenly you're nothing. This is annoying for the children. D. is jealous too, she just pretends she isn't. For example, let's say she's happy, then someone tells her he was with F., suddenly she's angry. Nothing is hidden, it's all open. Now I've crossed him out, he doesn't interest me."

Even today, F. and E. aren't speaking. They live on the same plot of land, their homes are adjoined within one building, all registered in Ahmad's name. Out of all of his wives, they are the only ones who did not get their own houses and remained captives of Ahmad and of each other. As long as they are considered his wives and live in his house, they are not entitled to National Insurance money. Their joint electricity and water bills are the focus for endless arguments.

E.'s house is small, containing two rooms for eight people. It is unfinished, has no furniture and no beds. F.'s house was recently renovated, containing a modern kitchen, ceramic tiles, and pleasing furniture. "I sold all my dowry for that," exclaimed F. Over the bed is an enlarged picture of F., aged 20. In her yard flutters the husband's washing, a sign of her status. In the past, E. recalls, whenever she herself used to hang out his clothes in her yard, F. used to scream at her. "Out of jealousy," E. concluded, "what a stupid jealous thing. Now she's a bit different. Never mind, when he was ill we all left him. He continues to come just to the two of us, to her more, but I don't care, I've got no desire to sleep with him, it's all by force. I'm fed up with it all. All this Bedouin life, all their customs, should go to hell."

Part 5

The defeat of the wives can be seen in the children. E.'s two sons, aged 17 and 15, have taken over her house. "They take on the authority of a father," she says, particularly the younger one, a small thin rickety boy, who terrorizes his mother and sister with blows. His 14 year old sister, who never stops smiling, is forced to serve him, to bring him his clothes, do his washing, and make his tea. If she refuses, he beats her. The two brothers decided to stop their sister going to school, though she was the only one who had reasonable grades. Nobody in the family had the authority or will to stand up to them, nor could the local welfare office intervene.

"This way is better for everyone. A woman doesn't need to learn," said the older brother, who didn't manage to finish primary school. "He's a good boy," his mother said, trying to defend him, "he understands me more. Just the younger one is terrible." When the girl recently tried to attend school, her younger brother lay in waiting for her on the way and fell on her with blows. The mother asked B.'s oldest son to beat him for her, and since then he doesn't speak to her. She tiptoes around her house, trying to soften his heart with money and caresses, but to no avail. She is particularly afraid that he will carry out a threat to set fire to the house.

Fear of their adolescent sons grows in the hearts of all of the wives who feel that their weakness and poverty stimulates the forcefulness of the men to whom they gave birth. D. quickly married off her two daughters "before their brothers grew up and told them who to marry." Even in F.'s renovated house there is not enough money for books or clothes for the children, and the curses and blows of her 13 year old son "make me weep." Her oldest daughter, aged 16, plump and with a passive expression on her face, recently confessed to her mother, to the latter's disgust, that she is in love with E.'s son. [Close-relative marriages are not uncommon in Bedouin-Arab society.] "Where did this love come from?" complained F. "E.'s son talks to her, persuades her to love him, just to destroy me. I won't let her suffer like me. Everyone knows he's a bad lot, always going with Jewish women. That's not love, that's stupidity. All the family loves her and wants him to marry her. She's on the wrong road altogether, she needs help. Love starts after the wedding, sometimes."

"It's hard for me," F. added immediately. "I've never felt warmth from anyone. Who loved me? Even my own child doesn't love me. I feel my daughter is in trouble, she's always feeling uncomfortable, something's always bothering her but I don't know what. She always wanted my love, but I haven't time for that. I'm always thinking about other things. I have no love in me, I'm completely empty. I'm not able to love my children, that's it, just worry about them all the time, in case anything happens to them. What a hard life we have, I only stay for the children."

Analysis: Four Themes

Several themes emerge from this case study. The first is the interrelationship of race/ethnicity, religion, gender, political status, and social class (Osmond, 1988) for women in polygamous marriages, placing them in situations of multiple jeopardy (Rao, 1996). Feminist scholar Samira Haj rightly calls into question whether Arab-Palestinian women, under occupation by the Israeli state and in the throes of the Intifada (a revolt begun in December 1987 by Palestinian Arabs to protest Israel's occupation of the West Bank and Gaza Strip), could experience "the family as the principal site of women's oppression" (1992, p. 778). While agreeing with Haj's analysis of Palestinian women at that time and place, this argument needs to be qualified in order to apply it to other Arab women. For example, the present case study demonstrates how women experience the family as both profoundly oppressive and as the locus of coping adaptations.

A second, related theme that has emerged from this study concerns the severe economic, emotional, and social depravation incurred by the wives and children of polygamous families. The literature confirms the association between polygamy and family conflict (Al-Krenawi et al., 1997). The data reveal ample evidence of the abuse of Ahmad's wives. These instances include, but are not limited to, verbal and non-verbal put-downs, physical assault, the threat of physical assault, marital rape, and economic deprivation (Carden, 1994; Shalhoub-Kevorkian, 1997). The children likewise experienced neglect in not having their psychological and instrumental needs met (Trocme, 1996), and several boys learned to intimidate other family members, demonstrating the aggressive behaviour that is common to polygamous families trans-culturally (Efoghe, 1990).

Additionally, it should be emphasized that several factors motivated Ahmad to have more than one wife, the third evident theme. Anthropologists distinguish between wealth-creating polygamy, wherein women's domestic labour generates wealth; and sororal polygamy, which aptly describes Ahmad's situation, wherein the husband's wealth allows for more than one wife (White, 1988b). Ahmad's culture was a "fraternal interest group," associated with higher incidences of polygamy, wherein "women" could be "import[ed]...from other communities" to live in male centred residences (White 1988a, p. 875). His culture encouraged polygamy, in part because of its perceived association with increased procreation and because it allowed tribal/*hamula*/familial networks to be extended (Chamie, 1986). Ahmad's tribal status also made polygamy possible where another man, with less wealth and status may have been precluded. Finally, the wives in the present case study perceived male sexual appetite as a principle motivation, contrary to the views of scholars who argue that this is a "simplistic" hypothesis (White 1988a, p. 871).

Polygamy, like other social institutions, is an organic construct, adaptable to the changing particularities of society, person, and place (Pringle, 1997). Ahmad clearly tested the limits of polygamy in Bedouin-Arab society. Islam holds that the maximum number of allowable wives is four (Koran, Surah 4, v. 3), but Ahmad married six. Islam holds that each woman is to be treated equally, but he clearly played favourites. Social and religious convention allows a man to have more than one wife if he has sufficient economic resources to care for them; Ahmad's advancing age, increasing family size, and his wives' worsening economic situations were positively related. And so the paradoxes and problems associated with Ahmad's polygamous family become particularly apparent.

A fourth preeminent theme is the paradoxical nature of polygamous marriage. A man's public rationale for seeking more than one wife is to enable a large and successful family that will carry on family honour. Sons, in this world view, are intended to marry into good families, to gain prosperity, and to retain high tribal status. Daughters are to marry into good families, to bear many sons, and to be effective mothers and wives (Al-Krenawi & Graham, 1997). Ahmad succeeded numerically, fathering 60 children. Unfortunately, his triumph ended there. The literature has long associated polygamous children with lower scholastic achievement (Al-Krenawi & Lightman, 2000; Cherian, 1990). Some of the 60 children were illiterate, and none had graduated from high school, despite community norms of secondary and (increasingly) post-secondary attainment. The literature also demonstrates that polygamous children experience more problems in psychological and social adjustment (Al-Krenawi, 1998b; Al-Krenawi & Lightman, 2000; Oyefeso & Adegoke, 1981). Two of the children had been diagnosed with mental health problems, several more had substance abuse problems, and incidents of son-to-sibling and son-to-mother intimidation were common. Moving beyond these findings, the sons were either unemployed or held low paying, manual labour jobs with low social status. Two daughters had experienced divorce, which is highly stigmatizing to Arab women (Brhoom, 1987). None of the children were seen as having married spouses of high community status.

This leads to a final theme: the elaborate coping mechanisms adopted by the six wives. As Kadiyoti (1988) insists, "women strategize within a set of concrete constraints that are identified as patriarchal bargains" (274). One of the most effective ways of analysing this process is systems theory (Goldstein, 1973; Pincus & Minahan, 1973). From the perspective of systems theory, Ahmad, his six wives, and their children, constituted one system. But within this main family system there were sub-family systems, consisting of each wife and her children. When Ahmad was in good health and enjoyed prosperity, the wives competed for his attention and for economic resources. When they were in conflict, each of the sub-family systems tended to clash as well. This acrimony in turn created its own dynamic of escalating tensions, increasing strife and causing violence between children from different sub-family systems. Intra-sub-family strain could be triggered by virtually any party (e.g., Ahmad not paying enough attention to a wife, wife-to-wife conflict, or children-to-children conflict). Ahmad rarely intervened in these instances, preferring to retain a neutral position. Similar to polygamous families in other societies, external resources, such as the wives' parental wealth, influenced marital behaviour (Mulder, 1992). The six wives were in similar economic circumstances, with the exception of D. who fared slightly better. Even so, autonomy became more of a possibility to the wives who had their own houses, and, as a result, an external source of income. The principal mechanism of change, however, was internal rather than external sources. The wives, who were given the opportunity for external resources, first had to find the courage and nerve to accept the funding.

Indeed, the family system changed decisively, and five of the six wives became closer and their conflicts reduced. Theorists have long distinguished between "power" and "authority." The former denotes an agent-object dynamic where exploiter dominates exploited; the latter term "refers to the subordination of human consciousness to a legitimate rule (and contingently to those who determine the rule)" (Asad, as cited in Nelson, 1997, p. 113). The changing family dynamics and the decline in Ahmad's authority were clearly interrelated.

In one sense, the change in his authority was gradual, corresponding with his dwindling wealth. A key turning point occurred 20 years previous, when the wives followed B.'s precedent of directly receiving their child allowance cheques. Increased economic autonomy had been preceded by growing social autonomy, each wife gaining her own home, and in D.'s case, a home under her own name. A particularly strong catalyst, however, was Ahmad's stroke. After the stroke, Ahmad's waning economic and social status was eclipsed by the ready evidence of his own mortality, and his declining physical prowess coincided with much diminished authority. The spouses openly concurred that they were less prone to "buy into" a construction of his authority; the reasons for competing for him, fearing him, and obeying him, had reduced in intensity. To paraphrase Paolo Freire (1971), they did not internalize the values of Ahmad, their oppressor, as readily, after the stroke. As one wife stated: "For us, he is dying now. He is worth nothing. God has punished him for what he did to us." This outlook at once influenced new behaviors, and in return was reinforced by these same new behaviours: new strategies of spousal coping and adaptation.

A new equilibrium emerged in the overall family system. In the old system, with six wives competing with each other, the fear of being perceived as weak precluded wives from sharing feelings and providing mutual support; such competition and jealousy is common to polygamous family structures (Al-Krenawi, 1998b; Bhugra, 1993). However, in the transformed family system, and given the commensurate reduction in Ahmad's authority and increase in his wives' autonomy, the wives had a safe context for empathizing with one another, providing mutual support, and experiencing ventilation, catharsis, and emotional release. The wives grew closer, recognizing common bonds of subjugation, and recovering the tradition of Bedouin-Arab tribal and familial feminine intimacy (Abu-Lughod, 1985b). They were able to universalize their problems, and in recognizing their common bonds of oppression, they could better validate their personal experiences (Shulman, 1984).

The experiences of these six wives affirm how polygamy, an admittedly heterogeneous construct (Kadiyoti, 1988; Mulder, 1992), can be highly malleable to changes from within. It is here that women negotiate within the family system and within their own historical and cultural contexts. By asserting themselves in this way, the women in the present polygamous case study can help scholars to better understand gendered power and authority relations among Arab peoples. Nelson (1997) rightly insists that such "dynamics.... are much more subtle than we have been led to believe" (p. 121). So, too, are they much less linear, and much less static.

The next section looks at the children of polygamous marriages, specifically, the children of the senior wife. This study is based on the notion that children in these situations are more likely to show behavioural problems than the children of monogamous parents.

CHILDREN OF POLYGAMOUS MARRIAGES

Data for this study was collected from three sources, all derived from a convenience sampling of 25 children attending one of ten Bedouin-Arab elementary schools in Rahat, a Bedouin-Arab city in the Negev and the largest in Israel (population over 40,000). The first source was the student files, which contained records of academic achievement and a comprehensive profile of the children's family background. The second source was the home room teachers of the 25 students; each was interviewed for one hour using a semi-structured questionnaire covering such topics as academic achievement, attendance, behavioural problems, dropping out, peer interactions, self concept, and stuttering. Several teachers had visited the homes of children and therefore could provide richer data than what appeared in the student files. The third source was a convenience sampling of 17 of the subjects' mothers, who were interviewed for an hour regarding their family functioning and its relationship to the student's functioning; this was collected by the school principal, one of the chapter's co-authors.

One hundred of the school's 600 children came from polygamous families. In order to provide a rich sense of sibling/half-sibling dynamics, the sample also excluded subjects who were "sole children" to a senior wife. Likewise, in order to provide as diverse a pool as possible, none of the subjects were siblings or half-siblings. The above selection criteria resulted in the selection of a sample of 15 boys and 10 girls, ranging in age from 6 to 12.

The sample children were born to the senior wife in families with two (but not more than two) wives. Families with more than two wives would have family dynamics beyond the scope of the present research and were therefore excluded from analysis. Although there is no well developed literature on the children of polygamous families, there was sufficient evidence to warrant differentiating between children born to senior wives versus those born to junior wives. No studies have compared the social and health functioning of "senior wife" versus "junior wife" children, but, as was discussed earlier in this chapter, a small body of research documents that senior wives are at particular risk of depression and somatization disorders (Al-Issa, 1990; Chaleby, 1985; El-Islam, 1975). Moreover, Bedouin-Arab fathers are known to pay greater attention to junior wives and their children compared to senior wives and their children (Al-Krenawi, 1995).

The school teaches children from kindergarten to grade six and represents children aged 5 to 12. There are no social workers on staff, no counsellors, and no psychologists, although the principal may make external referrals. Families are responsible for providing the student with their text books, pencils, pens, paper, and other supplies.

Findings

The average number of siblings related to each child, belonging to the senior wife, was five, and the average number of half-siblings, belonging to the junior wife, was three. Each subject belongs to the first of two sub-families (headed by a junior wife and senior wife) within the main family, under the authority of the father. The fathers of the subjects ranged in age from 25 to 40 and had 0 to 12 years of formal education with a mean level of education of a little over six years. One third had been unemployed over the past year, and two thirds were truck drivers or unskilled labourers employed in factories or on construction sites. None appeared to have serious health problems and all owned their homes. All lived in Rahat, and each belonged to a different family.

The senior wives ranged in age from 22 to 35. Levels of education varied from zero to eight years, with an average of 2.5 years. None had employment outside of the home. Each belonged to a different family. Two thirds co-habited the same house as the junior wife, but on different floors, and one third had a residence separate from the junior wife but in close proximity to it. Although the student files did not indicate whether any of the mothers had physical illnesses, all of the 17 interviewees had such somatic complaints as body aches, breathlessness, headaches, insomnia, or fatigue. All complained of *"assab,"* a nervous state including anxiety and tension. The normal stresses of daily living could exacerbate the *assab*, often impairing daily functioning and family harmony. All

17 complained of economic problems and described their spousal relationship as poor. They reported that their husband spent most of his time with the junior wife and her children and felt that the husband had little interest in the senior wives' children. The student files and home room teachers confirmed that none of the fathers had contacted the school to inquire about the children's academic record within the past year.

All of the 17 wives interviewed reported acrimonious relations with their husband's junior wife. It should also be noted that a common Bedouin-Arab term for a senior wife is "old wife," and for a junior wife is "young wife," with connotations of age and youth, respectively. Since youth and beauty are associated with femininity, the senior wives' self-esteem is consequently damaged by the term. Moreover, when a man takes on a second wife, the "senior wife" may be perceived as having been unable to fulfill her normal obligations as a wife.

All children had below average academic achievement and below average academic attendance. All sources of data revealed that the children of the senior wives had behavioural problems, difficulty concentrating in school, poor or sporadic school attendance, enuresis, or stuttering. Many showed low motivation towards academic achievement, poor follow-through with homework and in-class assignments, and poor peer relations. Because of their economic situation, many lacked, in part or in whole, school supplies such as text books, paper, or pencils.

These previous three sections offer nuanced insight into polygamous marriage in Bedouin-Arab society. But what should the helping professional take from them? This question will be addressed in the final section of this chapter, which looks at five principles which could be used to form the basis of helping professional practice with Bedouin-Arab polygamous families.

Implications for Helping Professional Practice

The first of the five principles mentioned above involves comprehending the significance of polygamy to the children, the senior and junior wives, the husband, and Bedouin-Arab society in general. This needs to be understood in the context of Bedouin-Arab gender construction, patriarchy, and cultural canons.

The transition from sole wife to senior wife is traumatic. Many senior wives believe that it leads to a reduction in status among her female peers and within the marriage itself, and this creates a loss of self-esteem. It is important to stress the frequent feelings of imposition: that the decision to take on a second wife is the husband's prerogative, and is made with little, if any, consultation with the first wife. Many senior wives reported feelings of betrayal, jealousy, and anger at the news of the husband's marriage to a second wife. As one senior wife put it, the existence of a junior wife entering the marriage created "a fire inside me." An Arabic term for a second wife, *darah*, ("one who makes trouble") says much about social attitudes towards a second wife. The junior wife is often younger than the senior wife, and as is the case among the subjects interviewed, is also perceived as the husband's favourite.

From a systemic perspective, polygamy can be a traumatic change to the family system. Some of the psychosocial impacts that the literature attributes to the Western experience of divorce were also encountered by senior wives' children in a polygamous context: academic problems (Bisnaire, Firestone, & Rynard, 1990), low self-esteem, and negative attitudes towards a parent (in the Bedouin-Arab case, the father) (Wiehe, 1984). Like Western children with divorced parents, how well a senior wife's child is coping may be related to how well the mother is coping (Kurtz, 1995). Finally, mourning the loss of a spouse, which is common in Western divorces, is also known to occur among Bedouin-Arab senior wives (Butler et al., 1995). When asked about the relationship with her husband, for example, one subject bitterly responded: "For me, he is dead." Another study confirms a tendency among senior wives to feel low levels of spousal affection. For example, during therapeutic group intervention with Bedouin-Arab widows, senior mothers adjusted to mourning more quickly and more easily than their junior wife counterparts (Al-Krenawi, 1996). This was demonstrated previously in chapter 2, case study three, in which we discussed group therapy intervention with respect to widows.

Although anthropologists note in some societies instances of cooperation, friendship, and amicably shared domestic labour responsibilities between co-wives (Adams & Mburugu, 1994; Borgerhoff-Mulder, 1992; Ware, 1979), this was not indicated among any of the Bedouin-Arab subjects. Indeed, the introduction of a junior wife is seen as splitting the Bedouin-Arab family into two sub-families. The senior wife may perceive that some of the husband's material resources are thus diverted from her and her children to the junior wife and her children. Competition often develops between the junior and senior wives, which in turn could create sub-family competition as the wives *and* their children compete for the husband's social and economic support (Dorjahn, 1988). Finally, as analyses of polygamy in other societies point out, such competition may reinforce an already pre-existing low self-concept among polygamous family members (Owuamanam, 1984).

The grievances a senior wife's children feel towards their father may be perceived on several levels. They may first experience the reduction of the father's social and economic support towards the senior wife and her children.

Secondly, the decline in the father's support towards their mother and in the quality of the parents' relationship often exacerbates the children's resentment towards the father. Thirdly, from a systemic perspective, the lessening of fatherly support is often, in turn, associated with an increase in reciprocal mother-to-child bonds, which in turn furthers the child's sense of commitment to the mother and anger towards the father. Finally, anger towards the father may be displaced towards the junior wife and her children. Indeed, it is common for children of two sub-families to perceive one another as "enemies" rather than as "brother" or "sister." This may be comparable to sibling rivalry in Western cultures in the context of remarriage and/or parental favouritism (Leung & Robson, 1991).

This leads to a second principle for helping professional practice: the necessity of understanding the relationship between the creation of a polygamous family and the social functioning of the senior wife's children (as previously discussed). Third, there are a variety of helping professional skills and resources that become necessary. It is important to work collaboratively with professionals in schools, and to involve them, where appropriate, in the treatment process. Teaching family members how to pay attention to children's emotional needs, and modeling such behaviour for the family members, is equally essential. Systemic thinking may also assist in carrying out effective interventions accordingly (Al-Krenawi et al., 1994). A helping professional needs to be able to read the family's ecological map: the two sub-families within the family, and the family's place in the extended family/tribe and community. It is likewise important to set realistic goals regarding the improvement of family and intra-sub-family dynamics, or the allocation of the father's resources towards sub-families. We argue that change is most successfully implemented with the active participation of the father, recognizing his considerable power over both sub-family systems. The husband's father is often respected by the husband, both wives, and their respective families, and in some cases may therefore be involved as a mediator or advocate.

Fourth, the helping professional should carefully select and target systems for intervention. Bedouin-Arab women, it should be emphasized, are socially encouraged to be loyal to their husbands. A wife who divulges family problems to anyone outside of the immediate family may be considered disloyal, and could incur the anger of her husband and/or extended family members (Mass & Al-Krenawi, 1994). Thus, it would be difficult to frame a helping professional intervention in the immediate context of meeting the wife's needs.

A far more appropriate target system is the children. *Both* parents' social status and future economic well-being are strongly dependent upon the size of the family; family honour is closely associated with the number of sons in a family and their future life successes. Thus, a helping professional intervention could feasibly be framed in the context of attending to the children's emotional, instrumental, and relational needs. The motivation to address these needs may be high, if a helping professional can help the family to appreciate the importance of their relationship to the children's social functioning at school.

Moreover, in focusing on the children's difficulties, other familial systemic issues may also be addressed. This allows for the consideration of the differential allocation of economic and social support between the two sub-families. Improvements in sub-family, half-sibling, and co-wife relations may be convincingly portrayed as interdependent. Junior and senior wives could be encouraged to perceive each other as partners, rather than opponents; half-sibling relations could improve in a similar manner.

Fifth, the value base of such interventions could be reinforced by the cultural canons of Islam. The Koran clearly emphasizes the husband's imperative to treat his wives equally: "Marry women of your choice, two, or three, or four; but if ye fear that ye shall not be able to deal justly (with them) then only one" (Koran, Surah 4, v. 3). Other Islamic ideals that are implicit to the interventions include harmony with others, peace in the family, and ensuring children's well-being.

CONCLUSION

Polygamy is a rare family-type, even when it is culturally accepted. This chapter outlined the consequences that this form of marriage has on the wives and on the children of polygamous families. Women who share a husband must deal with the dynamics and strain that this brings to their lives. Psychological strain is becoming more apparent the more this family unit is studied. The children are also affected by being in a polygamous family. They may fight with and become jealous of their half-siblings, do poorly in school, and have behavioural problems. Being aware of these consequences can assist in ensuring that this particular case is handled with sensitivity by helping professionals and other mental health care providers.

The present chapter is necessarily exploratory: a beginning point for conceptualizing the social significance of polygamy, particularly its impact upon children and the attendant prospects for successful helping professional practice. Much of the analysis, therefore, is embedded within the ethno-specific context of Bedouin-Arab society. Worthy topics for future research could focus upon longitudinal research, outcome evaluations, the perspectives of children born in polygamous families, and the practice of polygamy within societies other than the Bedouin-Arab. The next chapter analyses another important cultural experience in Bedouin-Arab society that will influence helping professional intervention: blood vengeance.

Chapter 5

HELPING PROFESSIONS IN THE CONTEXT OF BLOOD VENGEANCE

INTRODUCTION

The practice of blood vengeance, the obligation to kill in retribution for the death of a member of one's family or tribe, is illegal in most countries of the world. However, many traditional cultures – including some Bedouin-Arab – continue to practice this form of honour. This chapter begins by explaining the historical and social contexts for blood vengeance in Bedouin-Arab society. It then examines a case study in which a family is under the threat of blood vengeance and flees their tribe to ensure the safety of their tribesmen. Blood vengeance is quite literally a matter of life and death; the analysis pays particular attention to resulting, culturally appropriate helping professional intervention. A short section discusses the implications for children living under the threat of blood vengeance. The chapter closes with blood vengeance and its significance to culturally appropriate helping professional intervention.

A considerable body of research has developed among practitioners and scholars in Western societies, concluding that there are a finite number of ways to respond to conflict. One option is to dominate, wherein one side of the conflict attempts to impose its will through psychological or physical means. Another approach is capitulation, wherein one side unilaterally relinquishes its expectations or demands. A third option is withdrawal, wherein one side walks away from the conflict, refusing to be a part of it any longer. A fourth is inaction, doing nothing with the hope that the passage of time will result in changes that lead to a more favourable stasis. Negotiation is a fifth, and multi-faceted, approach that could involve a sixth related facet, mediation. Whether a conflict is settled (involving behavioural change among one or both sides) or whether it experiences a deeper level of resolution (involving a change in attitudes), may determine whether conflict will reoccur. Negotiation involves settlement, but does not necessarily result in resolution. It can only occur if there is interdependence among the disputants; if one side has everything it needs and there is nothing the other side can offer, negotiation will not be effective (Rubin, 1997, p. 6).

The present chapter will consider blood vengeance and traditional legal structures and their relevance to helping profession services. The next chapter will analyse traditional forms of mediation and their interaction with helping profession personnel. As we point out, the growing facet of modernization interacts with time-honoured modes of resolution. Notions long prominent within Islam – of the human and divine roles within the process of *Tahkim* (arbitration) – are, on some level, implicit to any practice of conflict resolution among the Bedouin-Arab (Moussalli, 1997). The Islamic *Shariah* (Islamic Law), and clear social traditions within some Arab communities, provide a set of guidelines for managing family conflicts (Faour, 1997). These guidelines may certainly be referred to within Bedouin-Arab communities of the Negev and could include principles, anchored in the Koran, that laud peaceful settlements and the avoidance of quarrels (Faour, 1997, pp. 180-3).

Helping professions typically construct vengeance as an individual or relational pathology and attempt to understand it in Western terms without sufficient ecological reference to multicultural systems (e.g., Gabriel & Monaco, 1994; Kirman, 1989; Stuckless & Goranson, 1994). Social work scholars Gabriel and Monaco, for example, refer uncritically to Karen Horney's notion of vengeance as "a neurotic solution, compulsive in nature, which had the power, if unaddressed, to become a way of life" (1994, p. 169). Likewise, these authors cite Searles' conception of vengeance as the "repression of grief and separation anxiety. It [vengeance] enables the person to avoid or postpone experiencing of both affects, because he has not really given up the other person toward whom vengefulness is directed" (1994, p. 170). Other authors, similarly, see vengeance as a reflection of narcissistic rage (Kohut, cited in Gabriel & Monaco, 1994, p. 170), and as family resistances requiring clinical intervention (Kirman, 1989, p. 95).

In contrast, to understand Bedouin-Arab vengeance is to appreciate it on its own, culturally-specific, terms. Blood vengeance is a long-standing Bedouin-Arab tradition, a form of collective guarantee provided by a given group to all of its members (Jabbur, 1995) in a society where communal duty is paramount. It evolved, in part, from the special needs of a nomadic, warrior people, wherein living in tents, without the benefit of solid walls in the sparsely populated desert, makes one vulnerable to attack by others. It therefore reflects the need for some system of justice in the absence of the formal methods, the legal specialists, or the police forces that are common to Western societies (Rieder, 1984, p. 134). Blood vengeance continues to occur in the Arab world, with a recent example being the occurrence of several killings in the Negev region of Israel in 2006 and 2008, as well as the 2007 killings in Jordan and Egypt (Personal Communication with a Jordanian social worker, 1996).

The Arabic term for vengeance, *"Thaar,"* is defined as "to ask for his blood or to kill the killer." In the Arab world, taking revenge is considered to be a person's right. As culturally acceptable behaviour, it is not condemned, providing that the circumstances are considered warranted (Al-Munjed, 1975). Indeed, the *Al-Thaar*, a person who seeks revenge on another tribe member under just circumstances, is often considered a hero within his own tribe.

Thus, unlike synonyms in the English language such as spite, malice, vindictiveness, envy, or rage, the Bedouin-Arab conception of vengeance is more than an emotional response to a perceived wrong: it is based on a perception of being in the right, and of restoring symmetry to an unbalanced social exchange (Rieder, 1984, p. 133). Indeed, the level of coercion that is initially perceived is directly related to the level of counter-aggression (Collins, as cited in Rieder, 1984, p. 142). The need to move from inequality based on the rule of the strong, to the balance of relative equals, figures prominently (Rieder, 1984, p. 139). Consequently, a vengeance relationship requires individuals, families, and tribes to avoid any hint of weakness, since impressions and deterrence count as much as reality, and since symbolic and physical attacks are closely linked (Rieder, 1984, p. 138).

Vengeance extends broadly across all areas of social life, rendering economic property, property of honour, and sexual property, homologous (Rieder, 1984, p. 138). If a male member of the group is killed, this is considered to be a crime committed against the group as a whole (Ginat, 1987) and economic hardship is expected to befall the victim's family. Likewise, if a man is killed by another tribe, a mark of shame (*Ar*) descends upon the aggrieved tribe that can only be removed by killing a member of the offending tribe in return (Al-Aref, 1944). If a female is killed, on the other hand, four males of the offending tribe would have to be killed to even the score (Al-Abaddi, 1973). If, however, the murderer is female, revenge should be at the hands of a female member of the aggrieved tribe (Al-Krenawi, A., Personal Communication, 1996).

Potential murderers know that in killing one individual, which may seem an easy matter, they are exposing themselves and their family, extended family, or tribe to the terrible threat of group vengeance. The status of *Al-Madmi* (a person who kills a man from another tribe), in this sense, can be extended to all members of the murderer's tribe. The act of murder may take generations to be avenged, for in the desert there is no statute of limitations (Ginat, 1987). From early childhood, a Bedouin-Arab learns that a murder is never forgiven. Even death does not bring forgiveness: if the murderer dies, another member of his group, though innocent, must pay for the crime (Arad, 1984). This custom is deeply rooted in the Bedouin-Arab culture, as the saying, "blood can only be erased by blood" attests.

THE RITUALS OF VENGEANCE IN BEDOUIN-ARAB SOCIETY

There are several factors that determine blood vengeance. One of these is the tribal concept of *kahams*, "the group formed by all descendants of one ancestor to the fifth generation" (Marx, as cited in Ginat, 1984, p. 80). If a killer and a victim are not members of the same *kahams*, then blood money (*diyya*) can be paid through the services of a mediator. There is generally a period of *'atwa* (a waiting period) prior to the agreement of a *diyya*. Its effective duration is not clearly defined, although it usually lasts at least one month, during which time, until the *diyya* has been paid, "every member of the murderer's co-liable [*kahams*] group lives in constant fear of death" (Ginat, 1984, p. 60). When no *'atwa* is reached, another member of the family, not necessarily the murderer, is likely to be killed. When members of the co-liable group understand that one of their members acted without due consideration of collective responsibility, he is likely to be expelled from the group.

If, however, a killer and a victim are members of the same *kahams* and tribal relations are relatively good, then the killer is exiled for several years, becoming a *meshamas*. Among some Bedouin-Arab, the killer's family gives his closest unmarried female relative (*ghura*) to the closest male kin of the victim. The *ghura* lives with this person until she gives birth to a male offspring. This is done in order to compensate for the loss of the male during the killing. After the birth, the *ghura* can return to her natal family. Usually, she marries the person who had taken her as *ghura*. If, on the other hand, a killer and victim are members of the same *kahams* and tribal relations are not relatively good, money is asked for. In these cases, similar conditions of *'atwa* and *diyya*, as per above, apply. Moreover, if *'atwa* is not met, then one person from the co-liable group is killed.

Another parameter that determines blood vengeance is tribal status. If, for example, the offending tribe is sufficiently powerful, the *sheikh*s of the aggrieved tribe may choose to substitute symbolic acts for death to expiate its shame. This occurs in a ceremony called *sulha* (a compromise between two parties in dispute) conducted by important community leaders, such as *sheikh*s, who are asked to intervene in order to settle a controversy (Landsman, 1988). In one instance, a person who had murdered a man from another family had visited the murdered person's family with tribally appointed mediators. He said to the *sheikh*, "Here I am, you can kill me." The day after, the *sheikh* of the tribe called the people in the area and said to that man, "I can kill you, but I am a man." The *sheikh* cut the man's hair in front of the people and said to the man "Go on your way" (Al-Krenawi, K., Personal Communication, 1996).

THE EFFECT OF BLOOD VENGEANCE ON CHILDREN'S MENTAL HEALTH

The literature has long recognized that social conditions such as poverty, unemployment, inadequate housing, poor health care, and low educational opportunities increase the incidence of child abuse and neglect (Doyle, 1996). Considerable progress has been made in discerning some of the culturally specific parameters of what may be perceived as abuse or neglect (Hogan & Siu, 1988; Krajewski-Jaime, 1991; Saunders Nelson, & Landsman, 1993). Authors have distinguished an *emic* perspective, the viewpoint of members of the cultural group in question, from an *etic* perspective, that is, one that is interpreted from an outside viewpoint (Korbin 1980, 1981; Korr, 1986; Lum, 1995). Some studies have looked into childbearing and childrearing practices in instances where *emic* and *etic* conceptions are in conflict and where they are in agreement (Beavers, 1986; Siegel, 1994). However, few cross-cultural studies have moved beyond the immediate family to consider the *emic* and *etic* perspectives in relation to broad societal factors that may be associated with abuse or neglect.

The following section examines how the widespread Bedouin-Arab practice of blood vengeance has serious implications regarding child neglect. For the purposes of this study, neglect occurs "when the basic needs of children are not met, regardless of cause" (Dubowitz et al., 1993, p. 10). It includes such criteria as a lack of parental/guardian supervision, nutrition, clothing and hygiene, physical health care, mental health care, and developmental/educational care (Trocme, 1996).

In order to illustrate our points, we will briefly examine a study published in *Child Abuse and Neglect* (Al-Krenawi, Slonim-Nevo, Maymon, & Al-Krenawi, 2001) to provide empirical data demonstrating that blood vengeance can be a horrific problem for children. The goal of this study was to investigate the well-being of Arab adolescents who live under the threat of ongoing blood vengeance, and to assess the impact of socio-demographic characteristics, cultural context, and family functioning as mediating factors. The sample consisted of 100 adolescents (aged 12-14 yrs) in grades 6-8. Self-reported standardized measures were used to assess the participants' level of self-esteem, mental health, and perceived family functioning. The participants of this study demonstrated higher levels of distress and symptomatic behaviour as compared to the Israeli norms. In a series of multiple regressions, General Family Functioning, as perceived by the participants, emerged as the major predictor associated with mental health. Female participants reported a higher anxiety level than their male counterparts. Male participants, on the other hand, were more willing to continue the feud of blood vengeance, as measured in subjective terms. These findings suggest that there are similarities among children and adolescents who live in war zones and those who live under the threat of blood vengeance. Family functioning appears as the major mediator of well-being (Al-Krenawi et al., 2001).

A CASE EXAMPLE

A man from a large and powerful tribe in the Negev was murdered, and although the murderer was arrested, Bedouin-Arab law and the custom of blood vengeance dictated that a male of equal rank from the murderer's tribe must be killed. The murderer came from a small, relatively powerless family. It was therefore clear that the man's sole brother, or one of the brother's male children, was essentially on "death row." Immediately, to avoid conflict with the tribe of the murdered man, and because the lives of the family members were in danger, senior members of the murderer's tribe, which his family had been a part of for two generations, told his brother to leave the tribe. Not knowing when or from whence the retribution would come, he and his family fled to an isolated part of the desert. For the past three years they had been living in extreme poverty and total isolation. The condemned family consisted of the man, aged fifty, his wife, forty-five years old, and six children ranging in age from six to sixteen.

Because they were of low social status, there was little possibility of mediation within the current social order or protection from a larger and therefore more powerful tribe. Moreover, having only been a part of the tribe for two generations meant that only the immediate family would be known to the offended tribe, thereby narrowing the target to this nuclear family.

The book's co-author, a helping professional of Bedouin-Arab ethnicity, worked with the family over a three month period of weekly sessions. The following is an analysis of the family's problems and the helping professional interventions utilized to help alleviate these problems.

Striking a Helping Alliance

Striking a helping alliance with this family required considerable culturally-sensitive knowledge and skill. At the first contact with the family, for example, the helping professional waited outside the tent and called *Yaa Raai Albit* (greetings), an acceptable address in Bedouin-Arab culture. He also provided numerous assurances that he was not going to hurt the family, and that no Bedouin-Arab tribe had sent him there. During the first contact, the father gave the social worker three cups of coffee; when he offered a fourth, the social worker declined, at which point the father remarked "That's right, you are a Bedouin." The cups of coffee were a test: a Bedouin-Arab does not drink more than three cups of coffee in succession. After this point, the father began to trust the social worker, and gradually divulged the circumstances leading to the family's current situation.

The helping professional was also able to connect with the father by understanding the significance of the latter's use of proverbs and metaphors (Al-Krenawi & Graham, 1996a; Al-Krenawi, Graham, & Maoz, 1996; Devore & Schlesinger, 1991; Landsman, 1988; Lieberman, 1990; Slattery, 1987). The father began explaining his situation, for instance, by citing the famous Bedouin-Arab proverb *Weish Izaak Ala Almor Ger Al-Amr Minh*, "the worst situation leads to an even worse situation." Rather than explicitly identifying feelings, he tended to rely on metaphors such as *Qlbi Lonh*, "my heart looks black, like the colour of these ashes" (in the fire by which they both sat).

The social worker was also able to interact with other members of the family. He understood the concept of gender separation, and once inside the tent, sat in the *Shiq* section, that area where men sit. The wife immediately left for the *Mahraham*, where women congregate in the event of a visit by a male visitor. The social worker did not ask to speak with the wife, for fear of compromising her, himself, or both.

The social worker observed and interacted with the children while they played games, discerning much, as will be seen, about their coping and feelings. He also participated in much of the family life, including their meals, the parents' conversations with their children, and the family's few recreational activities such as storytelling or music playing. By doing so, the social worker was able to gain the family's confidence more than might have been possible in a more formal professional relationship. The corresponding trust enabled him to discuss the family's difficulties in greater depth. Key to this engagement was an appreciation of and respect for the family's world view, and a concomitant impulse to integrate the social worker's own ideas regarding the family's problems with the familiar perceptions and strategies that the family members had developed on their own. Had he done otherwise, the social worker might have met resistance, if not outright expulsion from the family setting.

Poverty

The family's most pressing need was the resolution of their deep poverty. They lived in a simple tent near a rough track about five kilometres from the nearest road, without running water or toilet facilities. The tent was bare, save for a few simple cooking implements and sparse amounts of clothing. Family members wore ragged clothing and, although able to feed themselves, were obviously underweight and appeared malnourished.

Providing basic subsistence assistance required an understanding of the family's need for anonymity from those who might seek to fulfill their "obligation" for blood vengeance. Intervention, therefore, had to be informal and outside of the institutional setting, since the danger of identification would put the family at further risk. Once permission from the father was granted to bring food and clothing to the children, these were obtained for all members of the family from friends and a nearby *Kibbutzim* without revealing details of the case.

Addressing another need of the family, social security assistance was discussed with the father and a strategy was agreed upon. Since the females of the family were not in danger, the social worker made an appointment for the mother in Beer-Sheva (the main city in the Negev) and escorted her to the social security office. Within a month, the first payment was issued. From then on, the mother went monthly to Beer-Sheva to obtain welfare and to shop for necessities. Attending to basic survival needs alleviated some of the family's anxiety and allowed rapport and trust to deepen.

Mental Health

The parents' expectations that their eldest son, age 16, could take care of the family were tempered by the knowledge that, as the eldest, he too would be vulnerable to vengeance. The father also revealed at length his worries about the family's current and future problems, should he be killed. He often revealed his fears and anxiety by quoting Arabic proverbs rather than speaking of his despair outright. Cultural prohibitions restricted the extent of personal communication possible between the male researcher and the mother. Therefore, much of what was learned about her coping strategies came from observation at a distance and through commentary from the husband. The mother occupied most of her time with family chores and with caring for her family. She occasionally enjoyed periods of solitude, where she apparently cried and prayed to God to help them escape their hardship.

The children tended to talk little, but spoke freely once the social worker participated in their games. The girls did not talk very much about their uncle, although they said that their mother had told them that one of their brothers or their father might be murdered. During the social worker's participation in the boys' games, the eldest son indicated that all of the children understood the danger. He himself felt it acutely, knowing that he was a potential target of blood vengeance, and that should his father be killed, he would have to take full responsibility for the well-being of the entire family. Thus, in several respects, his former plans to prepare himself to take his place as an educated member of modern society had been replaced by fear, uncertainty, and helplessness. The resulting confusion was manifested in sleeplessness and fear.

When the social worker began to talk about the Bedouin-Arab custom of vengeance, the boys became angry, both towards the custom and their uncle. All of the children stayed close to the tent at all times, did not go to school, and had no friends for fear of being located. Two of the children wet their bed and one of the girls had a serious stammer. All appeared thin and physically underdeveloped. Although the eldest son was very active during the conversations, the other children talked little, lacking verbal and social skills. In Bedouin-Arab society, children learn social behaviour from their peers in large extended family interactions. Lacking such peer interaction, the younger children seemed socially underdeveloped.

The children had a peculiar way of speaking to each other, as if unable to communicate other than by crying, shouting, or calling each other derogatory names like *Abu Shaka* (one who wets the bed). The violent means of this social interaction appeared to be modeled after the father who, except when telling stories, communicated with his family members exclusively by shouting. The eldest expressed his culturally determined leadership position by ordering the others about in each of their activities. In their interactions with each other, the children acted angrily and violently, the slightest provocation making them nervous. The games of both the girls and boys tended to be aggressive, showing the stress that they were experiencing.

Coping Strategies

The family's socially marginalized status from its ordinary locus of social and economic support—the broader tribe—should not be equated with *psychological* marginality (Dickie-Clark, 1966). Indeed, the family exhibited numerous coping strategies, many of which provided solace and served as avenues for catharsis and venting. One such example was religion. The parents indicated that the ordeal had made them more religious. Both referred frequently to *Algder*, the Muslim conception of fate arising out of *Hakmat Allah* (God's judgment), and often prayed for the patience of Job (Al-Krenawi, 1996; El-Islam, 1982). While the children tended to blame their uncle for their situation, the father blamed Satan.

Music is often used in Bedouin-Arab culture to express psychological dilemmas (Har-Zion, 1988), and the father, often accompanying himself with the *Rababa* (a guitar-like instrument), sang sad Bedouin-Arab poems, venting his anger and sadness, bringing temporary relief from his suffering. In his song he said that he imagined himself walking in circles, as if in prison, with no possibility of exit.

While there was a lack of communication between the parents and the children, conversation being limited mostly to practical tasks, there were occasional opportunities for sharing stories that tended to be allegories for their current life situation. The father, for example, sometimes told his sons stories about a legendary hero from the past whose strength and power enabled him to survive incredible hardship. The mother told her daughters stories about the ideal woman who worked hard beside her husband, patiently enduring God's judgment.

The children's games, in a similar manner, tended to reinforce their coping strategies, as well as culturally-prescribed gender construction and gender separation in play and work (Abu-Lughod, 1985b; Al-Krenawi et al., 1994; Mass & Al-Krenawi, 1994; Peristiany, 1974). The boys often played *Al-Zaab Wa Al-Raee* (the wolf and the shepherd), each child assuming the role of a wolf, a shepherd, and the sheep herd. Over a period of an hour and a half, the wolf tries to trick the shepherd in order to capture the sheep, at which point he wins the game and becomes the shepherd. This game presents the male constructs of continual vigilance, strength, bravery, and cunning against potential threat to the family's property.

The girls played *Holetkin Yaa Banaat* (to encourage girls to dance), whereby two girls sit in a circle and sing, with a third dancing in the centre. One of the seated girls tries to slap the dancer; when the dancer is slapped, she stops dancing, and starts singing. The girl who stays dancing the longest without getting slapped wins the game, and the other girls carry her and sing for her. This game, like its male counterpart, emphasizes cunning, aggression, and vigilance against external threats.

The Role of the Helping Professional

Helping profession intervention in this case rests upon seven principal elements. The first is the capability of *not* being—nor being seen as—an authority figure. In the social worker's opinion, immediate seizure, or simply the threat of immediate seizure, of the children would have created more problems than benefits for both the children and parents. The family would have gone through the trauma of separation, and in the absence of culturally sensitive service delivery, the children themselves might have been exposed to a greater risk of vengeance retribution, since they would no longer be in hiding.

A second, related point is the necessity of striking a positive helping alliance based on acceptance, respect, trust, and validation of the family's current situation. This is inextricably related to a third facet, namely cultural sensitivity in appreciating the ecological context of, and significance to family members of, blood vengeance, as well as the family members' perception of their circumstances, problems, and resources. Indeed, the social worker was able to reiterate the parents' interpretation of the gravity of the family's predicament. He assured the children that retribution to the family was possible because of the vengeance circumstances.

And yet, to return to the second point, the social worker was able to provide empathy and understanding. He also had the opportunity to talk to the children about their bed-wetting, to provide information about its relationship to stress, and to work with the children, using several behavioural interventions to reduce the incidence of bed-wetting (Azrin, Sneed, & Fox, 1974). Likewise, the social worker treated the stuttering of one child, using shadowing and syllable-timed speech treatments (Cherry & Sayers, 1956; Kondas, 1967; Meyer & Mair, 1963).

Fourth, though the social worker employed a repertoire of sophisticated techniques, none were culturally inappropriate (an example of an inappropriate intervention might have been a formal family therapy session). Nor did he impose a social work physical setting upon the family: home visits were essential to establishing a professional relationship.

The fifth point was the social worker's participation in the children's games. This enabled him to build upon the children's strengths and current resources. This was related to the sixth point, being that participation in the children's games was an important culturally sensitive technique that allowed the social worker to develop trust and to better discern their situation (Sue & Zane, 1987). He was also able to assist the children in improving their communication by modeling and by having the opportunity to identify dysfunctional sibling communication and immediately suggesting and/or positively reinforcing more functional patterns. The children, in turn, applied this improved communication style to interactions with their parents, and in consultation with the social worker, were able to enhance parent-child communication.

Finally, perhaps most important of all, the social worker was able to provide many concrete services for meeting the family's basic needs, including providing clothing, food, school books, and toys, and enabling the family's access to monthly income security payments, which the mother had previously received in a nearby city. To the family, this assistance evidently signified the professional's sincerity, recognition of the family's most urgent needs, and capacity to be of help.

The helping professional broached the possibility of the children attending school at a future date. The significant distance from schools, the family's deliberate *in cognito* status, and the ever-present necessity of instant mobility precluded this for the time being. Instead, the younger children were being taught how to read and write by the oldest sibling, and were also instructed by the helping professional during his weekly visits.

Much of the success of the helping professional's role lay in his dual status as a helping professional and as a member of his clients' culture. In successfully applying helping profession practice to this situation and then describing how this was done, the helping professional has reinforced the growing helping profession knowledge base in supporting greater cultural sensitivity and inclusion in practice.

Implications for the Helping Professional Practice

Several implications for helping professional practice emerge from this discussion of blood vengeance. The first is that the cultural significance of blood vengeance, perhaps more than any other custom, points out the paradoxical role of the individual in Bedouin-Arab society. Bedouin-Arabs receive, from their family, extended family, and tribe, social support of considerable depth and breadth. However, as the blood vengeance example of the *Al-Madmi* demonstrates, these supports may suffer in return, due to actions of the individual. In this way, status within a tribe can create tremendous difficulties for individuals and families.

Vengeance can also help one to appreciate the Arab conceptions of individual and group rights, as well as what may appear to Western eyes as the seeming lack of reverence for individual life. The welfare of *Al-Madmi* children cannot be understood without reference to blood vengeance. In some cases, *Al-Madmi* children may be neglected; blood vengeance can therefore put the children at risk, increasing the probability of poverty and cognitive and behavioural problems associated with neglect (Erickson, Egeland, & Pianta, 1989; Gove, Hughes, & Galle, 1983; Martin & Walters, 1982; Sandgrund & Gaines, 1974). Because vengeance is the pivotal force behind the problems identified, helping profession interventions with a condemned family must be collaborative, supportive, non-condemning, and highly sensitive to context. In order to effectively mobilize a family's resources rather than impede them, the social worker should be a helper rather than a representative of a potentially judgmental authority. A deeper familiarity with central indigenous practices such as blood vengeance can provide a beginning point that can lead to this desired end.

There are several areas where helping professionals could effectively operate in the above vengeance contexts. Social workers could broker, mediate, or find members of the Bedouin-Arab community to determine the timing or amount of a *diyya* payment, to negotiate an *'atwa*, a *sulha*, or other non-violent alternatives to blood vengeance, to select the location, duration, and other contexts of a *mashama*, or to decide the terms of a *ghura*'s relationship with the aggrieved family prior to and after the birth of a male successor. Social workers could assist the offending family in bearing the emotional, financial, and potentially mortal costs of an *'atwa*. They could counsel or advocate on behalf of individuals who have become *mashamas* or *ghura* and could advocate on behalf of an offending family to the aggrieved family, or, if this is unsuccessful, to other powerful families that might provide greater leverage. In the case of an unresolved *'atwa*, the social worker could attempt to mediate between the "traditional" conception of justice, which could lead to the death of a male member of the offending family, and the "modern" justice system which would view this death as a punishable offence.

However, these roles, and other similar roles, have not been documented, in large part because of the limited contact of modern helping professions with this traditional culture. The continued settlement of the Bedouin-Arab, however, and their integration into "mainstream" modern Middle Eastern societies, increases the likelihood that Bedouin-Arab people will interact with the helping professions. To this end, the preceding case study provides an opportunity to begin considering how best to approach the Bedouin-Arab concept of vengeance.

CONCLUSION

Blood vengeance was both the cause of this family's private trouble—their economically and socially marginalized status—and a public issue that transcended the immediate range of the family's life (Mills, 1963, pp. 395-396). This chapter clearly demonstrated that being under the threat of blood vengeance has harmful and negative effects on children's behaviour and mental well-being. The social worker in the present case study advanced clinical services directly to the family. In order to address the structural causes of the family's plight, however, further community development work could find a helping professional in the role of advocate, broker, or mediator (Budman, Lipson, & Meleis, 1992; Weidman, 1982) in order to continue to bridge the gap between non-Western cultures such as the Bedouin-Arab (the *emic*) and the helping professions (the *etic*).

Chapter 6

TRADITIONAL MEDIATION AND CONFLICT RESOLUTION: COLLABORATION WITH SOCIAL WORKERS AT THE LEVEL OF THE COMMUNITY

INTRODUCTION

In order to treat clients successfully, a helping professional must have an understanding of the client's social background and a way of understanding and interpreting his/her environment. The way in which clients conceptualize and articulate their problems can vary significantly across cultures and may be misunderstood by practitioners, particularly those from different cultural backgrounds than their clients (Al-Issa, 1970, 1982; Bilu & Witztum, 1993; Westermeyer, 1993). Misunderstanding clients due to a lack of cultural sensitivity may create barriers to access, or provide occasions for misdiagnoses/misassessments as well as the selection of inappropriate approaches to intervention (Fabrega, Ulrich, & Mezich, 1993; Kilgus, Pumariega, & Cuffe, 1995).

Several resources can be utilized in order to avoid these negative consequences. Collaborative relationships, of which there are several types, are perhaps one of the most important of these resources and will be discussed in detail below. Also imperative, as has been stressed throughout this volume, is understanding a culture from that culture's viewpoint. In a Bedouin-Arab society, traditional beliefs are usually paramount, and although they are sometimes utilized in collaboration with western ideas of mental health treatment, they should not be understood in the same ways. Rituals, which are discussed further on in this chapter, are one method used by this community to mediate situations. Understanding and being sensitive to the long tradition and significance of these rituals is crucial in being perceived as a culturally sensitive outsider. This is one reason that relationships must be created and that a bridge between cultures must be established.

This chapter points out the strengths and weaknesses of several types of collaborative relationships. It also explores a case study in which the use of a cultural mediator is discussed and analysed. Finally, it looks at one case study in which a traditional ritual, the *Bisha*, is utilized.

COLLABORATIVE RELATIONSHIPS AND CULTURALLY SENSITIVE PRACTICE

Helping professionals can develop culturally sensitive practice by utilizing available resources. In the Bedouin-Arab community, there are a number of ways that a helping professional can communicate more effectively with his/her client. The following section discusses several of these options. Recent literature discusses numerous ways in which other personnel can be used to enhance a practitioner's cultural competence. The first class of these personnel is cultural interpreters. Content from the proceeding several paragraphs was derived from social work as well as such allied helping professions as psychiatry, nursing, and psychology.

Cultural Interpreter

Interpreters are bilingual people who orally translate communication between individuals and their clinicians (professionals who provide mental health service) (Cheng, 1987). They are often people who are chosen because of convenience or availability (such as other clients waiting to see the clinician, direct care staff, etc.). However, sharing a common language does not guarantee understanding, because if the bilingual interpreter has no knowledge of or background in the ethnic culture of the help-seeking individual, translations that may be literally correct may not convey the essence of an ethnic individual's response (Singh, McKay, & Singh, 1999). In addition, interpreters focus on translating only the spoken word and fail to "translate" the very important nonverbal cues that are emitted by the individual. In many cultures, normal social interactions rely very heavily on nonverbal communication (Singh, McKay, & Singh, 1998). Family members and relatives may also, on occasion, be asked to provide interpreting services. This practice is most inappropriate for many reasons. For example, being inexperienced interpreters, family members may minimize potentially embarrassing information about the individual seeking mental health services, thereby depriving the clinician of relevant diagnostic information (Glasser, 1983). Further, in some cultures, particular family members are designated to receive any important information affecting the family first, and that member has the decision-making power to disclose the information to whichever other family members he or she sees necessary (Pottinger, Perivolaris & Howes, 2007). Using family members as interpreters does not show respect for these, and other, common cultural norms.

Having an interpreter does not necessarily remove cultural barriers to therapeutic communication between the individual and the clinician. Even when interpreters have been trained in Western mental health concepts, they will still need to be trained in the ethnic individual's cultural concepts, rituals, beliefs, and mental health practices to be able to understand culturally bound attitudes towards diseases and disorders, culturally-bound etiologies for diseases and disorders, and 'culture-bound' diseases and disorders themselves (i.e. diseases or symptoms considered to be a recognizable illness only within a particular cultural or ethnic group). Clearly, although bilingual capacity is necessary, it is not sufficient for a person to be an effective interpreter (Singh, McKay, & Singh, 1999).

Cultural Broker

Cultural brokers may provide an effective alternative to interpreters in the delivery of mental health services to people from minority cultures. Cultural brokers are people who are acculturated in one or more minority cultures *and* the mainstream culture (Herzog, 1972; Paine, 1971). They are able to straddle multiple cultures, and function as linguistic and cultural bridges between cultures. Cultural brokers are in the unique position of being able to communicate the nuances and values of a minority culture to the majority culture, as well as communicate the nuances and values of the mainstream culture to the minority culture (Singh, McKay, & Singh, 1999). They are different from bilingual interpreters in that they not only make communication possible between speakers of different languages, but also enhance the interaction and understanding between people of different cultures.

The term cultural broker was introduced in the area of mental health by Weidman (1975) to refer to an intermediary who works with therapists from the mainstream culture and clients from other cultures. The cultural broker facilitates the understanding of the clinician regarding the nature of the problem or psychiatric disorder, as perceived by the individual who is seeking the mental health services. The cultural broker also helps the individual to understand how the problem or disorder is viewed and treated by the clinician (Singh, McKay, & Singh, 1999). There are often differences in the mental health ideologies and practices of the ethnic individual seeking services and the clinician providing them. Further, both lack information about each other's expectations, particularly those related to the treatment process.

Given the different cultural backgrounds of the clinicians and the individuals seeking services, it is likely that their expectations for each other may only partially overlap. One of the roles of a cultural broker is to increase this overlap by changing the expectations of both the clinician and the individual through informal education. The clinician does not have the necessary background or cultural experience to correctly interpret the ethnic individual's responses. It is the combination of linguistic, cultural, and mental health knowledge and skills that constitute the cultural broker's unique expertise in identifying relevant information for the cultural aspects of the ethnic individual's mental illness (Singh, McKay, & Singh, 1999). A cultural broker has a comparative understanding of how the mental health system in the ethnic culture differs from that of the mainstream culture, and is able to clearly explain these differences to both the ethnic individual and the mainstream clinician. Cultural brokers may also be useful with ethnic individuals who speak the majority language by facilitating cultural communication.

Cultural Consultant

Budman et al. (1992) used the term cultural consultant to describe the involvement of an Arabic-speaking consultant, a nurse-sociologist, in the case of an Iraqi-American adolescent who was admitted to a psychiatric inpatient unit. The cultural consultant could be defined as one type of a cultural broker, who is, in addition to being acculturated in the minority culture and the majority culture, a mental health practitioner. As such, the cultural consultant can not only translate or interpret the interaction between the clinician and the help seeking individual, but can also take an active role in the process of diagnosing and treating the individual. In the case study described by Budman et al. (1992) the cultural consultant helped in three areas: cultural interpretation, suggestions to improve psychiatric care, and primary care before and after the patient's hospitalization. In general, the cultural consultant's role is to bridge the gap between the clinician on one hand and the help seeking individual (and, on occasion, his/her family) on the other hand. S/he does so by helping to clarify the explanatory model used by each side to the other. Therefore, the cultural consultant needs in-depth knowledge of the worldviews of both the health care providers and the patient and family.

With the goal of helping each to understand the other's framework without favouring or alienating either, the cultural consultant should have cultural maturity. Ideally, the cultural consultant should have experience or training in the psychiatric field and should be bicultural and bilingual. Awareness of one's own identity, behaviour, and biases is also important. The cultural consultant in mental health can serve as a broker and a diagnostician, helping the therapist to determine the patient's problem or disorder. S/he can help the mental health professional to answer the question "is the patient's behaviour normal?", a question that lies at the heart of cross-cultural psychiatry, a field that must determine normality in its cultural context.

Cultural Mediator

The cultural mediator's purpose is to mediate between two cultures that represent different perceptions and ways of reaching the same goal—promoting personal and social welfare in the community. The role of the cultural mediator is based on motives of cooperation rather than conflict, which stands in contrast to the purpose of "regular" mediation: mediating between two sides that represent different interests (Shemer & Bar-Gay, 2001). In order to facilitate cooperation, the cultural mediator's role is to "translate" the ways that different cultures define a conflict, how they attempt to solve it, and how they behave towards one another (Fry & Fry, 1997). Besides being a cross-cultural translator, the cultural mediator also functions as a buffer between cultures that helps to maintain the unique identity of each side (Al-Krenawi & Graham, 2001b).

The importance of the cultural mediator in the community lies in his/her ability to encourage the empowerment of different groups in the community that are deprived of access to the power centers in the society. The cultural mediator, therefore, is not perceived as a neutral third side, but he/she is expected to promote social justice in the community and improve cultural sensitivity (Schellenberg, 1996).

The analysis of social work in one Arab community in the Middle East advocates for collaborative work with this long-standing cultural tradition well predating the profession. The cultural mediator (CM), in this case, provides insight into how social work might begin to interact with an Arab community in Israel that has only recently begun to encounter helping professionals. The authors do not profess to offer the only means to this end, but rather a starting point that could be used as the basis for future culturally appropriate interventions and research.

The social work-CM interface is far from perfect. However, in its current format, it has the potential to render interventions more culturally appropriate, bridge gaps between the cultural and professional canons, and promote helping profession's role in communities that have only a negligible understanding of the vocation. As we elaborate, CM methods of settling disputes involve culturally appropriate forms of communication, understanding conceptions of victimization and forgiveness, appreciating attitudes towards conflict and the role of the individual in society, kinship, family, and patriarchy, and the maintenance of individual, group, and family honour (Irani, 1999). First, the CM is explained, including its development in the Bedouin-Arab community, its significance to and encounters with social work practice, and its potential trans-cultural applications. As is stressed in the conclusion, future helping professional research and practice should focus on further enhancing women's choice making opportunities in this patriarchal culture.

The next section discusses the role and meaning of mediation within the Arab community. A case example follows, which includes a description and analysis of the cultural mediator project which took place in Rahat, Israel.

MEDIATION IN ARAB SOCIETY

Throughout the Arab world, mediation practices have existed to resolve individual, familial, and group conflicts (Salem, 1997). Typically, people implementing traditional forms of conflict resolution have not required training credentials or higher education. With this in mind, strictly speaking, such mediation tasks cannot be described as indigenous helping professions. At the same time however, as Canadian expert Edward Kruk contends, mediation has been applied to areas conventionally analogous to social work and the human service fields. Significant potential exists for further application of mediation as a practice model, as well as the more informal incorporation of mediation skills into everyday social work practice (Kruk, 1997). These insights, we argue, have bearing on the type of Arab conflict resolution we discuss.

Among Arab peoples, the *sulh* (settlement) is the society's major reconciliation ritual, in which other traditional mediation functions are involved: the *musalaha* (reconciliation), the *tahkeem* (arbitration), and the *wasta* (patronage-mediation) (Irani, 1999; Khadduri, 1997). These traditional mediation roles reflect Muslim values. According to Islamic Law, the *sulh* is a contract (*akd*) that is legally binding on the individual and community, the purpose of which is "to end conflict and hostility among believers" and to promote Islamic norms of harmonious individual and community relations (Khadduri, 1997, p. 845). The Jordanian government recognizes the *sulh* in its legal codes, and it is widely practised among Palestinians and Arabs in Israel, Lebanon, and Syria (Abu-Nimer, 1996; Irani, 1999).

The following section concentrates on one such mediation function, the *wasta*, an Arab word meaning mediation and derived from the literary phrase *wastat al-kalada*, the precious stone in the middle of a necklace (Al-Munjad, 1975). This term emphasizes the centrality of the stone, flanked on either side by other beads (Farrag, 1977; Witty, 1980), suggesting an inter-relationship between all parties and highlighting the well-respected status of the *wasit* (mediator). The *wasta* is a centuries old tradition within Arab society. The *wasit* are usually well respected, senior men within the collective who initiate interventions in times of dispute within or between families, extended families, *hamula*, or tribes. Their ascribed status is based on several cultural values. The first value is respect for age, providing legitimacy and credibility for intervention in a social conflict. The second is familiarity with the history of the city, region, and people. A third related value is knowledge of the community's customs and social fabric. A fourth is high community status and considerable power, based on kinship connections, political position, religious merit, and previous mediation experience (Abu-Nimer, 1996; Landsman, 1988; Rothenberger, 1978; Witty, 1978). A fifth is the pre-eminent role of the family in all aspects of Arab life. A sixth, as will be elaborated, is the *wasta*'s gendered function of leadership within a patriarchal social structure.

The Cultural Mediator Project

Rahat

This project was initiated in Rahat, Israel, the largest Bedouin-Arab city of the Negev, and the largest in Israel. As elaborated in chapter two, unemployment rates are high, the population is very young, and family size is large. The modern and traditional architectures co-exist. Constructed houses exist side-by-side, with traditional tents, and livestock kept both within and outside of city limits (*Rahat City Annual Report, 1998*). The Social Service office in Rahat, which is funded by the federal Ministry of Social Affairs (75%) and the city (25%), is mandated by national legislation but administered by local authority. It was opened in 1982, with 1 social worker on staff. At the time of running the mediator project, it employed 13 social workers, 6 of whom were Bedouin-Arab and 7 of whom were Jewish; 7 were women and 6 were men. All had BSW-level training from Israeli universities, official certification, and practice experience ranging from 1 to 15 years. Since federal legislation deemed that the ratio of populace to social workers should be 1,000:1, Rahat was under-serviced by a total of 20 social workers. Caseload records in 1996 indicated that the social service office had a caseload of 934, including addictions, child welfare, family counselling, income maintenance, and youth-at-risk services (*Rahat City Annual Report, 1997*).

Planning the Project

The book's first author formerly practiced in Rahat, and more recently had provided clinical supervision in the Rahat agency. He chaired a weekend workshop and round-table forum for local social workers. The professor, like the workers, had become increasingly aware of the problem-solving role of well-respected community members in clients' lives. The workshop therefore concentrated on developing further social work collaboration. The session was followed by a round table meeting initiated by the mayor, at the professor's prompting. The professor and workers proposed a list of 35 well respected, male community leaders, allowing each of the tribes, *hamula*, and major families to be represented. Most of the 35 had collaborated previously, on an ad hoc basis, in local social work interventions as *wasit* and were traditional healers, *sheikhs*, religious leaders, or other respected men.

For two reasons, the 35 *wasit* are hereafter called "cultural mediators (CM)": on one level, as will be shown, they mediated between the community (the cultural canon) and local social workers (the professional canon), while on a second level, their *wasit* role invariably involved mediation between two or more parties.

The literature confirms, in a preliminary sense, the CMs' potential contributions. In the West, as a non-adversarial conflict resolution procedure, mediation provides an alternative to litigation, allowing disputants to retain authority and negotiate an agreement with the help of a third party in divorce and child custody cases, civil disputes, juvenile cases, and criminal cases (Galaway, 1988; Irving & Benjamin, 1987). Research into community mediation programmes in the West likewise demonstrates how disagreements may be resolved between neighbours, victims and perpetrators of crimes, and other parties (Galaway, 1988; Payton & Tedesco, 1982). Moreover, preliminary evidence demonstrates the significance of individual and community mediation to such non-Western communities as individuals of Asian and Korean backgrounds, in addition to

Arab peoples (Abu-Nimer, 1996; Hirayama & Cestingok, 1988; Landsman, 1988; LeResche, 1992; Merry, 1989; Norell & Walz, 1994; Witty, 1978, 1980).

The application of mediation principles to helping professions has been longstanding. Many basic helping profession skills contribute to the mediation process and assist mediators in their effectiveness. These skills include attention and focus in early stages of the process, developing and utilizing questions effectively, summarizing, reflecting, and intervening (Kruk, 1997). There are also other, more specific, skills that are required for successful mediation. These include "normalizing, reframing, shifting the parties from position- to interest-based negotiation, mutualizing and emphasizing the common connectedness between the parties, future focus, task focus, conflict management, establishing and maintaining ground rules, pre-empting, confrontation, reality testing, and caucusing" (Kruk, 1997, p. 8).

Studies have long concluded that the helping profession's recent exposure to the Arab world has not been trouble-free (Al-Dabbagh, 1993; Al-Krenawi, 1998a; Al-Krenawi & Graham, 1996a). Helping professionals often develop poor working relationships with families in need. "Husbands," one scholar notes, "usually refuse to deal with the social worker" (Irani, 1999, p. 10). The reasons are myriad, and have been discussed in previous chapters; gender dynamics, culturally biased interventions, and etic understanding all serve as examples. However, in Israel, an additional dynamic prevails. The helping professional operates within federal legislation. Most are trained within Israeli universities and work in agencies that are likewise funded by the state. The worker, in several respects, may therefore represent the state, and any interaction necessarily places the worker – regardless of ethno-racial background – and Arab client into the broader universe of Middle East political conflict. In part because of these contextual factors, and due in part to long-established precedent, Bedouin-Arab peoples tend to refer to local religious or political *zaim* (leaders) within their own community. The latter are very similar to the CM in Rahat, and provide assistance with such domestic issues as child custody, family violence, separation, or divorce (Irani, 1999; Khadduri, 1997).

At the first meeting, social workers introduced their field of practice and geographic jurisdiction, and each CM identified his tribal/*hamula* status and corresponding neighbourhood. Several ensuing meetings elaborated on the nature and scope of local social services. Learning was reciprocal. The CMs heard about client autonomy, client confidentiality, the emotional needs of children, the psychosocial needs of mothers, and the significance to individuals and families of such problems as addictions, family violence, intra-family disputes, and marital discord. The social workers learned more about the CMs' informal roles in mediating between individuals and families over a wide spectrum of issues (as will be discussed).

On the basis of common CM-social worker concerns, all agreed to establish a project that would integrate the CMs, in a voluntary capacity, with current social service programmes. The project was intended to:

- provide information about social services to CMs
- increase social workers' cultural sensitivity
- increase collaboration between the modern social welfare system and the CMs
- develop social service community relations and enhance community use of social services.

During the project's first 12 months, 1997-1998, the CMs collaborated with the social workers in 120 cases. These included situations of blood vengeance, child abuse or neglect, divorce, family violence, marital problems, miscellaneous family problems, out-of-wedlock pregnancy, polygamous marriages, and youth at risk (Al-Krenawi & Graham, 1997a). Client participation in the project was voluntary, and the client was free to relinquish CM participation at any point in the intervention and proceed solely with the social worker, or, if the received services were not mandatory, terminate social work services. This approach, reflecting the professional canon, had certain assumptions about client power, control, and autonomy, and intersected with a CM model that was closer to the cultural canon, and as will be seen, could be more proscriptive and authoritative.

In four respects, this approach can be distinguished from one advocated in a family services clinic for Arab peoples in Jaffa, Israel (Savaya & Malkinson, 1997). First, CM participation was "bottom up," integrating already well established modes of community intervention, rather than being a top-down strategy implemented and conceived of by a social service agency. Second, whereas the Jaffa project was initiated by Jewish practitioners for Arab peoples, the present project was initiated by and for members of the Arab community, albeit with the participation of some Jewish social workers. Third, we disagree with how previous research portrays Arab community leaders. Far from "an elite group not in touch with the feelings of the population," the CMs had an abiding understanding of, and commitment to, the well being of their communities (Savaya & Malkinson, 1997). Finally, the present project was initiated with considerable reference to strategic community leverage points, including, for example, the support and participation of municipal leaders. It certainly reflects patriarchal power relations within Bedouin-Arab families.

A Case Example

The present case example illustrates the demonstration of project objectives. The example was provided by one of the social workers at a monthly meeting of the social service agency and was presented for other agencies in the region. The case begins with a dispute between a husband and wife who had been married for six years. The wife had a disagreement with the husband's mother over the latter's involvement in her daily life. Because of it, the husband retained his five children and insisted that the wife return home to her parents. The husband's immediate family cared for the children, ages one month to five years. Theirs had been an exchange marriage: where two men are married to each other's sister. The same day that the wife's brother learned of his sister's plight, he, in turn, retained sole custody of his children and insisted that his wife (the first husband's sister) be sent home to her parents. This reciprocal action was seen as having retained power symmetry between the two families, and hence preserved the integrity of his family honour.

These actions immediately precipitated tensions between the two extended families, both of which were within the same tribe and were of comparable social status. Within 20 days of the initial husband sending home his wife, a third husband, in response to increased intra-family tensions, decided to retain custody of his children and insisted that his wife go home to her parents. Theirs, too, was an exchange marriage, leading to a fourth husband immediately insisting that his wife go home to her parents in response to the third husband's actions. The actions of the third and fourth husbands further increased tensions between the two families. There was an increasing likelihood that all communication between the two families would be cut off, and that the four marriages would end in divorce. The first wife visited a general practitioner physician with complaints of anxiety, depression, fatigue, and various stress-related somatic symptoms. The physician, who was not an Arab, in turn referred the woman to one of Rahat's social workers for counselling. The social worker was a Bedouin-Arab from a family of comparable social status to the other two families, and within another of Rahat's tribes. He held bi-weekly sessions with the woman and conducted a visit to the husband's home, where he met the husband, the husband's father, and other male relatives. The social worker explained to the men that he was legally obligated to have the children immediately returned to the mother, according to Israeli law, and that if they did not agree to this plan, the police would have to get involved (it should be noted that Islamic law insists that young children be in custody of a mother, if she is well). The men were angered by the social worker's intervention, and sent a family delegate to the social worker's family, explaining to the family *sheikh* that further involvement from the social worker would create a dispute between their extended family and the social worker's.

Male elders within his extended family and tribe met with the social worker, and insisted that he not involve himself in the case. The social worker explained that his job legally obligated him to do so. The elders responded that the man should either desist, or quit his job, since the integrity of their family and tribal relations was the greatest priority. The social worker thus had a major dilemma between the cultural and professional canons.

In consultation with his supervisor, the social worker met with four CMs, one from each disputing family and two from other families not involved in the dispute but within the tribe. Together, the social worker and CMs developed three goals. The first and most immediate was to return the children to their mothers. The second was to consult with the four women to determine if they wanted to return to their husbands, and the third was to restore positive relations between the two families.

The CMs met separately with powerful representatives from both families. They heard both parties' stories, allowing for the expression of anger and frustration, ate with members of each side, and used cultural stories, such as those that correlated bravery with forgiveness. In discussing the children, the CMs did not appeal to legal explanations. Rather, they utilized two other arguments. The first was that it was important to keep the problem within the tribe and to not have a member from an outside tribe, or legal apparatuses such as a social worker, the police, or courts, involved. The second was an appeal to benefits of returning the children to their mother. Both arguments provided common ground upon which all parties could agree. Based on the strength of their reputations, the CMs were able to provide sufficient assurances that the children would be well cared for upon their return to the mothers. The CMs would also act as mediators, were any concerns to arise over the children's well-being while in their mother's care. Also because of their standing, the CMs were able to take a directive stance and insist that the children be returned before any further discussions occurred. Within two days of initial contact, the CMs had personally delivered the children to their respective mothers. Over the course of this stage of intervention, the social worker had been apprised of the process.

Turning to the second objective, the CMs had conversations with the first wife, her parents, her mother-in-law, and powerful leaders on both sides. The CMs obtained assurances from the mother-in-law that she would not interfere in the wife's day-to-day affairs as much as she previously had. Afterwards, having obtained consensus among these parties, the wife apologized to the mother-in-law in the presence of the CMs and agreed to respect and obey the mother-in-law, just as she would her own mother. These two compromises led the wife, accompanied by the CMs, to return to her husband. The same day, the other three wives returned to their husbands, accompanied by the CMs.

Stage three, which occurred within 30 days of the initial incident, was a *sulha*, in which powerful male members of each extended family met in the house of the tribe's *sheikh*, one of the CMs. The men shook hands, ate a meal, and agreed that the entire matter would be dropped. With this ritual completed, the social work case was closed.

It should be noted that all four women were asked by the social worker and the CM if they wanted to return to their homes, and all said that they did. All had expressed concerns about their families and children. The researchers remain unclear as to the extent of the women's choice-making capacities here, as well as in the first wife's apology and subsequent return home; in these respects we propose that further research and practice developments should be examined, as we elaborate shortly. For their part, the CMs and social worker were highly motivated to bring the dispute to an end. Recent social work research emphasizes the importance of community involvement in all aspects of child protection (Barsky, 1999). These same principles certainly apply to the present community. If the social worker and the CM had not been involved, it is possible that the intra-family and inter-family disputes may have been experienced with greater intensity or duration, and that the period of non-maternal contact with children may have been longer. Divorce or the creation of a polygamous marriage as a result of such conflict is not uncommon (Al-Krenawi & Graham, 1998, 1999a). Although somewhat provisional and tentative, the present case study nonetheless provides some insight into how social workers and other helping professionals might intervene with such a non-Western society.

Analysis

The CMs' involvement in the case adhered to the following cultural principles:

1) Patriarchy is a core theme. The patriarchal nature of Arab (Chekir, 1996; Joseph, 1996; Makhlouf-Obermeyer, 1979) and Arab-Palestinian families (Al-Haj, 1987; Haj, 1992; Hiltermann, 1991; Rockwell, 1985) has long been evident. Gender roles were both reinforced and potentially challenged by the CM-social work interaction, as was previously discussed. This is a theme that will be revisited in the conclusion.
2) Emphasis is placed on the group, since this unit of organization-(especially the family- (and not the individual)), forms the basis of

Arab culture (Barakat, 1993; Sharabi, 1975). The definition of problems and the processes leading to their solution are invariably referenced to, and involve, the group. Individuals experiencing problems do not choose between alternative courses of action in isolation from others. Help seeking is often collaborative, involving family members at every stage of intervention (Al-Krenawi, 2000a; Al-Krenawi & Graham, 1999a). The importance of the group is reinforced in daily interactions. Rather than adopting Euro-American ideals of conjugal isolation and withdrawal from the extended family, Arab social structures are dominated by daily interaction with near and extended kin (Holmes-Eber, 1997).

3) Since they are from the same cultural background, CMs are able to work with disputants to frame problems and solutions in the context of religion and culture, using metaphors, idioms of distress, and proverbs that are familiar and accessible. Stories and experiences that are related to similar events help to enable participants to universalize their problem and to appreciate potential solutions.

4) The concept of pride is key to Arab life, and when *Ar* descends upon an individual, family, or tribe, the restoration of pride is key to the integrity of all. Thus, CMs emphasize the preservation and protection of honour among all parties, along with other cultural values such as forgiveness, tolerance, respect, and social status, and frequently refer to them as a way of pressuring the other side.

5) Intervention is immediate, spontaneous, and quick, and can occur without the request of the disputant parties, in contrast to the sometimes slower initiation processes, the legal formality, and the preceding consent of disputants that can occur in the West.

6) Intervention is often directive. Advice is given and settlements are strongly advocated, to the point of nearing imposition.

7) Disputes are often resolved without face-to-face bargaining or negotiation, as that could be perceived as antagonistic or as a further state of humiliation. The process usually allows parties to present their story separately to a third party, engendering catharsis, ventilation, and the expression of disappointment and frustration.

8) Conflict is negative, threatening, and disruptive, and needs to be settled quickly or avoided. A CM would focus on the need to quickly terminate the damage and destruction brought about by conflict.

9) Disputes restore social order rather than change power relationships or the status quo and are based on the need to keep families, *hamula*, and tribes unified. All areas of Arab familial, *hamula*, and tribal life are in-

terdependent, be they economic, marital, social, or political. Instability in one area has immediate repercussions for others, thus amplifying the need for immediate and complete redress.
10) Mediation references the impact of immediate tension on the future. This reflects the cultural value that the life of the individual and collective should create a positive environment for the next generation. There is, therefore, a high impetus to avoid present-day disputes from disturbing future harmony.
11) Strong community pressure to obtain a settlement occurs in light of the above factors.
12) Priority is given to people and relationships rather than to tasks, structures, or tangible resources. Energies are concentrated on the relationship and social status between parties, rather than on concrete, substantive compensations.
13) If a payment is to occur, the third party is responsible for arranging and delivering it in the *Sulha*, which includes the two parties involved and is witnessed by other community members.
14) Age, gendered status, tribal affiliations, and other ascribed roles are the CMs' point of entry; the helping professionals may lack some, if not all attributes.

This project highlights several themes. CM participation revived the social work role in several ways. By collaborating with the social workers, the CMs learned about the function of social work, discovering that it was not just instrumental, and heard more about the various fields and some social work strategies. It should be stressed that Arab peoples underutilize helping professional services (Savaya, 1998). With their increasing awareness, the CMs were able to become ambassadors of the profession within the community, promoting its role and bringing cases to workers in many instances. These facets led to still greater sensitivity among CMs to the difficulties faced by social work clients, particularly women and children. They shared this knowledge with others, helping to promote greater community sensitivity regarding the needs of women and children. These indigenous strategies, operating within cultural assumptions, are perhaps a more resonant vehicle for women's empowerment than imposing strategies from the outside.

Women, in bottom-up social relations, played an important role in identifying a problem, leading to a social work intervention that in turn precipitated the use of top-down male authority within the community. In that respect, the interaction reinforced prevailing gender-based community power dynamics. However, in a second respect, the collaborative intervention of the social workers and the CM helped to address a problem involving women, and may have, in a small way, cultivated community awareness of women's empowerment and problem resolution. Future research could delve deeper into the extent to which women were involved in, and consented to, the imposition of such top-down authority.

A growing feminist ethnography demonstrates an elaborate and nuanced pattern of female social relations, and a considerable capacity for women, in their roles as mothers, spouses, daughters, aunts, grandmothers, and cousins, to assert influence upon men, especially in private and informally (Abu-Lughod, 1985b; Haj, 1992). While beyond the scope of this chapter, the wife in the first marriage, by resisting the interference of her mother-in-law and the requirements of the traditional culture which she is expected to meet, may be seen as having resisted the imposition of patriarchal relations upon her. We emphasize that Bedouin-Arab gendered social relations are neither linear nor static, but rather are organic constructs, potentially malleable to transformation from within. Social work was implicitly part of that resistance process, both in relation to the immediate intervention and to community education and other interventions that could further enhance women's rights. Future innovation in practice and research should build on social work's nascent role within the community in these respects, and should do so in reference to other international work intended to empower women.

This case also reveals that modern and traditional approaches to helping can be used successfully, in parallel. They can be mutually complementary (Al-Krenawi & Graham, 1996a; Chi, 1995; Edwards, 1986; Schwartz, 1985). Moreover, rather than grafting cultural awareness on to prevailing structures of social work practice, the professional canon can be more truly adapted to, and changed by, the cultural canon (Devore & Schlesinger, 1994). The present community is a small, under-serviced minority group with high levels of unemployment, poverty, and social problems, outside of the core of mainstream Israeli social, political, and economic life. This lack of autonomy could exacerbate widespread "fear," present throughout the Arab-Islamic world, "of losing an indigenous 'authentic' Islamic-Arab culture" (Ahmad, 1992 as cited in Shalhoub-Kevorkian, 1997). The CM, an indigenous construct, counterbalances these influences, helping to sustain the culture.

The CMs involved in the case scenario provided an important buffer between the modern Western system, which was seen as intrusive and threatening, and a traditional system based on kinship relations, gender constructs and other cultural norms. On the other hand, the CMs shared much with modern social work practice: they operated systemically, could read a family's ecological map, were able to identify and utilize leverage points, and had a sophisticated repertoire of one-to-one and group process skills. Their identification of, and collaboration with, authoritative family and tribal members was widely seen as a key factor leading to success. As one CM remarked, "only the powerful people in a family can bring about change." Another likewise said, "if you don't choose the right person, you are wasting your time," A third concurred: "change occurs from the top to bottom, not the other way around." This reinforces the importance of the CM role, as their status is culturally proscribed, and based on gendered community status. Alternately, social workers are trained at universities and rely on a professional canon for status and skills. The two forms of status are thus not parallel in the type of respect given by the target culture. Thus it is not necessary for a CM to undertake university training in social work to be instrumental in situations requiring conflict resolution, and, as was previously discussed, social workers can learn from the CM how to render interventions more culturally appropriate.

Another theme that has become apparent is the importance of social workers' ability to successfully function in two mutually competing cultures: the social work profession and the local culture of Rahat. At a critical stage in the case intervention, it appeared as though community leaders might have forfeited any possibility of the worker's participation. As he later divulged: "I was frustrated. I didn't know what to do. On the one hand, I had a commitment to my profession and its ethics. On the other hand, I was worried that my job would endanger my family's reputation, and would lead to grave problems for the people I love." Almost paradoxically, his society provided the answer to his dilemma. By using the social work skills of resource mobilization, advocacy, collaboration, and facilitation, the social worker was able to work with the CMs, ultimately resolving the child custody disputes within the wider nuclear familial and extended familial structures that had created the disputes. By discussing the case with the CMs, the social worker was able to provide insight into the psychosocial and developmental significance of the scenario to the children. By working together to devise a set of intervention goals, he was able to help the CMs to partialize the problems, prioritize them, and conceptualize them in a holistic manner. More broadly still, the social worker-CM collaboration empowered all parties, ensuring a successful social work intervention, sustaining the public reputation of the CMs, and creating stability within the community.

BISHA RITUAL

The following section uses a case study to examine the practice of *Bisha*, or ordeal by fire, which the Bedouin-Arabs use throughout much of the Middle East to resolve various forms of disputes. Far different than institutionalized methods used by helping professional personnel, this is a method in which a traditional ritual is used to resolve individual conflicts.

A ritual is an authoritative mode of symbolic discourse, having reference to mystical beings or powers, and evoking those sentiments from which society is constructed (adaptation of Lincoln, 1989, p. 53; Turner, 1967, p. 19). This section introduces a conflict-resolving ritual, combining the previously developed "redressive" (Turner 1967, p. 270) and "reconciliation" rituals (Collier, 1984, p. 133), as defined below. Like classical perspectives, the analysis provided focuses on how a ritual reflects the social order, reinforces conformity to collective values (Durkheim, 1965), and deters behaviours that deviate from culturally acceptable norms (Gluckman, 1954, 1963). Beyond this, the analysis is influenced by Geertz (1973), Turner (1969), and other anthropologists (Furman, 1981; Pilgrim, 1978), who affirm a ritual's capacity to transform social structures.

A reconciliation ritual transformation occurs in two ways. The first involves resolving conflicts that occur between two or more people in order to reinstate a sense of mutually agreed upon justice (redressive). The second involves restoring stability, order, and harmony to social relations (reconciliation). Conflict-resolving rituals thus need to be understood systemically (Pincus & Minahan, 1973) and ecologically (Germain & Gitterman, 1980) in their reciprocal relationships between the individual, small group, community, and society.

The following section outlines the context and practice of the Bedouin-Arab ritual of the *Bisha*. Next it discusses the individual, community, and social significance of a case example, and it concludes with a discussion of the implications for modern mental health and social service practitioners working with such societies as the Bedouin-Arab. The data comes from two sources. The case example is derived from an open-ended interview with members of two tribes, the traditional healer, and the *sheikh* mediators who were involved in the case.

The Ritual

The *Bisha* is one of a variety of traditional rituals that are practised by lay people and by traditional healers in Bedouin-Arab culture (Al-Krenawi & Graham, 1996a, 1997a; Al-Krenawi et al., 1996). Fire has a wide spectrum of representation among indigenous societies. Some associate it with mysticism, others with the sacred flame on a sacrificial altar (Freeman, 1981), others with a source of joy (Lewis & Dowsey-Magog, 1993), others with a god (Bonnafe, 1973), and others, such as the Bedouin-Arab, as a revealer of truth (Abu-Khusa, 1993; Kazaz, 1989). Several societies incorporate such ordeals by fire as fire-walking, licking boiling milk, passing hooks through the skin of the back, or passing hot skewers through the tongue (Freeman, 1981; Lewis & Dowsey-Magog, 1993). Like these rituals, the *Bisha* involves the licking of a red hot metal tool as an unchallengeable means of substantiating an accusation or erasing a stain of shame upon an individual, family, or tribe (Kazaz, 1989). The Bedouin-Arabs usually apply the *Bisha* ritual to disputes with a civil or criminal origin, or in any situations where there is a suspicion of wrongdoing (Abu-Khusa, 1993; Kazaz, 1989).

The man who administers the *Bisha* is known as *Mobashshi*. Only two Bedouin-Arab tribes are known to have the *S'er*, the divine secret necessary to pass the *Baraka*-inspired (blessing from God) *Mobashshi* from father to son (Kazaz, 1989). The first is the Al-Ayadi tribe, situated in Al-Ismaliah, Egypt. The second is the Bili tribe, whose sphere of influence extends to the Hedjaz, Najd, and some parts of the trans-Jordan (Abu-Khusa, 1993; Al-Aref, 1944; Kazaz, 1989).

The process of performing the ritual includes several elements. First, the *Mobashshi* listens to both parties and tries to convince them to not request the ritual. If he concludes that reconciliation is impossible without it, he pronounces that the ritual will be performed and that both parties must accept its results (Al-Aref, 1944; Apshtin, 1973).

Necessary conditions for the *Bisha* are fire, a group of people who serve as witnesses, and a metal tool—a ladle about four inches in diameter with a long iron handle. The ladle end of the tool is inserted into a hot, well-stoked fire. Before taking the tool from the fire, the healer gives the accused some water. The accused rinses his/her mouth and spits the water onto the ground. He/she then pokes his/her tongue out for general inspection to show there is nothing on it, and that it is in its natural state (Khamis Al-Krenawi, 1996 Personal Communication). The *Mobashshi* takes the metal tool from the fire and shows the witnesses that it is red hot. He orders the accused to put his/her tongue out, and the accused must lick the metal tool. The tongue is then examined by the *Mobashshi*. If he finds it harmed, he declares the accused guilty; but if the metal tool has left the tongue unharmed, the accused is declared not guilty (Abu-Khusa, 1993; Al-Aref, 1944; Kazaz, 1989).

A Case Example

This case involved a 45 year old man who had been accused of stealing sheep from another tribe. He belonged to a large tribe of about 500 individuals, and became embroiled in a disagreement with a second tribe of comparable social standing, also numbering about 500 people. Early one morning, members of the second tribe noticed that several sheep from their field had gone missing. They followed footsteps from the field leading directly to the accused man's house. He and his tribe denied knowledge of or involvement in the incident. The disagreement became the rallying point around which each tribe expressed its honour and claimed that, if left unresolved, the situation would perpetuate *Ar* (mark of shame). The accused side could not withstand the continued accusations of wrongdoing against one of their members. The aggrieved side felt with equal intensity that the theft had been a grave humiliation upon their tribal pride. For several days, tribal members on both sides refused to talk to each other. Tensions mounted between each side. There were several reported brawls between young men of each tribe, and members on both sides had generalized feelings of anxiety.

Cultural norms prohibited contacting the police. Instead, an informal mediation system was initiated shortly after the incident once three *sheikh*s from different tribes learned about the misunderstanding and decided to mediate separately with important tribal members on each side. After hearing declarations from both sides, they declared a *wajah*, a three day period of amnesty that each side was obligated to agree to by virtue of cultural customs. During the *wajah* period, the mediators continued to talk with members of the two tribes, and in the process became the conduit through which dialogue occurred. The *wajah* could have been extended for two or more additional periods, if both sides agreed to the extension. An extension was not necessary, for near the end of the first *wajah*, the aggrieved tribe proposed a *Bisha* ceremony, to which the accused side shortly agreed.

A departure to a *Mobashshi* in Egypt was immediately arranged for the accused man, along with his relatives, members of the other tribe, and the three mediating *sheikh*s as witnesses. A *Bisha* was performed; the participant later divulged that he had no fear in undertaking the ritual. The man was pronounced innocent, and the *Mobashshi*'s declaration was immediately embraced by the *sheikh*s and by tribal members on both sides. The accusations were immediately withdrawn, and within a week of the initial incident, the final stage of resolution occurred with the *sulha*. Tribal leaders from both sides met, shook hands, ate a meal together, and agreed to drop the matter entirely.

The *Bisha* needs to be understood on several levels, the first being societal. The ritual reflects the need for some system of justice within the Bedouin-Arab community in the absence of its own formal process, legal specialists, or police forces as we understand them in the West. Had the Israeli police been involved in the above case, with dissatisfying processes or results to either side, the consequences may have been grave, as discussed below. Indeed, ethno-specific rituals of conflict resolution such as the *Bisha* may be added to "negotiation," "adjudication," and other recently analysed forms of dispute-resolution procedures such as "mediation, avoidance, shaming, denial of reciprocity, fighting, and so on," as examined in Western contexts (Collier, 1984, p. 109).

The introduction of a third party is key to the *Bisha*'s function. In Arab society (Budman et al., 1992; Weidman, 1982) and trans-culturally, "there is an underlying "social logic" to triads as a means of resolving conflict, and an assumption pervades much of the literature in this area that some form of "stranger" third party is the most desirable way of handling conflict if escalation and violence threatening to the social order is to be avoided" (Yngvesson, 1984, p. 251). In the case study, the *Mobashshi* acted as a neutral third party. *Sheikh*s were additional necessary third parties who provided important pre-*Bisha* mediation, and who ultimately facilitated the *Mobashshi*'s involvement.

From the individual's perspective, the *Bisha* had several layers of significance. Perhaps most importantly, participation in a ritual can change a person's social status, or their relationship with others. The ritual gives a culturally-prescribed form, structure, and meaning (Rando, 1985) to the resolution. It also integrates parts of the self and binds individuals with their communities and histories (Hoch-Smith & Spring, 1978). It enters participants into a common physical and symbolic space in which a shared history and culture are implicit throughout the process. Moreover, the very act of agreeing to a mediation ritual, we argue, creates a predisposition towards reconciliation, just as the involvement in a ritual of healing creates a predisposition to be healed (Csordas, 1983). Likewise, the process of submitting to the transcendent power of a ritual reduces estrangement between two people by allowing both to participate in an activity, to accept its consequences, and implicitly to adhere to the social order and hidden powers that the ritual represents. These aspects are further reinforced by the presence of witnesses who validate the temporal aspects of the ceremony and also its social ecology and ultimate mystery.

Rituals provide unique opportunities for communication and ventilation, necessitating the behavioural expression of thought and feeling (Rando, 1985). This "acting out" moves the individual from passivity, helplessness, and emptiness towards integration as an actor in the change process. Rituals, being a right brain activity, touch the unconscious more quickly than verbalization. This mind/body congruence also enhances the process of working through any emotion or problematic condition that inhibits change (Rando, 1985). Similarly, rituals such as the *Bisha* promote healing. In the case example, the resolution of disputes avoided personal distress, marital and family dissolution, violence, and even death. In their stead, the ritual engendered catharsis, psychological release, and improved social functioning on both sides. This, in turn, led to social harmony and cohesion, further reinforcing a cycle of individual-to-social healing.

According to systems theory, all social relations constitute systems that have boundaries, that change by moving from disequilibrium to equilibrium, and that are influenced by external factors or inputs (Pincus & Minahan, 1973; von Bertalanffy, 1971). In the case example, the two tribes may be seen as separate systems experiencing a disequilibrium-equilibrium transformation; they too were part of one transformative system overall, the immediate Bedouin-Arab city where both tribes lived.

CONCLUSION

The Bedouin-Arab practice of *Bisha* has been analysed as a conflict-resolving ritual that has reciprocal relationships between the individual, small group, community, and society. The case study demonstrates that the ritual reflects the social order, reinforces conformity to collective values, deters behaviours that deviate from culturally acceptable norms, and transforms social structures by resolving conflicts between two or more people and by reinstating a sense of mutually agreed justice.

In modern helping professional practice, various aspects of rituals have been incorporated in the process of treatment: in dealing with bereavement (Al-Krenawi, 1996; Bolton & Camp, 1989; Rando, 1985), family dysfunction (Child, 1996; Friedman & Pettus, 1985), incest healing (Winslow, 1990), multiple personality disorders (Versper, 1991), and post-traumatic stress disorder (Obenchain & Silver, 1992), to cite five examples. Indeed, some mental health professionals assert that the very act of treatment may be viewed as a ritual (Rando, 1985; Wyrostok, 1995). Modern practitioners may likewise appreciate the healing significance of rituals such as the *Bisha*, and where appropriate, may validate traditional rituals and incorporate traditional healing in alliance with modern therapy (Al-Krenawi & Graham, 1996a, 1996b). So too might future research consider how police and court systems undertake their functions in parallel process with informal mediation systems such as the *Bisha*.

Ultimately, whether the *Bisha* ritual in the present case study was based on actual or contrived techniques is not the pivotal question. What is significant is whether it worked within the context of a particular problem requiring mediation. In the case example, the ritual restored stability, order, and harmony, in the context of a social transformation, since Bedouin-Arab society saw it as the only valid way to get at the absolute truth and so re-establish equilibrium between people. Rituals are not relics of our ancient past. Rather, they are persistent and successful human adaptations that remain vital across time and culture (Wyrostok, 1995), and are particularly salient to such indigenous populations as the

Bedouin-Arab. As such, the *Bisha* can assist helping professionals to understand the complexities and prospects of ritual mediation among cultures such as the Bedouin-Arabs.

Turning to the CM project, the literature has considered the role of helping professions as cultural consultants/brokers in front-line services (Budman et al., 1992; De Santis & Ugarriza, 1995; Eisenbruch & Handelman, 1990; Fandetti & Goldmeier, 1988; Weidman, 1982). The CM project demonstrates that CMs themselves are a further extension of this brokering process, helping to bridge gaps between social work and a traditional community. While beyond the scope of the above example, CMs could provide valuable consultation for social workers regarding community norms, values, opinions, and beliefs. Several non-Arab social workers that were involved in the project emphasized how often they had consulted community CMs during all stages of intervention. One remarked that "without the help of one CM, I would have created a lot of damage in a delicate treatment process." Another, providing addictions treatment, consulted a CM and learned who was the most relevant person within the client's family with whom to consult.

Even the Arab social workers had varying understandings of their culture. Some, like their non-Arab counterparts, learned more about the helping significance of the cultural canon. Many community members extensively use various traditional healing rituals, such as meal preparation and consumption during family mourning, or visiting saints' tombs in times of anxiety or psychosocial problems (Al-Krenawi & Graham, 1996a). Likewise, myriad traditional healers, such as the *Dervish*, or the Koranic healer, provide direct help to some people with mental health or psychosocial problems (Al-Issa, 1990; Al-Krenawi, 2000a; Al-Krenawi & Graham, 1999a, 1999c, 1997b; Al-Krenawi et al., 1996; Al-Safi, 1982; El-Islam, 1982; Gorkin & Othman, 1994). Workers also learned new terminology used widely by members of the community to describe their psychosocial problems, such as *halit sarah* (a person attacked by an evil spirit, causing confused behaviour) and *markob* (spirit possession). The CMs also provided interpretations of Islamic religious law regarding divorce, the raising of children, adoption, foster families, and other matters.

CMs personify the importance, in Arab culture, of an individual's reference to the group. People see themselves foremost as extensions of the *hamula*, extended family, and nuclear family (Al-Haj, 1987; Al-Krenawi & Graham, 1997a, 1997b). Authoritarian and collective principles prevail over the democratic or individualistic, as does social stability over social change. The Arab family is *the* source of economic, social, and emotional support. If traditional values are rejected, an individual faces complete ostracism. Problems of the individual, so strongly linked to the group, are also solved by the group. We suggest that a helping professional who does not operate in this systemic context will face minimal success.

Turning to broader structures beyond the Bedouin-Arab in Rahat, had the CMs *not* been utilized, the police may have become involved, hostilities might have escalated, the welfare of the children may have been further compromised, and marital, family, and extended family stresses might have been amplified, perhaps leading to divorce. Agency policies and practices should appreciate the significance of CMs, and enable them to resolve community problems.

In today's context of globalization, where Western values permeate virtually all areas of the world, the Bedouin-Arab, like other communities in the Arab world, remain close to the cultural/religious values that differentiate them from the West. Within a generation, the community has been transformed from nomadism/semi-nomadism to sedentarism and from a time-honoured agrarian economic base to growing participation in the market and more generally in modern Israeli life. The CM helps to bridge the tensions that necessarily exist between localization and globalization, and the norms/values of Israel and those of the Bedouin-Arab community, in any social work intervention.

The cultural mediator project in Rahat is necessarily exploratory and preliminary. Future research should consider how to enhance women's choice-making opportunities in this patriarchal culture. Other research could include outcome evaluations of CM-helping professional collaboration, as well as greater empirical and ethnographic analysis of the perceptions of clients, social workers, CMs, and other members of the community. Perhaps the use of community mediation, while innovative and new, reflects some good things about social work practice at a deeper level given that the profession has always had a commitment to mobilize community resources towards the solution of the client's problem and the promotion of the client's welfare.

There remains, as well, an essential practice imperative. While working with members of traditional cultures, modern professionals should understand the meanings that traditional resources—particularly belief systems—have for the client and his/her community. They should also be prepared, under certain circumstances, to work concurrently with traditional helpers (Al-Krenawi & Graham 2003). This is not to say that social work should appropriate traditional practices into "modern" modes of intervention. At the same time, a helping professional must realize that historical and ethnographic evidence reveals considerable common ground upon which both the traditional helper and modern helper stand. The next chapter discusses a variety of topics related to traditional healing in the Bedouin-Arab culture.

Chapter 7

CASE STUDIES IN CULTURAL AND RELIGIOUS HEALING PRACTICES

INTRODUCTION

In 1991, a Bedouin-Arab woman who had never before received psychiatric treatment was identified as a possible social work client and sent to a Negev mental health clinic. At the intake assessment, she appeared suspicious of any intervention, asking repeatedly "which type of doctor are you?" and when she would be prescribed medication. Refusing to engage with the social worker, she grew more and more adamant that this was to be her first and last encounter with psychotherapy. The session abruptly ended when she terminated the treatment, refused to contract for further appointments, and rejected the social worker and what he was attempting to do, dismissing the entire process as "nothing more than talking."

On one level, such an experience may be interpreted as client resistance, a common aspect of the helping process which can be a result of cultural stigma surrounding mental illness. More than this, however, it typifies two culturally-specific realities which influence many Bedouin-Arab's experiences of Western forms of helping. The first is the frame of reference through which mental health interventions are perceived. It must be emphasized that psychiatric treatment is new and in many ways foreign to this traditional population, having been initiated only in the last thirty years in the form of predominantly pharmacological treatment by psychiatrists, most of whom are Jewish and thus of a different cultural background (Al-Krenawi, Graham, & Al-Krenawi, 1997). "Talking therapy," which is even newer, was first introduced in 1981 by a Bedouin-Arab psychiatric social worker, one of the co-authors and the protagonist of the story above.

The second reality has to do with the limited development of literature addressing helping professional practice with respect to traditional populations such as the Bedouin-Arab. Recent research concurs that helpers have to respect and accept the client as a representative of his/her culture (Ben-David & Erickson, 1990; Sue, 1990). To this end, it is argued that traditional healing should be integrated into interpersonal practice with people of various cultures (Kelley & Kelley, 1985; Kissman, 1990; Morrissette et al., 1993; Schindler, 1993; Waltman, 1986). However, research has not yet considered how to operationalize these principles in order to apply them to a Bedouin-Arab population. As the following chapter will demonstrate, a beginning point is through understanding the Bedouin-Arab notion of "rituals." A wide body of literature (Drever, 1956; Eliade, 1957; Halifax, 1982; Scheff, 1977; Van Gennep, 1960; Winick, 1956) defines rituals, in this sense, as "prescribed formal behaviour for occasions not given over to technological routine, having reference to mystical being or powers" (Turner, 1967, p. 19).

This chapter outlines the importance of the helping professionals' understanding of the culture in which they are working. It first looks at the significance of Islam to traditional healing, and then turns to three Bedouin-Arab rituals which can be applied to the development of culturally-specific helping profession interventions: *Zurah* (saint's tomb visiting), *Rahamah* (memorial ritual for the dead), and *Dhikr* (invocating God's name) – the latter-most ritual with the purview, or facility, of the *Dervish* traditional healer. The chapter then analyses the Koranic traditional healer, and concludes with strategies for creating a helping alliance between professional helpers and traditional Bedouin-Arab communities.

THE HEALING SIGNIFICANCE OF ISLAMIC THOUGHT

The following case examples reflect longstanding Bedouin-Arab cultural traditions. All, on some level, are inextricably linked with Islam, the religion of Bedouin-Arab communities in the Negev. Religion is central to Muslim self-conception and has been found to promote either emotional health or emotional strain in times of crisis or disease (Al-Krenawi, 1995; Azhar, Varma, & Dharap, 1994; Reisher & Lawson, 1992; Rizvi, 1989). People with a strong religious background consider divine intervention to be a part of the healing process of mental illness (Lederach & Lederach, 1987; Shilon, 1981); as well, Umoren (1990) points out that Muslim explanations of illness and treatments are related to a world view that can best be described as strongly religious.

The philosophy of traditional Muslim medicine draws its strength from a reliance on one of the basic tenets of Islam: the belief in fate, that all things that happen to a person, both good and evil, are the will of God. According to Islam, both health and illness are caused by Allah through the natural and supernatural powers created by Him (Al-Krenawi, 1996; Al-Krenawi et al., 1996; El-Islam, 1982). Devoted Muslims must therefore accept their fate with strong faith, courage, and great patience. One Islamic Arab point of view is that mental illness is the result of an interaction between human beings and evil spirits, and is therefore either the fatalistic result of a defective relationship with God, punishment from God, or God's will (Al-Krenawi, Maoz, & Shiber, 1995; Eikelman, 1968). Generally, Muslims believe that a person consists of two aspects: the physical and the spiritual (Qutib, 1967; Tabarah, 1977). Those who practise Islamic principles and are obedient to God's will and to the Prophet's traditions achieve a good relationship with God, and thereby balance the two sides of themselves. They are thus likely to secure good social relationships and are protected from diseases (Najib, 1982; Rizvi, 1989).

In the framework of the Islamic religion, there are two types of spirits. The first are good, by virtue of having been converted to Islam by Muhammad. The second are bad and follow *Iblis*, the fallen angel who had been expelled from the Garden of Eden (Koran, Surah Al-Hijr, v. 28-40). The latter attack and seduce mankind as punishment for their sins to Allah, and are the source of much mental, physical, and psychosocial suffering (Al-Juhri, 1991; Ibn-Taymeh, 1957). In either case, there are three forms of spirits in the world: those that fly through the air, those that appear like animals such as cats or dogs, and those that stay on the earth and move from place to place. The latter category of evil spirits is prominent in garbage dumps, toilets, and other undesirable areas, while others exist within human beings (Al-Jamal, 1983; Al-Jzari, 1987; Ashoor, 1989; El-Shamy, 1977). It is believed that God created angels from light, human beings from clay, and the *Jinn* (evil spirits) from fire (Boddy, 1989; Kennedy, 1967). The *Jinn* constitute a world of supernatural beings with greater power than humans, but less than that of angels (Ashoor, 1989; El-Shamy, 1977; Ibn-Taymeh, 1957).

Muhammad himself began to treat people who suffered from what we now call "mental illness" (Al-Ataar, 1989; Navdi, 1983), saying that these diseases are caused by *Iblis* and his assistants (Ashoor, 1987; Badawi, 1992). Muhammad's friends learned these skills and techniques from him, and a tradition of "prophetic medicine" developed from them (*Al-Tibb an-nabawi*) that was passed from generation to generation (Al-Nasimi, 1984; Salim, 1986; Sherif, 1972). Out of this tradition, the contemporary phenomenon of Koranic healing was derived–as elaborated in subsequent pages. The following sections look at several traditional healing practices that have potential relevance to modern helping professions.

Traditional Healing in Context

Generally speaking, when working with any traditional culture, helping professionals must appreciate the helping significance of rituals, giving greater latitude to the concurrent use of traditional and modern models of helping within the client's community, recognizing that the two helping systems are distinct, yet potentially related (Bilu, Witztum, & Van der Hart, 1990; Lambo, 1978; Rando, 1985; Rappaport & Rappaport, 1981). Given that cultural sensitivity is so central to the helping profession identity, the helping professions may lead the way in research looking into the helping benefits of healing rituals.

A number of researchers have examined the significance of rituals to the helping process among non-traditional societies (Cf. Abramowitz, 1993; Bolton & Camp, 1989; Frey & Edinburg, 1978; Gutheil, 1993; Hoch-Smith & Spring, 1978; Kobak & Waters, 1984; Rando, 1985; Winslow, 1990). From them, one can infer rituals' potential utility within a Bedouin-Arab helping context. As Frey and Edinburg point out, an appreciation of rituals "may help prevent helping professionals from engaging in practices that negate their client's ability to work out their own solutions to problems" (Frey & Edinburg, 1978, p. 89). Rituals integrate parts of the self and bind individuals with their communities and histories (Hoch-Smith & Spring, 1978). Rando (1985) notes that they give form, structure, meaning, and allow unique opportunities for communication, ventilation, and culturally appropriate acting-out throughout all of social life. As such, they "can be created to function in therapy as they function in other parts of life" (Rando, 1985, p. 239). Rituals are fundamental to the community's cultural canon, are inextricably linked with its strongly Islamic basis of living, and are a non-stigmatizing and legitimized aspect of its natural helping systems and traditional forms of physical and mental healing. Most Bedouin-Arabs who are illiterate or not verbally skilled might prefer traditional healing rituals to modern, more discursive counselling techniques. To many, they have greater community sanction than Western forms of helping (Al-Krenawi & Graham, 1996a).

Three Healing Rituals

Three Bedouin-Arab rituals will be discussed in further detail: *Zurah, Rahamah* and *Dhikr*. Data for this study is derived from interviews with Bedouin-Arab tribal members in the Negev, Israel (Al-Krenawi, 1992; Al-Krenawi, 1993), and in the context of the practice and life experience of one of the co-authors, including his active participation in the community's ritual performances. For clarity's sake, because they have different contexts, processes, and purposes, each ritual will be analysed separately in relation to the individual(s), his/her family, and the wider community.

Saint's Tomb Visiting (Zurah)

Islamic saints are found among most Muslim Arab communities. Living saints as well as dead saints have the power to perform miracles through the *Baraka* (religious insight bestowed upon people highly favoured of God) (Al-Krenawi, 1992; Geertz, 1968; Sharafeldin, 1983; Trimingham, 1949). Saints are seen as "a particular kind of friend of God, one whose special closeness to divinity [is] mediated between the ordinary faithful [people] and [an] all-powerful and distant deity" (Eliade, 1987, p. 2). Dead saints' tombs are holy places, associated with stories of relieving personal anxiety, healing physical and mental ailments, and mediating requests to God (Bazzoui & Al-Issa, 1966; El-Islam, 1967; Kline, 1963).

The family in Bedouin-Arab society is linked closely by economic, emotional, and social ties, encouraging individual problems to be perceived as problems of the entire family. Many instances of personal distress occasion visits to tombs by the nuclear family, and often by parts of the extended family and members of the tribe. It is not unusual for several Bedouin-Arab families to visit the same tomb at the same time, on behalf of unrelated supplicants. Some precipitating reasons for visits include disease, economic hardship, or minor and major mental health issues identified by the *Dervish* (traditional Bedouin-Arab healers) as induced by evil spirits. Examples of the latter are *Khriah* (anxiety), *Mlmus* (fear), *Nfs mn Al-Jinn* (depression), and *Mrkob* (violence and confusion due to the devil's possession) (Al-Krenawi, 1992).

At the tomb, *Koran* verses are read, candles and incense are lit beside the grave, and white cloth is hung on the tomb itself. Vows are meant to appease the saint's soul, and special requests are made to prevent tragedy or illness from striking the supplicant, his/her children, or the family's property. Prayers are said corporately and individually; additional supplications that do not address the initial reason for the visit often arise. After all requests have been made, a lamb is led around the grave and is slaughtered as a symbol of a fulfilled vow, cooked and eaten. This is followed by readings from the first chapter of the *Koran*, and by a final supplication where all address God, through the saint's soul, and ask that their prayers be granted. When the supplicant and his/her family return home they are met by other members of the tribe and by friends, who say *Mbrock Alzuarah*, (congratulations), a symbol of their wish that God has accepted the visit and has provided assistance to the supplicant.

Throughout this ritual, the individual supplicant(s) puts him or herself under the supernatural power of the saint, giving rise to intense feelings and often to outwardly emotive forms of prayer and crying. For most supplicants, the ritual creates a strong element of self-expression, catharsis, ventilation, self-satisfaction, and psychological release. It is arguably due to this internal satisfaction that some individuals emerge from the ritual with an altered outlook and a predisposition to interpret subsequent life events as a consequence of the ritual, and thus external objectives are achieved as a consequence of internal intrapsychic achievement (Al-Juhri, 1991). One can infer from psychodynamic theory that particular success with this ritual will be experienced by people whose psychological need to submit to a parent figure plays a dominant and dynamic role in their character structure (El-Islam, 1967). Transference of these needs to the saint, and their satisfaction through the saint-visiting submissive ritual, offers a feeling of internal fulfillment, in spite of the ritual's apparent lack of logic, objectively speaking (the saint is deceased).

The ritual provides a strong group therapeutic context in several respects. At one level, the extended family and tribe act as a supportive network during the ritual process, and indeed throughout the course of the supplicant's problem. To borrow from the Milan group of strategic family therapy, the visit to the tomb culminates in a "family ritual. . . . an action or series of actions, usually accompanied by verbal formulas or expressions, which are to be carried out by all members of the family" (Palazzoli et al., 1978, p. 95).

On another level, in the immediate context of being at the tomb, the ritual generates a natural helping group, providing opportunities for the expression of negative feelings and information about the problem, the sharing of coping strategies, and the universalizing recognition of common problems. When several families visit the tomb at the same time, helping networks are expanded, spontaneous acts of mutual support often take place, and the families have the experience of sharing these group activities.

Memorial Ritual for the Dead (Rahamah)

When an individual's deceased relative or friend appears in a dream, the result is often a memorial ritual for the dead. In one such example, a dead husband appeared in a Bedouin-Arab widow's dream and indicated that he wanted to take her to where he is. She became fearful, interpreting the dream as a sign that her husband wanted her to enter the afterlife (Al-Krenawi, 1993). A memorial ritual is performed to address the dream and make peace with it, preventing negative consequences from occurring.

The Bedouin-Arab term for this memorial is *Rahamah*, which in direct translation means "to obtain food for the dead person's soul and to invite people to eat the food" (Al-Krenawi, 1993). This ritual is always held on a Thursday, the day before the Muslim Sabbath, and begins with the dreamer's daytime visit to the deceased's grave, accompanied by relatives, while other family members and friends obtain and prepare food at the dreamer's home. That evening, a dinner is held to which extended family and friends are invited. The meal starts with the reading of the *Koran*, which is intended to prevent the soul of the dead from re-appearing. Next, the person who had the dream reveals its content to the group and, as a consequence, the conversation is directed towards the subject of the deceased. Feelings are raised, support is given, and the after-life is much discussed. Once the group has perceived that sufficient validation and support have been given, food is brought into the room. After the meal is consumed, a final prayer is said on behalf of the deceased's soul.

On an individual level, the therapeutic value of this type of ritual is suggested by none other than Breuer & Freud (1955). In their case reports of the treatment of Fraulein Elizabeth Von R. Freud, Elizabeth is instructed to visit her sister's grave, although no reasons are cited for this intervention (Breuer & Freud, 1955). More recent bereavement literature has extrapolated upon the therapeutic significance of grave-visiting (Rando, 1985; Whitaker, 1985). In the case of the Bedouin-Arab woman introduced above, the visit to the grave precipitated emotional responses of crying, talking to the dead person's soul, and other manifestations of anger, sadness, ventilation, self-expression, catharsis, and psychological release.

The meal itself provides opportunities for the dreamer and the entire group to express and share feelings, to give support, and to provide closure to outstanding issues associated with the deceased, or with such emotions of mourning as anger, depression, guilt, or the fear of death. Religion is central to this process, providing individuals and groups a sense of meaningfulness to life, which may in turn promote support and consultation in the context of sorrow and tragedy; religion's relationship to the transcendental realm also provides a sense of security and self-worth (O'Dea, 1966). Individuals often emerge from the ritual with an increased acceptance of the death.

It also should be noted that the preparation of food for the evening's dinner provides friends and family members with an opportunity to discuss the deceased, their feelings, and any unfinished business which may be associated with the death. Conversation does not have to be solely attentive to the emotional needs of the relative who is visiting the grave—that is, by virtue of the dream itself, the person who may be perceived as the most bereaved. This particular group dynamic provides members of the dreamer's support network a distinct opportunity to share their own feelings and thoughts.

Invocating God's Name (Dhikr)

The *Dervish* are religiously-imbued traditional healers who continue to enjoy great status in the Bedouin-Arab community and who have responded to mental health and social problems in the context of Islamic religion and its concomitant rituals for centuries (Al-Krenawi 1992; Geertz, 1968). One of the rituals which the *Dervish* use to this end is the *Dhikr*, an invocation to God literally meaning "to remember, recall, mention, or utter" (Al-Ghazali, 1950). This ritual, originally emerging from the mystical *Sufi* movement in Islam, became incorporated by the Bedouin-Arab *Dervish* for religious purposes, and evolved over time into a means of ameliorating psychosocial and mental health problems (Geertz, 1968; Schimmel, 1975).

An example of a psychosocial or mental health problem is a *Baraka*—defined by researchers as a sort of mental breakdown. This must be determined by a well-recognized *Dervish* to have been a *Baraka* for it to be the case. In order to heal individuals found to have had a *Baraka*, specific remedies/rituals are prescribed. The *Khabit* produce amulets that are worn on the body to ward off evil spirits. Only men become this type of healer; usually the tradition is passed down from father to son, as long as the latter is perceived to have sufficient literary skills and acceptance by the community. Treatments are based on ancient practices found in books originating from Egypt and Morocco. Fortune-tellers, practising a craft that is ordinarily passed down from mother to daughter, are able to predict the future by reading the dregs remaining in a patient's coffee cup. The *Dervish* can also include Koranic healers, who use religious principles stemming from the Koran, after having intensely studied the Koran and the traditions of the Prophet Muhammad at a university or college, in order to treat patients who have been attacked by evil spirits (Al-Krenawi & Graham, 1996a; 1996b; Al-Krenawi et al., 1996; Gorkin & Othman, 1994; Graham & Al-

Krenawi, 1996; Morsy, 1993). The *Dervish* are often central to many of the traditional healing rituals used in Bedouin-Arab society.

In addition to being helped in problem identification and in receiving individual counsel from the *Dervish*, it is common for Bedouin-Arabs with mental or psychosocial problems to join with a *Dervish* on a weekly basis in meditation. Groups ordinarily meet at the *Dervish*'s house in the early evening on Thursdays, the day before a Muslim holy day. The ritual takes place separately for men and women, in reflection of the norms of Bedouin-Arab culture and Islamic religion (Mass & Al-Krenawi, 1994). This also positively affects the group process, giving permission for group members to express feelings and actions, through ecstasy and meditation, that otherwise might be inhibited in a co-gender context.

The sessions begin in silence, with participants sitting in a circle. The *Dervish* facilitates the group, initiating group conversation regarding members' problems and coping strategies. During the next stage the group stands, the *Dervish* enters the middle of the circle and initiates prayer. Prayer is ended with the *Dervish* singing a hymn, accompanied by two group members repeatedly beating large drums in loud monotonous rhythm. At this point, the transition is made to the group meditation stage in which members focus on the power of God and sway to the drum beat in a trance while repeating the phrase *Allah He* (God is alive). This stage often culminates in individual members reaching a state of physical and emotional ecstasy. The *Dervish* ends the ritual by leading group prayer, in which all members ask for God's forgiveness (Al-Krenawi, 1992). A silence is maintained, individual requests to God are made, and the session ends with members silently departing from the *Dervish*'s home.

From a religious perspective, through the invocation of God's forgiveness, the purpose of this ritual is to cure and clean the body from sins. The point of ecstasy is seen as personal experience of a Divine presence (Schimmel, 1975). From the vantage point of helping, the ritual induces a state of hypnotic trance, a process that much research indicates has therapeutic value (Cassanas, 1992; Witztum, Buchbinder, & Van der Hart, 1990). On an individual level, the transition from the subjective reality of personal experience to the irrational world of the Divine leads to feelings of satisfaction, confidence, catharsis, psychological release, self-expression, and, above all else, resolution to deal with one's problems. On another level, group members give emotional support, universalization, and a network of support outside of the ritual. The ritual process itself provides a further sense of union with other members participating in that ritual, reinforcing greater group cohesion (D'Aquili, 1985).

The *Dervish* is a tangible symbol of religious strength, an authority figure conveying empathy, understanding, and acceptance. Because of their faith, the participants believe in the power and the capacity of supernatural powers, imparted through the *Dervish* via the ritual. This increases their expectation and resolve to work out their problems (Frank & Frank, 1991; Kennedy, 1967; Torrey, 1972). The principles of psychodynamic theory indicate success will be experienced in relating to the *Dervish* if this relationship mirrors a dominant character need to submit to a parental figure (El-Islam, 1967).

Integration of Traditional Healing with Modern Methods of Helping Professional Practice

The following examples are taken from cases derived from clinical records at the Soroka Hospital, the Negev region's main medical centre and largest mental health care facility, during the late 1990s. Any Bedouin-Arab in the region requiring specialized forms of psychiatric or somatic treatment is generally referred to the Soroka by their general practitioner from a primary health care clinic in the patient's community. During the three month period of data collection, there were 60 Bedouin-Arab patients in the Soroka's mental health clinic. From this population, subjects who were diagnosed by the biomedical system as psychotic were eliminated, as were subjects who did not utilize both traditional and biomedical healers. From the resulting sample pool, 20 participants were randomly selected in order to render an equal number of male and female subjects.

The participants from both sexes represented the wider population's younger to middle age adults with respect to such criteria as age, occupation, religiosity, marital, tribal, and parental status (for a more comprehensive discussion of Bedouin-Arab demographic characteristics, see Jabbur, 1995). The male patients ranged in age from 24 to 40, with an average age of 27. Five said they regularly practised Islamic religion; the other five considered themselves only somewhat religious. The female patients ranged in age from 17 to 46, with an average age of 35, and all indicated that they practised Islam regularly.

Of the psychiatrists who worked at the Soroka Hospital, five were Russian Jewish immigrants to Israel, one was a Jewish Israeli of Romanian origin, and the other was a Jewish Israeli psychiatrist-in-training. Among the traditional healers, five were *Dervish* healers, five were amulet writers (*Khatib* or *Hajjab*), six were fortune-tellers (*Al-Fataha*), and four were Koranic healers (*Moalj BelKoran*).

An analysis was conducted looking at the experience of the 10 male and 10 female non-psychotic Bedouin-Arab psychiatric patients selected who utilized both the biomedical psychiatric system and traditional healers (hereafter referred to as a traditional mental health system). The findings of this analysis revealed that the men were more familiar with the biomedical system. However, it is misleading to infer that women therefore had few resources at their disposal, for the female subjects were more knowledgeable about the traditional system than were the males. This differential pattern of knowledge reflects several culturally specific realities that affect utilization patterns and differ between the two sexes. These factors include individual versus collective decision making, geographic mobility, the construction of mental health problems, a system's ability to strike a therapeutic alliance, modes of diagnosis, and outcome satisfaction.

The 20 patients were diagnosed with psychiatric disorders other than psychosis by the biomedical system, including anxiety disorders, depression, phobias, posttraumatic stress disorder, social adjustment disorders, and social problems. It was also the case that all 20 selected patients were likewise considered by the traditional healers *not* to be possessed by evil spirits (as opposed to the more severe category of possession); diagnoses included *Amaal* (sorcery), *Hariah* (anxiety), *Hassad* (the evil eye), and *Nufs Mn Al-Jinn* (air from evil spirits).

In this comparative study, clarity of communication requires the use of terms such as "patient," "symptom," and "diagnosis" in describing the biomedical *and* traditional healing systems. The terms themselves, however, are commonly attributed to the biomedical system and should not imply that the traditional system incorporates them from a biomedical perspective. A traditional healer may describe the people he sees as *"marid"* (sick person), a comparable term to "patient." He may likewise tell a patient "you have the evil eye." For brevity's sake, the manuscript refers to this as a diagnosis, even though the traditional healer never used the term "diagnosis" or "symptom".

Four points bear particular emphasis. First, it is essential to consider all conclusions in the context of the diagnoses. The traditional healers may have been less effective, and the biomedical practitioners more so, had the diagnoses been of a more psychotic nature (Al-Krenawi & Graham, 1996b; Okasha, 1966).

Second, much of the analysis of the biomedical system in Israel reflects its current rather than its potential state, and is far from representing Western medical psychiatry. Most of the psychiatrists in the present study are recent immigrants from the former Soviet Union who were hastily retrained in Israel. They, like many Israeli mental health practitioners, do not speak Arabic. The delivery of psychiatric services in Israel has been significantly affected by rapid immigration of mental health practitioners to Israel from the former Soviet Union, among other countries (Popper, 1993; Popper & Horowitz, 1996). All of the psychiatrists participating in the study admitted to having little cultural familiarity with the Bedouin-Arab community. Many, with non-Western training, may have strength in organic practice, but less knowledge of cross-cultural practice and psychotherapeutic processes (Shuval, 1985, 1990). Future research might consider how Bedouin-Arab patients relate to Arabic speaking, but non-Bedouin-Arab psychiatrists in Israel or elsewhere.

Third, the present analysis is a case study of one society, with findings that could generalise to other cultures where traditional and biomedical healing systems co-exist. Just as they would in other ethno-specific contexts, issues of power, social hierarchy, and cultural differences influence Bedouin-Arab patients and their Jewish practitioners (Gorkin, 1986). Similarly, the limited fluency in Arabic among biomedical practitioners in the present study is only one factor, and not the primary one, defining help seeking patterns. While the present study uses the terminology "help seeking patterns/processes", it should be acknowledged that some recent literature employs such terms as "pathways to care" (e.g., Rogler & Cortes, 1993). Language is a point of entry and marker for the more profound distinction between insiders and outsiders. The healers are insiders who are sought for ailments that are locally construed as being dependant on the social world. The biomedical practitioners are outsiders. They may be considered inept or out of place in the local social world, but they operate within a biomedical system and so possess a technical efficacy that extends both to access to treatments of the body in a highly mechanical sense, and to political control.

Therefore, it is not only cultural variations, but power differentials that motivate the patient's help seeking behaviour. Any encounter that occurs between a non-Bedouin-Arab biomedical practitioner and a Bedouin-Arab patient necessarily enters the two into the wider symbolic universe of Middle Eastern politics. Here, the contexts of power and political relations between a dominant Jewish population and a minority Muslim/Arab community become implicit, if not explicit, to any helping process (Al-Krenawi & Graham, 1996b). Beyond these considerations, the sociosomatics of how "culture infolds into the body (and, reciprocally, how bodily processes outfold into social space)" is critical to our understanding of help seeking patterns (Kleinman & Kleinman, 1994, pp. 710-711). As outlined in the first chapter, the Bedouin-Arabs are a high context society which, in turn, further amplifies the differences between Bedouin-Arab and Israeli societies, with commensurate influence upon help seeking processes (Gorkin, 1986).

Finally, it is important to emphasize that both the traditional system and the Bedouin-Arab culture in which it exists are heterogeneous phenomena. "The local contexts of social experience are both shared and fragmented. Gender, age, cohort, political faction, and biography inflect local worlds so that they are plural" (Kleinman & Kleinman, 1994, p. 712). While recognizing some of the merits of the traditional system, the researchers also sought to understand its ambiguities, paradoxes, and the full range of assistance—from minimal to maximal—that it was capable of providing.

Common Patterns and Common Perceptions of Mental Health Care Utilization

Members of many recently modernizing traditional societies utilize the traditional health care system only after the biomedical system has been attempted (Al-Krenawi et al., 1996; Bilu & Witzum, 1993; Waldman, 1990). Likewise, among the Bedouin-Arab sample, all patients adhered to the following pattern of help-seeking behaviour: they first turned to their family and friends, then went to a general practitioner (GP) within the biomedical system, then to a traditional healer, and then were referred to the psychiatric system by the GP. After this point, noticeable differences emerged between the two sexes, as will be discussed.

Researchers have emphasized that the way that one perceives a problem/disease strongly influences the person's degree of suffering and efforts to seek help (Cf. Chirsman, 1977; Christensen, 1987; Chung & Lin, 1994; Kleinman, 1982). In many ways, Bedouin-Arabs hold biomedical health practice in high regard and tend not to find contact with GPs stigmatizing (Fabrega, 1991). Psychiatrists, however, are perceived differently, and need to be utilized in ways that are perceived to be less stigmatizing. Somatic symptoms, particularly pain, provide *the* major precipitating reasons for a Bedouin-Arab to seek medical attention. Somatic symptoms are readily comprehensible.

All patients, when they visited a GP, insisted that interventions be restricted to the physical realm. The doctors tended to be somatization-oriented, like their patients, prescribing numerous laboratory, radiological, and "modern" tests. Two physicians admitted to the researcher that the principal function of some of these interventions was to reassure and strike a therapeutic alliance with their patient.

Absent from many treatments was any emphasis on the possibility of a psychiatric problem, as distinct from a strictly physical one. When psychiatric referrals were made, they were invariably to the Soroka, a general hospital that is perceived as being less stigmatizing than a psychiatric hospital, and a place where somatic treatments prevail. As a result, the patient, assuming that the problem was strictly physiological, tended to focus on physical complaints over the course of the psychiatric encounter.

It should be noted that the overall process of multi-stage referrals tended to increase patient anxiety by raising the suspicion that he/she suffers from a disease that is either unknown or unduly complicated. Many patients, as well, experienced high expectations for successful and quick treatment, and consequent disappointment when this was not realized (West, 1987). Some of the examined patients, for example, were prescribed medications and returned the following day, complaining of side effects and of the medication's inability to improve the underlying condition.

Gender Differences in Health Care Utilization

There are several implicit codes that produce gender differentials within the health care field. This section outlines six areas in which gender differences are particularly relevant within the analysis of the dual-use of traditional and western methods of healing.

Collective versus Individual Decision Making

Male utilization patterns tended more towards the individual's decision making. Among the female patients, in contrast, the family, as distinct from the patient by herself, was responsible for major utilization decisions. As a result, the men had greater licence to choose between the two systems. The women, for gender-specific reasons, were more inclined to choose the traditional healer. The female patients and their families were universally aware of the stigma associated with contacting the psychiatric system. Among unmarried women, the stigma could damage their marital prospects (Okasha & Lotaif, 1979). Among married women, the label of psychiatric illness could be used by their husband or his family as leverage for him to divorce or remarry (Bazzoui & Al-Issa, 1966; Chaleby, 1985). Most women also gave the impression that marital therapy would have been indicated. None, however, pursued this option. Several were fearful of consequent harm to their marriage, a finding that is consistent with previous research into Arab women's attitudes towards marital therapy (Savaya, 1995).

Geographic Mobility

Geographic mobility was an equally powerful factor in utilization decisions. The women were largely restricted to seeking treatment from biomedical and traditional systems in close proximity to their homes as they were not allowed to leave their immediate community. The men, however, were more mobile: many visited traditional healers from outside of their communities, and others were able to consult psychiatric and general practitioners within or beyond their home communities.

Symptomatology, Perceptions of Etiology

Regardless of gender, the Bedouin-Arab patients presented complaints that were more easily comprehended by the traditional system than the biomedical. Their distinct somatic idioms of distress (Ben-Ezer, 1992; El-Islam & Abu-Dagga, 1992; Good, 1977; Pliskin, 1987) were based on the head (which, according to Arab culture, governs and integrates all body activity) and the heart (the centre of all feelings). These, in turn, were controlling metaphors that operate on the social, bodily, and psychic levels all at once (Good, 1977; Kleinman & Kleinman, 1994). Bedouin-Arab patients could complain of giddiness when they felt incapable of proper social functioning, and of heartache when having pent-up feelings of emotional distress. These symptoms could easily be misunderstood or missed by a clinician outside of the Bedouin-Arab culture. Both sexes presented somatic complaints at different levels. Males complained of fatigue, physical pain, and weakness. Females, in contrast, described how pain travelled in their bodies, and often referred to the heart. The women also tended to rely more heavily than men on metaphorical language to describe subjective feelings.

Both sexes appeared concerned with how the disease decreased social functioning within the family and tribe, and so were highly motivated to seek successful treatment, regardless of biomedical or traditional health care utilization decisions. As has been demonstrated in previous studies on high context patriarchal societies, men were particularly concerned with their ability to function as the family breadwinner and to fulfil tribal social obligations, and by doing so, preserve the integrity of the family name (Pliskin, 1987; Zola, 1973).

Men and women often had different perceptions of the causes of their ailments. The educated men were apt to think of etiology in terms of *Mn Allah* (Divine Will and Punishment) (El-Islam, 1994); the less educated and illiterate men were more likely to focus on *Al-Jinn* as causes. The male patients examined, like their counterparts in other Arab cultures, tended to show no association between levels of education and the inclination to embrace supernatural explanations of mental illness (Caliph, 1989; El-Islam & Abu-Dagga, 1992).

The female patients emphasized spirit causes, but tended to frame these in the context of human agency. Many saw sorcery—the harmful, evil spiritual forces of other people—as an important etiology. This concurs with research conducted among other cultures, into the relationship between witchcraft and illness (Cannon, 1957; Ruiz & Griffith, 1977). Several patients experienced the evil eye; that is, they claimed to be the subject of another's envy, and consequently suffered psychiatric difficulties (El-Islam, 1978; Morsy, 1993).

Women also experienced another cause of distress, the *Kabsa*, a phenomenon common to Arab society (Boddy, 1989; Early, 1993; Inhorn, 1994), literally translated as a "raid" or "surprise attack," in which a woman recipient is forced, by the evil spirit possession of another woman, into a state of infertility or sickness. In one such example, shortly after she had returned home with her newborn son, a woman had become distressed after her husband's second wife had visited her; within several days, the woman experienced patterns of nightmares and headaches. She enlisted the advice of a fortune-teller, who concluded that the second wife had deliberately visited during a state of *"Njsh"*; that is, she had not bathed after having had sexual relations with the husband and thus brought impure spirits into the first wife's house, which were seen as being capable of harming the mother and the newly born son.

The above gendered differences had a significant impact upon health care utilization. On the level of symptomatology, human agency among the women was more strongly associated with their spirit-derived illness. Not surprisingly, then, on the level of utilization, women were more likely then men to exercise agency upon their illness. When they acted upon their illness, they were also more inclined than their male counterparts to turn to traditional healers.

Despite living in a patriarchal society, Bedouin-Arab males, it must be remembered, tend to be fearful of women's magical powers as expressed by such forms of sorcery as magic beads and stones (Bar-Zvi, 1988; personal communication with amulet writer and fortune-teller, 1996). Women are more familiar with, and are more frequent users of, traditional Arab healing systems (Al-Issa, 1989; Al-Sabaie, 1989; Dickson, 1949; Nelson, 1974). Moreover, in responding to various forms of disadvantage, women become knowledgeable about spirit-type phenomena. For example, women in polygamous marriages encounter a higher incidence of psychiatric problems (Chaleby, 1985) and are particularly adept at sorcery as a way of coping with being one of many wives (Bazzoui & Al-Issa, 1966).

Therapeutic Alliance

Patient-psychiatrist relationships tended to be formal; over the course of follow up with the researcher, most of the female patients examined, and many of the male patients, could not even recall their psychiatrist's name. Language barriers were observed in the encounters with the psychiatrists. In part because they tended to be better educated and in part because they interacted with a greater number of people outside of the immediate home community, the male patients were conversant in Hebrew. The female patients, in contrast, spoke only Arabic. The male patients, therefore, had a greater probability of being able to communicate with the psychiatrists, all of whom spoke Hebrew and were unable to communicate in Arabic. When the women interacted with the psychiatrists, however, a translator/chaperone was needed, usually a member of her immediate family which could also have significant implications for the patient/psychiatrist relationship, as shown below.

Direct communication between the female patient and psychiatrist was thereby inhibited, particularly when discussing issues of familial functioning that may have been related to the diagnosis and other personal topics that the female patient may have perceived as compromising. This inhibition was exacerbated by the patients' expectations surrounding the prescription of medications or receipt of physical examinations rather than talk therapy; this problem was apparent for both sexes. Patients were therefore reluctant to divulge information which they felt was personal, unrelated to the treatment, or inappropriate information to convey to someone outside of their culture. Because of the resulting gulf between biomedical practitioner and patient, misinterpretations, misdiagnoses, and mistreatments (Budman et al., 1992; Lipton & Simon, 1985) were all common. The example of the male patient, whose case was described in chapter 3, illustrates this point. He was initially misdiagnosed and treated as a paranoid schizophrenic. But as was demonstrated above, the biomedical mental health care system correctly understood the "form" of the patient's symptoms, auditory and visual hallucinations, but it did not initially appreciate the "content," or cultural significance, of these symptoms. A traditional Bedouin-Arab healer, the *Dervish*, exorcised the patient, after which point the symptoms decreased, the patient was re-diagnosed by a senior psychiatrist as a neurotic, and both biomedical and traditional systems were successfully continued for several months in follow up treatment before the patient was discharged (Al-Krenawi & Graham, 1997).

The traditional healers tended to strike closer alliances with the patients. Healers and patients often visited at each others' homes for several hours and sometimes several days at a time, whereas interactions with psychiatrists tended to be for only a few minutes. Families allowed their daughters to stay with healers for prolonged periods of time, up to several days, in the healer's home. Moreover, women were accompanied by family members – female and male - during biomedical treatment.

Healers, as religious people, tended to refer to their patients as "my son/my daughter," and in many respects, including nomenclature and content, the patient-healer relationship took on a quasi-familial demeanour. Having such a close relationship helped to reinforce the patient's trust and belief in the healer's supernatural capacity (Graham & Al-Krenawi, 1996; Kiev, 1964; Prince, 1976; Torrey, 1972).

The traditional system provided opportunities for the patient to communicate with the healer in a confidential manner. Because the healer and patient shared the same world-view, language, religion, and culture, patient-healer communication tended to be more effective than with biomedical psychiatrists. Traditional terminology, because it is embedded in local systems of meaning, was more understandable and thus less anxiety-producing than the biomedical terminology. Moreover, when problems in perceptions arose, the healer and/or the patient's family were able to elucidate in the patient's mother tongue.

The healer, reflecting Bedouin-Arab culture, also tended to promote the active involvement of family members, thus activating a natural support network that was far more vigorous than in the biomedical model. The traditional system, in contrast to the biomedical, also tended to build informal networks of support beyond the level of the family. For example, a traditional healer may treat a patient using rituals, such as visiting a saint's tomb, in which family and community members are active participants (Al-Krenawi & Graham, 1996a).

The biomedical system tended to sustain stronger therapeutic alliances when the patient was active with the therapist: able to articulate their needs succinctly and to reveal their problems over the course of talking therapy. Conversely, in the traditional system, the healer took on a more active, authoritarian role, while the patient was more passive and dependent, looking at the healer as a *hakim* (wise person). As several authors point out, this dynamic is consistent with expectations often observed in Arab societies (Al-Krenawi & Graham, 1996a; Budman et al., 1992; West, 1987).

Diagnosis/Analysis of Dreams

None of the patients examined were able to state the name of their psychiatric diagnosis, let alone its meaning. In part, this was because of a tendency to defer to the psychiatrist's authority and to assume that the patients therefore did not need to be concerned with these aspects of treatment. Biomedical diagnoses, as well, were made either in English or in Hebrew, neither of which are the patients' primary language. Given that they did not speak either of these languages, this was a particular problem for the female patients. Likewise, as will be discussed, the psychiatrist was often precluded from entering the patient's symbolic universe, by virtue of cultural differences. Even if a patient had been told the diagnosis, its meaning might remain ambiguous at best. This is not to imply that the patients did not ask questions. Most were very interested in learning about the nature of the treatment (for example injections versus oral medication), as well as the disease's prognosis and its degree of severity.

Among traditional healers, in contrast, dream interpretation was one of the most significant means of diagnosis, and was used by all healers under examination (El-Islam, 1982; Gorkin & Othman, 1994). Other techniques, depending on healer type, included dialogue with spirits and various rituals, including reading coffee dregs, reading from amulet writing books, or reading from Koranic healing books. According to the patients and healers, all traditional healer types—save for Koranic healers—frequently guessed patients' symptoms, often correctly.

The traditional diagnoses themselves were made in culturally specific terminology, in the patient's language and in their shared world-view (Abu-Lughod, 1986; Frank, 1973; Torrey, 1986), and were thus familiar and accessible to the patients. Traditional healers highlighted external loci of control, particularly supernatural powers, in contrast to psychiatric explanations emphasizing internal loci according to psychodynamic or psychophysiological models (Bilu & Witztum, 1995). Because of the traditional system's emphasis on transcendent powers, there was less of a tendency for the patient to think that their problem was their own fault (Grotberg, 1990), thereby removing associated stigma and shame.

Rather, the healer persuaded the patient to construct problems in terms of accessible, shared world-view symbols, and to attach emotions to these symbols. They then worked with the patient to manipulate the symbols "to help the patient transact his/her own emotions" (Dow, cited in Bilu & Witztumm 1995, p. 163). For example, one of the female subjects was anxious and suffered from insomnia. In her coffee dregs, there appeared the symbol of a snake, which a *Fatah* told her symbolized an enemy. In order for her to reduce her anxiety and insomnia, the *Fatah* read verses from the Koran and then told the woman to reconcile with an acquaintance with whom the woman had admitted to having a falling out. Once this reconciliation took place, the snake no longer appeared in her dregs, and her somatic problems were solved.

Outcome Satisfaction

Among both genders, biomedical practitioners were able to help many patients with issues of pain and symptom reduction, prescribing medications as treatment. Psychiatrists also provided patients with letters in support of applications for income security programmes and for sick leave; this was particularly important among male patients, all of whom were familial breadwinners. In many instances among patients, especially women, informal networks of help were cultivated with other patients. Men were inclined to build networks among members of their own family, tribe, neighbourhood, or wider ethno-community. Women's social networks extended to females from different tribes and to Jewish patients, such as Moroccans or Yemenites, who spoke the same language and/or who were familiar with Bedouin-Arab culture. The women's encounters with Jewish patients allowed the provision of information regarding traditional forms of Bedouin-Arab healing and the receipt of information and advice regarding access to social services.

Although the traditional system did not address as many physical complaints as the biomedical system, it nonetheless dealt with more non-physical symptoms such as nightmares and delusions. Many of the healers' treatments focused on dreams, feelings of fear, or anxiety symptoms such as breathlessness, lack of energy, or headaches. Patients often described their personal difficulties via proverbs, which resonated with the traditional healer but often seemed foreign to the biomedical clinician. For instance, rather than telling a practitioner that he felt utterly alone and abandoned, one male patient said that he wanted to "cry like a little camel who was left alone in the desert." Rather than saying that she was in despair and felt completely hopeless, a female patient simply divulged that "my eyes are blind and my hand is shorter." Female patients, in particular, frequently used similes and metaphors common to Arab culture to indirectly convey highly subjective feelings (Al-Krenawi, 1997). Rather than describing her feelings directly, a woman who typically dressed in completely black garb said that she felt "like ashes, just like my clothing."

Both genders believed equally that the traditional system helped them more than the biomedical. One gender difference of note was that females appeared to be more inclined than their male counterparts to use the biomedical system for somatic medical examinations.

Much of the underlying dissatisfaction with the biomedical psychiatric system stems from a lack of familiarity with the basic tenets and objectives of this form of practice. The term "psychiatry" was strange to many of the patients interviewed, especially the less educated women. When asked, only a few of the men attempted to define it, and most of these tended to confuse it with the treatment of physical maladies. Two of the subjects who were educated defined psychiatry in terms of a "psychological complex," but were unable to explain the term more fully. The traditional system, in contrast, used idioms of diagnosis and treatment that were more fully discernable to the patients (Bilu & Witztum, 1995). Further, as discussed earlier, the traditional system often located the source of suffering as outside of the patient's control, thereby lessening the patient's felt shame or stigma.

Female patients were more inclined to believe that improvements in their situation were the result of the traditional intervention; this was also true of male patients, but to a lesser extent. In part, this was because they attributed any improvement in their non-physical symptoms to the traditional intervention rather than the medication, and also because the traditional system is culturally familiar. It is true that some of the educated male patients reported that the medications reduced pain, but most of the other male patients interviewed, and virtually all of the females, were less confident in the benefits of prescribed medications. One female patient expressed her surprise that "the doctor gave me medications" without any preceding "physical examination."

Patients were also less disappointed with the traditional system's rate of change, given their underlying belief in God's justice and goodness. Islamic thought emphasizes that material and spiritual well-being are achievable only through a profound submission to the will of God. Those who fail to submit are in a state of conflict and, it is thought, their personalities begin to disintegrate (Rizvi, 1989). According to the Koran, a life without faith is a state of spiritual non-being in which one loses touch with his/her true self (Koran, Surah 49, v. 19). From some Islamic points of view, the concepts of well-being, satisfaction, salvation, self-realization, and achievement are linked to the belief that an individual's performance in this life determines their ultimate outcome in the hereafter (Rizvi, 1989).

THE KORANIC HEALER

Koranic healers are a further healing tradition found in Bedouin-Arab society. They exist in Arab communities outside the Bedouin-Arab. The following section focuses on how one becomes a Koranic healer and how one utilizes his knowledge of the Koran in the treatment of mental illness. This is done by describing the three stages of mental illness from a Koranic point of view and is illustrated with a case study concentrating on the experiences of several Koranic healers.

Those Arab Muslim healers, called *Sheikhs* or *Moalj Bel-Koran* in Arabic, base their work on the Koran and *Hadith* (the tradition of the Prophet Muhammad, based on what he said or did). The Koranic healing movement, in particular, has significantly increased within the past half decade and is found among virtually all Muslim societies (Bali, 1993). It also enjoys legitimacy, in both public reputation and in its sanction by many Islamic scholars (Al-Jzari, 1987; Ashoor, 1987; Bali, 1993). As will be demonstrated, Koranic healing, moreover, provides a point of entry into a value base that is vital to many Muslim helping profession clients but which challenges the values of many, if not most Western helping professionals. It reflects, first, a patriarchal social structure, where men dominate leadership authority in the economy, household, polity, and religious institutions. It also holds, second, that the spiritual world is both active in the day-to-day affairs of individuals, and requires the intervention of traditional healers. In this sense, greater understanding of Koranic healers allows for both the possibility of dialogue between the two value bases, as well as greater cultural sensitivity towards Muslim society. As Al-Dabbagh (1993) insists, if helping profession practice, which is a Western construct, does not possess sufficient cultural and religious sensitivity in working among Muslims, it is destined to fail.

Healer Characteristics and the Process of Becoming a Healer

Over a three-month period, through semi-structured interviews and tape recorded observations, the healing activities of a number of Arab Muslim Koranic healers and the treatment of several Israeli-Arab and Gaza Arab/West Bank individuals were studied. The six healers who were examined for this book were male, aged 25 to 45, and married with children; two were Bedouin-Arab living in the Negev, two were Arabs from the Gaza Strip, and two were Arabs from the West Bank. The two Gaza Strip healers had undergraduate degrees from the eminent Islamic institution Al-Azhar University in Egypt, and were school teachers. The two West Bank healers had diplomas from Hebron College and were, respectively, an *imam* (prayer leader) of a Mosque and a teacher. One Bedouin-Arab had graduated from the Islamic University of Gaza, and was also a school teacher; the other was a student at an Islamic college in an Israeli Arab city. All had majored or were majoring in Islamic religion and thought.

Islamic teaching holds that women are more readily influenced by *Iblis* (the devil) than men are. The Koranic story of Adam and Eve describes Eve as more easily succumbing to the enticements of *Iblis*, and hence her female descendants are weaker and more corruptible than men (El-Shamy, 1977; Ibn-Taymeh, 1957). Because they menstruate and give birth, they are thought to be less pure than men and hence vulnerable to attacks from evil spirits. Physically attractive women, or those around them, are particularly prone to attacks (Bali, 1993; Boddy, 1989; Grotberg, 1990; Kennedy, 1967). It is based on these beliefs that women cannot become Koranic healers, although women are prominent in other healing activities, especially *Fatah*.

A man becomes a Koranic healer by first possessing extensive scholarly knowledge of Islam. He is then expected to contact an experienced Koranic healer, who becomes a supervisor for the new healer over a period of up to a year, teaching him from appropriate books and from his own experience, and providing extensive support and encouragement. The senior healer is also available for post-apprenticeship consultation. Koranic healers appear to enter their craft differently than do other forms of Muslim Arab healers, such as *Khatib* (amulet writers), or *Fatah*. These latter healers tend to attribute their status to divine will; "fate somehow led them to become healers. . . . as they conceive it, there is generally a religious meaning to their career choice" (Gorkin & Othman, 1994, p. 223; See also Al-Krenawi et al., 1996). Although they are profoundly religiously imbued, Koranic healers, in contrast tend to choose their career paths based on personal choice, as opposed to divine inspiration.

Al-Jzari (1987) and Al-Daramdash (1991) note some major characteristics of Koranic healers. They are:

1. The healer has to believe in God, and practice the Islamic pillars as written in the Koran and *Hadith*.
2. The healer must follow the Prophet Muhammad's Koranic treatment processes, as personified by the saints of Islam.
3. The healer has to believe that the Koran can influence evil spirits.
4. The healer has to be a righteous person and do nothing that is forbidden by Islam.
5. The healer must have knowledge of the evil spirits' world.
6. The healer must know how the evil spirits enter the human body, and what traditions can influence them to leave.
7. The healer has to know which Koranic chapter(s) to use in a given treatment.
8. The healer must be mindful of God throughout the treatment process and after it, in order to avoid infiltration by evil spirits.
9. The healer must have a sense of goodwill, which is the basis upon which he helps people who have been attacked by evil spirits.
10. The healer has to be married, on the assumption that he therefore will not be distracted by the sexual dynamics of the treatment process.

Stages of Mental Illness Treatment by Koranic Healers

There are three stages of treatment: pre-treatment, diagnosis, and treatment. They are outlined in detail below.

Stage One

The first stage of treatment, pre-treatment, creates the proper treatment atmosphere by eliminating any distractions as well as any items that are not in strict adherence with Koranic healing. All musical instruments and any golden jewellery are removed from the room where treatment is expected to take place. The healer also removes all pictures from the room, which is believed to allow angels to enter. If the client has hung an amulet, a tool used by a different healing tradition, it has to be put it in a fire and destroyed.

As with other Arab-Muslim healers (Gorkin & Othman, 1994), Koranic clients tend to travel to a distant healer rather than visit a local one. "The emotional preparation involved in making a longer trip," as other scholars have observed in relation to other healers' clients, may contribute to "patients' readiness and hopefulness for a cure" (Bilu, Frank, & Kakar, referred to in Gorkin & Othman, 1994, p. 225).

Men are allowed to observe the treatment, but women are not. If the client is a woman, she has to cover her body with *hijab* (a long dress), in accordance with Islam. The healer cannot treat a woman by herself; male relatives, such as her husband, father or brother, have to accompany her in treatment.

The healer begins the process by telling the client and family about God's power, that everything happens by God's will, and that the healer is only a mediator between them and God. He also emphasizes that other forms of traditional healing—including *Khatib* and *Sahharin* (sorcerers)—collaborate with evil spirits and are therefore not acceptable to Islam and should not be utilized (Al-Daramdash, 1991; Al-Jzari, 1987; Ashoor, 1987; Bali, 1993).

Stage Two

The second stage is the diagnosis. Helping profession clients and Koranic healers' clients are very similar. They both typically present a wide range of psychosocial and/or psychiatric problems. These can often have psychosomatic manifestations. In the case of the Koranic healers' clients, standard symptoms of possession include one or more of the following: the client keeps their eyes closed or covers them with their hands; there is strong shaking in the body, hands, or legs; the client shouts or cries; the spirit says its name. Single or multiple spirits may be in the body. Sometimes, spirits are able to communicate with the healer through the client. The healer might ask what kind(s) of spirit(s) they are, what their religion and sex is, the reason that they have entered the client's body, whether there is one or multiple spirits inside the client, where they are located, and whether the spirits work alone or with magical healers such as *Sahharin*.

If, however, the spirits are silent and the healer cannot communicate with them through the client, he then asks the client (as opposed to the spirit[s]) several questions about recent dreams. These may include whether the client saw any animals in their dreams, and if so, whether they followed the individual, how many there were, and what type of animal(s) appeared. The healer also asks whether the client had any dreams that were frightening, that involved falling from a high place, or that involved going somewhere that seemed frightening. The dream questions help the healer to determine how many spirits are inside the client and what kind of spirits they are. For example, two snakes in a dream are interpreted as two spirits within the client.

Once the healer has determined the diagnosis, he cleans himself and his surroundings and asks the people in the room to do the same. This is according to the *Hadith* in which Islam is considered clean, and so individuals and their surroundings also have to be (Farsy, 1964).

Stage Three

The third stage, treatment, is the most difficult for the healer, since he has to confront the spirits and exorcise the client. The healer begins this process by covering the client's ears and getting the client to lie down on a bed. He then puts a hand on the client's head and reads the first chapter from the Koran (*Surah Al-Fatiha*) into the client's ear. He continues to read verses from other chapters, such as *Surah, Al-Baqara* v. 1-5; 163-164; 255-257, and *Surah, Al-Jinn* v. 1-9, as are appropriate for the type of spirit involved (Al-Ataar, 1989; Al-Jzari, 1987; Badawi, 1992). Every healer has a library of books on Koranic healing, which he consults in order to determine which verses to read and overall approaches to take.

The reading of Koranic verses agitates the spirits in the client's body, allowing the healer to communicate with the spirits and ultimately, to entice them to leave the client's body. While still in the body, if the healer recognizes a spirit as a non-Muslim, he tries to convert it to Islam (Al-Jzari, 1987; Bali, 1993). If, during the course of Koran readings, the spirits leave the body, there is no further need to communicate with them. As the Prophet Muhammad said, "Do not hope to meet the enemy" (Salim, 1986). If, however, the spirits initially refuse to leave the client's body, the healer communicates with them until they either leave the client or refuse to leave. The dialogue between the healer and the spirits can take more than one hour, depending on which type of spirit is in the client's body. If the spirits are "*Halat Sarah*" (in a confused state) and refuse to leave the client's body, they are considered beyond the healer's power. In this case he refers the client to another Koranic healer. *Halat Sarah* spirits are deemed especially dangerous and difficult to treat.

Another technique of treatment is an *Al-Taharh* purification ritual, wherein water that has been run over Koranic verses on a plate, is either consumed or used for washing. The ritual's purpose is to clean the body and the spirit from sins (Al-Ataar, 1989; Al-Dramdash, 1991; Al-Sabaie, 1989; Badawi, 1992; Bali, 1993; Ibn-Tymiah, 1957; Sanua, 1979). A different healing technique involves the use of honey, which is believed to be good for the body and soul, and *Habat Al-Baraka* (black cumin seed; or as the healers call it, "the blessing seed"). The two are mixed together and fed to the client, as recommended by the Prophet Muhammed (Abdul-Aziz, 1989; Ashoor, 1987). The oil of the black cumin seed can also be applied as a body lotion before going to sleep.

Koranic healers routinely lecture their clients about the power of God, and that they consider themselves merely tools in God's hands; everything happens to them only by the will of God. They recommend that their clients practise the principles of Islam. They often pray with their clients, and after the prayer, give a lesson about the power of prayer and religious devotion in general.

Homework assignments are common. The healers recommend rituals such as *Aqiqa*, where a meal is eaten with family and friends and where the Koran is read. Another ritual is *Mulad*, where religious songs and Koranic verses are cited and a meal with others is consumed. The healers also recommend praying in groups and going to the mosque for *Salat Al-Jumah* (the prayer of Friday), the Muslim holy day.

Although Koranic healers pride themselves in rapid cures, it should be noted that clients remain in contact with the healers, and consult with their healer regarding psychosocial problems, religious matters, or any troubling life events. Unlike other forms of Arab Muslim healers that can be stern in therapeutic approaches (Gorkin & Othman, 1994, p. 230), the Koranic healers under examination all assumed a supportive stance.

Koranic healers are known by public reputation and are referred by word-of-mouth. Moreover, they are actively involved in outreach activities with biomedical practitioners. Koranic healing activities are, for example, known to have been tape recorded and disseminated to biomedical practitioners, in order to help the latter to appreciate the significance of Islam to mental health and psychosocial functioning. Indeed, Koranic healers pride themselves, particularly in the area of mental health, in being able to treat problems that biomedical modalities have not been able to successfully treat.

CONCLUSION

A number of important factors can be used to further improve aspects of helping professional practice with a non-psychotic Bedouin-Arab population. The first involves striking a positive therapeutic alliance between patients and practitioners. It must be stressed that medications, as a helping professional form of treatment, have considerable sanction in Bedouin-Arab culture (Al-Krenawi et al., 1994). Patients enter helping professional therapy with the expectation of being treated medicinally. Comparable to what has recently been written about on the striking of therapeutic alliances with a western patient population (Burgess, 1993; Sarwer-Foner, 1993; Southwick & Yehoda, 1993), prescriptions in a Bedouin-Arab context provide a very good basis for striking a therapeutically beneficial relationship between the patient and the clinician. In order for helping professionals to be more successful in this enterprise, it is necessary to gain greater familiarity with Islamic theology, culture, and gender constructions, and their inextricable relationship with the Muslim conception of psychosocial and mental health problems. Future research might examine how Koranic healing can be integrated with helping profession practice for the benefit of all parties, helping profession clients included. For example, where appropriate, helping professionals could refer clients to Koranic healers. They could also consult with healers in order to cultivate greater cultural sensitivity in their practice. By mutual observation and mutual dissemination, each could provide the other a basis for improved practice.

Second, in order to maintain the alliance, greater knowledge of, and sensitivity towards, traditional modes of helping and the Bedouin-Arab culture is necessary. Helping professional practitioners need to learn more about informal community resources, cultural perceptions, belief systems, and practices (Beiser, Gill & Edwards, 1993). This was particularly true for the helping professional practitioner subjects described in this chapter. Such knowledge will provide a clinical basis for mutual trust, understanding, and respect. It also provides an important tool for gaining access to the patient's main problems or conflicts, as these are frequently expressed by way of bodily symptoms, proverbs, and nonverbal language. Koranic healers, in fact, share with modern counterparts such as the helping profession, systematic procedures of assessment and treatment, a complex canon of professional theory learned at universities, a period of training, ongoing professional consultation and professional supervision, and a system of professional ethics. Koranic healers also utilize a sophisticated repertoire of skills that are similar to those used by clinical helping professionals, including techniques such as suggestion, persuasion, and manipulation (Ruiz & Langrod, 1976). Central to the traditional healer's success is the client's belief in the healer's knowledge and techniques (Murphy, 1973); these beliefs raise expectations that in turn positively influence treatment outcome (Marica, Rubin & Efran, 1969; Rappaport, 1972). By involving family, and sometimes extended family members in treatment, the healer activates an extensive support network which the client can utilize during aftercare (Al-Krenawi et al., 1995; Al-Krenawi & Graham, 1996b; Al-Krenawi et al., 1996; Heilman & Witztum, 1994; Rappaport & Simkins, 1991; Speck & Attneave, 1973).

A third factor that is important to successful treatment is the clinician's ability to read a patient's ecological map, or the human environment in which a patient interacts (Hartman, 1978, 1979). The ecological map comprises ineffably subtle aspects of Bedouin-Arab culture: power relationships within family structures, familial interdependency in all aspects of patient illness (Al-Krenawi et al., 1994; Bott & Hodes, 1989; Kim, 1995), and the implications of illness labels to family honour, to cite some examples. The observed patients' illnesses could reflect and/or reinforce dysfunctional family patterns. The "sick" label, as an example, is known to have provided the patient with greater familial attention and in some cases indicated such emotional issues as avoiding an arranged marriage (Al-Krenawi et al., 1994). It is essential for helping professional clinicians to appreciate the cultural nuances behind these family patterns which can represent the problem behind the somatization (Kleinman, 1986).

This leads to a fourth factor, namely the clinician's ability to make inroads into the Bedouin-Arab community. Striking an alliance with powerful members of the patient's family undoubtedly furthers the treatment goals of the helping process itself (Heilman & Witztum, 1994). As an example, clinicians can help to strengthen instrumental family support systems by writing letters of support for patients regarding social service applications. Or, as another example, a clinician's alliance with the patient's family can promote the patient's more effective use of prescribed medications (Bassett et al., 1986). On another level, such clinician-family work also allows the helping professional system to gain greater community acceptance.

Fifth, helping professional practitioners are affiliated with a state-financed and administered medical system. On some level, therefore, they may be seen as representing the Israeli state (Jakubowska, 1992), and their clinical activities most definitely cannot be seen outside of "the context of geopolitical/ethnic cleavages between a dominant Jewish population and a minority Muslim/Arab community in the Negev" (Al-Krenawi & Graham, 1996b, p. 248). The present text advocates a model of helping professional/traditional integration through which power is more differentially shared by the patient/their community, the helping professional system, and the traditional system. In this sense, integration offers the potential for local helping professional, and therefore state, power structures to be adapted favourably towards the Bedouin-Arab, and for the creation of patterns of dialogue and reciprocal learning between helping professional and traditional systems.

However, in order for this to occur, helping professional clinicians must be aware of the cultural meaning of traditional practices (Al-Krenawi & Graham, 1996a, 1997; Atkinson, 1987; Grotberg, 1990; Sanua, 1979; Van der Hart, Witztum, & de-Voogt, 1988; Ward, 1984) and be open to acknowledging their potential therapeutic success. This knowledge not only promotes a stronger therapeutic alliance, it also allows the helping professional clinician to learn from the patient, since the client is an excellent information source regarding traditional practices and Bedouin-Arab culture. Any dialogue between modern and traditional healers in this cultural context must be undertaken with great sensitivity to process. If members of another culture were to supervise a traditional healer's activities, for example, suspicion and hostility could arise. Creating greater opportunities for mutual referrals, on the other hand, may well be productive: the patient would stand to experience higher quality care, and the practitioners, self-improvement. Informal discussions between biomedical and traditional healers may also have potential merit, particularly if the modern healers were of a Bedouin-Arab, or at least a similar, cultural background. One should emphasize, however, that mutual notions of collegiality may be a distant realization, although mutual respect is a valid objective over the shorter term. Finally, and perhaps foremost, the modern and the traditional healers must both recognize their own limitations. Modern practitioners, for example, may not be familiar with Bedouin-Arab cultural and religious beliefs; and traditional healers may be far more limited than their modern counterparts in dealing with psychotic illnesses, among other chronic or acute medical conditions.

An individual who receives treatment from a traditional Bedouin-Arab healer may do so on a variety of levels. First, there is the need to address the precipitating problem, whether it is, for example, somatic, psychosocial, psychiatric, or a combination of the same. Beyond this, there are obvious resonances between a traditional healer and the person seeking help. Some are cultural, since the healing rituals incorporate familiar religious, community, regional, or tribal praxes. Some are interpersonal, in the sense that the healer is either known in person or by reputation. Some are normative, in that the healing rituals enjoy community sanction. Some are experiential, in so far as previous rituals have been directly observed and have provided evidence of a certain utility. And some, implicitly at the very least, are political, in the context of the geopolitical climate. Bedouin-Arab healers are of the same cultural background as those who seek their help, and are therefore apt to be trusted. By the same token, any encounter between a non-Bedouin-Arab modern practitioner and a Bedouin-Arab patient necessarily enters the two into the wider symbolic universe of Middle Eastern politics.

Exposure to the psychiatric system, even if for only one session, provided the opportunity for the patients interviewed to relinquish several misconceptions: that psychiatric services are for "crazy people" only, that patients ought to be blamed for their mental illness, and that medications work virtually instantaneously. The helping professional system, on the other hand, has much to learn from the traditional system (Torrey, 1972). The traditional model's insistence on intense and continuous involvement of the family should provide a framework for the helping professional system to develop forms of strategic family therapy with this population (Al-Krenawi et al., 1994). The helping professional practitioner's explanation of diagnosis could be assisted by insights from the traditional model's use of culturally relevant terminology. The helping professional practitioner could also learn much from the traditional system's sophisticated approach to therapeutic alliance. However, as has been demonstrated, the helping professional practitioners were viewed by the patients as being less aware of traditional practices, less respectful of them, and less capable of learning from them. This stands in contrast to the traditional healers' considerable knowledge of the helping professional system, their willingness to integrate the two systems, and their relative respect for helping professional practices. In their search for models of traditional/helping professional system integration, scholars would benefit greatly from turning to the patients themselves, who are currently experiencing such integration in their daily lives.

Chapter 8

CONCLUSION

This book began by overviewing the state of localized helping professional theory and methods through the prism of one of its professions, social work. It then turned attention to better understanding the social, economic, and historical circumstances of the Bedouin-Arab peoples, generally and in the Negev. Case study examples provided insight into helping professional practice with individuals, families, and groups. Helping professional literatures have had little to say about the cultural practices of polygamous families or blood vengeance. Ours is the first book to provide insight into how helping professional intervention in Bedouin-Arab communities needs to be culturally situated in order to be effective. Practices that are also new to helping professions are discussed in relation to cultural mediation, conflict resolution, and traditional healing. We have learned how practitioners understand localized ways of providing helping professional services, and in particular the relationship between local cultures and helping professional theories and methods.

Recent helping professional literatures have grappled with the nature of localized helping professional knowledge. Concepts of local culture, or of helping professional theory, can never be linear, static, or monolithic: they are always changing, and are best seen as a dialogical outcome between people. Helping professionals—whether they are members of a cultural community or outsiders—represent helping professional practice. They may be significant mediators between a local culture and the professional skills and values that constitute the professional's frame of reference. Any interaction is in this sense a blending of professional and cultural ways of knowing—situated through the unique time and person centered prisms of individual, community, and place. Older notions of universal standards of professional knowledge and intervention are giving way to more nuanced and culturally situated approaches to practice. The present book, as part of this enterprise, has disseminated some practices that have been occurring among Bedouin-Arab communities over the past 15 years.

Conclusion

A cursory tour of recognized and unrecognized Bedouin-Arab villages of the Negev provides ample evidence of how helping professional structures reproduce broader, societal inequalities. The extent to which helping professions can be instruments of community and individual empowerment is closely aligned to how professional and cultural ways of knowing intersect. Is the former hegemonic over the latter? Can alternate ways of knowing assist helping professions to work with communities in order to deliver services in culturally respectful and inclusive ways? To what extent do helping professional practices impose principles that are external to communities and that ultimately alienate community members from their communities, contexts, and potentials? In an era of globalizing communication technologies, the transfer of knowledge between the Global North and Global South is paradoxical. Bedouin-Arab peoples own television sets, satellite dishes, telephones, computers, internet, and may have a ubiquitous experience of Northern culture. At the same time, there can be profound dissonances between Bedouin-Arab cultural traditions and values that are transmitted through the structures of globalization. Local cultures across the world simultaneously experience and resist these broader forces. The rise of Political Islam is one example of cultural resistance that has been occurring in the Arab world over the past 30 years. Any Bedouin-Arab consumer of helping professional services is ipso facto a part of these broader processes.

There are many ways of looking at these macro forces of post-colonialism, globalization and the historic transfer of knowledge and technology from the Global North to the Global South. Some observers see globalization as creating interdependence, prosperity, modernity, and progress (Martin, 2000), while others see it as contributing to poverty, corruption, and marginalization (Midgley, 2000). How can we better understand the forces of globalization? Five components are especially important: the increased movement of capital, products, and labour across territorial borders; the liberalization of trade; the universalized spread of world objects across the world; the westernizing or modernizing of cultures across the world; and the reconfiguring of geography such that time and space are not as significant as in previous eras (Waters, 2001). Some international actors such as the World Bank have sought to promote the liberalization of trade and the profusion of global technologies, while other actors, seeking to resist the economic and social dependence created by global capitalism have been part of worldwide social movements resisting the onslaught of globalization. Helping professionals in communities such as the Bedouin-Arab, as throughout the Global South, straddle two mutually contradictory spheres. On the one hand, they are a product of global processes of colonialism. Globalization, in that sense, appears to prevail. On the other hand, their practitioners may seek to ally with social movements that are allied with those communities that often have the least to gain, and the most to lose, from the forces of globalization that have produced increasing income and social inequalities within and between societies. The neologism "glocalization" has been coined to capture those local forces at work, throughout the world, that are deliberate attempts to resist the worst forces of globalization and to capitalize on the best.

How then, might this imperative occur among such Southern cultures as the Bedouin-Arab? How, indeed, might helping professions be more locally relevant, such that they can bring out the best of the Global South communities within which they work? Within Bedouin-Arab communities, there are religious and culturally bound strategies and personnel that can be used to enhance social work practice, making it more effective. One of the authors, Alean Al-Krenawi, conveys his personal and professional story as a Bedouin-Arab who received undergraduate and advanced studies at universities in Israel and Canada. After his first degree, he practised for eleven years. Especially early in his career, he felt a strong dissonance between his professional training and the culture of his home community: the Bedouin-Arab of the Negev, with whom he worked daily. He made mistakes and had many failures, his ability to create and sustain a helping alliance was often limited, his assessment of client problems, and clients' own understandings, were often in mutual conflict. His ability to decode client communication, and to understand what client's were intending to say, was poor. Clients expressed dissatisfaction with quality and outcome of his proposed interventions, and they terminated prematurely. Alean talked to his father about his difficulties who responded in metaphor. Pointing to the sky, Alean's father said "You are there with the airplanes." Pointing to the ground, Alean's father continued, "the rest of us are walking on our feet." The message was immediately clear. Alean's training had placed him in a different epistemological frame of reference than that of his fellow Bedouin-Arabs, who were his clients. This was an epiphanal moment. Alean became a lot more comfortable intervening according to the principles of his own culture; the training he had received in helping professional practice, based on culturally incongruent assumptions from the North, were no longer the first frame of reference, nor the final factor in determining how, why, where, or when to intervene. Alean increasingly saw himself as the conduit through which dialogue could occur: a dialogue between local and global knowledge. His success with intervention improved, so much so that he ultimately determined he would return to school and research the changing requirements of professional practice with his community (Al-Krenawi, 1998a). Chapters in this book are entirely congruent with Alean's lived experiences.

There are helping professional practices that can be problematic but also salutatory: in the hands of thoughtful practitioners, learning centered agencies and professional approaches, these shortcomings can be the basis of learning, and of improvement. We learn from our mistakes, and as the present book points out, we can learn from our successes. The case studies in our book provide evidence of an interaction – an ongoing dialogue between local practices and the global forces of the helping professions, which in the best instances could bridge gaps between local and global conceptions of helping. The local and the global are integrated, and in that process a new, and more appropriate basis for intervention with the Bedouin-Arab, occurs. Other helping professionals, in turn, may learn from these new approaches, build upon them, and further improve the knowledge base. Indeed, learning from success is a continuing effort that never really ends—no more so than would the changes and evolution of any living entity.

To be fair to the helping professions, attempts have been made to render professional intervention and service structures less culturally oppressive. Assumptions of universal are giving way to the particular; but professional regulators may continue to insist upon minimum standards of professional competence—of knowledge, skills, and values that are, in this sense, some attempt to retain notions of professional practice that may transcend time, place, and community. Whether it is social work practice in northern Canada (Brownlee & Graham, 2005), psychological practice in parts of China (Ho, 1998), or occupational therapy practice in the Global South (Yeoman, 1998), helping professionals have been working at localizing professional knowledge bases. Writing on China, Ho defines "indigenous psychology" as "the study of human behaviour and mental processes within a cultural context that relies on values, concepts, belief systems, methodologies, and other resources indigenous to the specific ethnic or cultural group under investigation" (1998, p. 94). Indigenous psychologies, in this enterprise, need to "demonstrate how they are informed by, rooted in, or derived from their respective indigenous cultures." Also significant, and to some authors, "more demanding[,].... is to demonstrate how they may enrich" mainstream helping professional theories (Ho, Ping, Lai, & Chan, 2001, p. 926).

A very wise way to develop inclusive professional theory is to learn from multiple societies (Hwang, 2005). The innovations that occur, for example, among Bedouin-Arab communities may be usefully extrapolated to other collectivist communities – for example, indigenous peoples in North America, or in Southern Africa. Psychologists introduce the notion of a knowledge landscape, "a metaphor describing the ever-changing potential knowledge peaks and valleys that surround each one of us" (Roos & Oliver cited in Jackson, 2005, p. 55). Climbing peaks can be analogous to taking risks, carrying out interventions differently, or applying alternate methodologies to test an idea, thus optimizing current practices. "Once the gains from incremental developments become small, the sensible option for further progress is to jump far away within the knowledge landscape" (Jackson, 2005, p. 55). In this metaphor, knowledge construction is continuous; knowledge landscapes are very open systems that are highly receptive to new ideas. Options for potential practice may be developed, ideas that had been previously scattered and viewed separately may be combined together, and new methods and research tools may be derived. Further enlightenment can be found with another metaphor: valleys may be setbacks, from which we learn, and from which knowledge generation may be improved. Various peaks in multiple landscapes may be examined; practitioners and scholars need to be able to envisage the very big scope of multiple peaks, and to learn from the different vantage points they represent (Jackson, 2005).

But much remains to be done. The examples we raise can profitably integrate helping professional practice with indigenous cultural practices. This is not to ignore the historic presence of the helping professions, nor the considerable refinements and sophistication they can represent. Rather, we advocate a balance between cultural practices and social work – an integration of paradigms, which the professional carries out in practice methods and which could lead to the ongoing emergence of a newer epistemology, better anchored to the needs and realities of Bedouin-Arab, or other, communities. There are religious and culturally bound strategies and personnel that can be infused to enhance social work practice. The suspicions of the helping professions and their tenuous relationship with Arab traditions introduce an imperative of localizing knowledge bases. The helping professions may indeed be useful conduits for conveying social problems, for developing a social conscience within Bedouin-Arab communities for their resolution, and for the development of social services for vulnerable peoples, but only if helping professional theory and practices continue to evolve in a manner that is culturally respectful.

REFERENCES

Abdelrahman, M. (2004). *Civil society exposed: The politics of NGOs in Egypt*, Cairo: The American University in Cairo Press.

Abdul-Aziz, K. M. (1989). *The black seed, treats every pain*. Cairo: Maktabat Ibn-Sina (in Arabic).

Abou El Azayem, G. A., & Hedayat-Diba, Z. (1994). The psychological aspects of Islam: Basic principles of Islam and their psychological corollary. *International Journal for the Psychology of Religion, 4*, 41-50.

Abramowitz, L. (1993). Prayer as therapy among the frail Jewish elderly. *Journal of Gerontological Social Work, 19*(3/4), 69-75.

Abu-Khusa, S. (1993). *The tribal judgement system*. Amman: Al-Matbah Al-Watania (in Arabic).

Abu-Lughod, L. (1986). *Veiled sentiments: Honor and poetry in a Bedouin society*. Berkeley: University of California Press.

———. (1985a). Honor and the sentiments of loss in a Bedouin society. *American Ethnologist, 12*(2), 245-261.

———. (1985b). A community of secrets: The separate world of Bedouin women. *Signs: A Journal of Women in Culture and Society, 10*(4), 635-657.

Abu-Nimer, M. (1996). Conflict resolution approaches: Western and Middle Eastern lessons and possibilities. *American Journal of Economics and Sociology, 55*(1), 34-51.

Abu-Rabia, S. (1999). Towards a second-language model of learning in problematic social contexts: The case of Arabs learning Hebrew in Israel. *Race, Ethnicity & Education, 2*(1), 109-126.

Abu-Rabia, S., Al-Bador, S., & El-Atawna, F. (1996). The Bedouin education survey in the Negev. *The Israel Equality Monitor, 5*, 1-31. (in Hebrew).

Abu-Saad, A., & Lithwick, H. (2001). *A way ahead: Development plan for the Bedouin towns in the Negev*. Beer-Sheva: The Center for Bedouin Studies and Development; Negev Center for Regional Development, Ben-Gurion University.

Adams, B., & Mburugu, E. (1994). Kikuyu bride wealth and polygamy today. *Journal of Comparative Family Studies, 25*(2), 159-166.

Achte, K., & Schakir, T. (1980). Jealousy in various cultures in the light of trans-cultural psychiatry. *Psychiatria Fennica*, 33-44.

Al-Abbadi, A. Y. (1973). *The Bedouin women*. Amman: Al-Matbah Al-Wataniah (in Arabic).

Al-Aref, A. (1944). *Bedouin love, law, and legend*. Jerusalem: Cosmos Publishing Co.

———. (1934). *Sevti ha-Bedowim be-machoz, Beer-Sheva* (The Bedouin tribes in the Beer-Sheva district). Jerusalem: Bostnai.

Al-Ataar, A. (1989). *The treatment according to the Koran*. Egypt: Daar Al-Astesphaa Bel-Koran Press (in Arabic).

Al-Bostani, M. (1988). *Studies in Islamic psychology*. Beirut, Lebanon: Daar Alblaah Press. [in Arabic].

Al-Dabbagh, A. (1993). Islamic perspectives on social work practice. *The American Journal of Islamic Social Sciences, 10*(4), 536-537.

Al-Daramdash, H. (1991), *The Koran as a treatment tool for people who are attacked by Satan*. Egypt: Daar Wali Al-Islamih (in Arabic).

Al-Fuaal, M. (1983). *The structure of Bedouin societies*. Cairo: Al Garib Press (in Arabic)

Al-Ghazali, A. H. (1950). *The revival of religious science*. Cairo: Issa Al-Babi Al-Halabi Press (in Arabic).

Al-Haj, M. (1989). Social research on family lifestyles among Arabs in Israel. *Journal of Comparative Family Studies, 20*(2), 175-195.

———(1987). *Social change and family processes*. London: Westview.

Al-Hamamdeh, M. (2004). *From the treasures of the forefathers: Bedouin meaningful tales*. Retrieved October 16, 2005 from: http://w3.bgu.ac.il/bedouin/Bedouin%20Tales.pdf.

Al-Issa, I. (1995). *Handbook of culture and mental illness: An international perspective*. Madison, CT: International Universities Press.

———. (1990). Culture and mental illness in Algeria. *International Journal of Social Psychiatry, 36*(3), 230-240.

———. (1989) Psychiatry in Algeria. *Psychiatric Bulletin, 13*, 240-245.

———. (Ed.) (1982). *Culture and psychopathology*. Baltimore: University Park Press.

———. (1970). Culture and symptoms. In C. Costello (Ed.), *Symptoms of psychopathology: A handbook* (pp. 27-45). New York: John Wiley & Sons.

———. (1969). Problems in the cross-cultural study of schizophrenia. *Journal of Psychology, 71*(1), 143-151.

Al-Jamal, A. M. (1983). *The spirits world in the shadow of the Koran and Sunna (Tradition)*. Cairo: Daar Al-Marif (in Arabic).

Al-Juhri, M. (1991). Mental illness in the Egyptian folklore. In S. Ottman, N. Addul hmeed and F. Abdul Rahman (Eds.), *Health and illness* (pp. 271-335). Alexandria: Daar Al-marif Al-Jameeh Press (in Arabic).

Al-Jzari, A. (1987). *Methods for prevention of Jinn and Satan.* Cairo: Islamic University Press (in Arabic).

Al-Krenawi, A. (2004). *Awareness and utilization of social, health/mental health services among Bedouin-Arab women, differentiated by type of residence and type of marriage.* Retrieved October 17, 2005 from: http://w3.bgu.ac.il/bedouin/Awareness%20and%20Utilization%20of%20Social-2004.pdf.

———(2000). *Ethno-psychiatry among the Bedouin-Arab of the Negev.* Tel-Aviv: Hakibbutz Hameuchad (in Hebrew).

———(1998a). Reconciling Western and traditional healing: A social worker walks with the wind. *Reflections: Narrative of Professional Helping, 4*(3), 6-21.

———. (1998b). Family therapy with a multiparental/multispousal family. *Family Process, 37*(1), 65-82.

———. (1997). *Speaking through proverbs: Bedouin-Arab patients communicate their distress in the psychiatric clinic.* Paper Presented at the International Multiculturalism Conference: From Theory to Practice, Jerusalem, Israel.

———. (1996). Group work with Bedouin widows of the Negev in a medical clinic. *Affilia: Journal of Women and Social Work, 11*(3), 303-318.

———. (1995). *A study of the dual use of modern and traditional mental health systems by the Bedouin-Arab of the Negev.* University of Toronto: Unpublished doctoral dissertation.

———. (1993). *The group as a tool for the development of social networks and social support for Bedouin widows.* Paper Presented at the Symposium XV Social Work with Groups: New York.

———. (1992). *The role of the Dervish as a mental health therapist in the Negev-Bedouin society: Clients expectations from these treatments and the extent of materialization.* MSW thesis. Jerusalem: Hebrew University Jerusalem (in Hebrew).

Al-Krenawi, A., & Graham, J. R.. (2007) The provision and use of social services among the Bedouin-Arab indigenous population in Israel. *Social Development Issues, 29*(1), 100-118.

———. (2006a). A comparison of family functioning, life and marital satisfaction, and mental health of women in polygamous and monogamous marriages. *International Journal of Social Psychiatry, 52*(1), 5-17.

———. (2006b). Health and mental health awareness and utilization among female Bedouin-Arab from recognized and unrecognized villages in the Negev. *Health Care for Women International, 27*(2), 182–196.

———. (2006c). Psychosocial therapy with Arabs in the Israeli context. In J. Kuriansky (Ed.), *Psychotherapy in a turmoil region: The Israeli-Palestinian experiences.* (pp. 217-227). New York: Wadsworth.

———. (2004). Somatization among Bedouin-Arab women: Differentiated by marital status. *Journal of Divorce and Remarriage, 42*(1/2), 131-144.

———. (2003). Social work in the Arab world. *Arab Studies Quarterly, 26*(4), 75-91.

———. (2001a). Polygamous family structure and its interaction with gender: Effects on children's academic achievements and implications for culturally diverse social work practice in schools. *School Social Work Journal, 25*(3), 1-16.

———. (2001b). The cultural mediator: Bridging the gap between a non-Western community and professional social work practice. *British Journal of Social Work, 31*, 665-685.

———. (1999a). Gender and biomedical/traditional mental health utilization among the Bedouin-Arabs of the Negev. *Culture, Medicine and Psychiatry, 23*(2), 219-243.

———. (1999b). The story of Bedouin-Arab women in a polygamous marriage. *Women's Studies International Forum, 22*(5), 497-509.

———. (1999c). Social work and Koranic mental health healers. *International Social Work, 42*(1), 53-65.

———. (1998). Divorce among Muslim Arab women in Israel. *Journal of Divorce and Remarriage, 29*(3/4), 103-119.

———. (1997). Spirit possession and exorcism: The integration of modern and traditional mental health care systems in the treatment of a Bedouin patient. *Clinical Social Work Journal, 25*(2), 211-222.

———. (1996a) Social work practice and traditional healing rituals among the Bedouin of the Negev, Israel. *International Social Work, 39*(2), 177-188.

———. (1996b). Tackling mental illness: Roles for old and new disciplines. *World Health Forum, 17*(3), 246-8.

Al-Krenawi, A., Graham, J. R., & Al-Krenawi, S. (1997). Social work practice with polygamous families. *Child and Adolescent Social Work Journal, 14*(6), 445-458.

Al-Krenawi, A., Graham, J.R., & Ben-Shimol-Jakbson, S. (2006). Attitudes toward and reasons for polygamy differentiated by gender and age among the Bedouin-Arab of the Negev. *International Journal of Mental Health, 35*(1), 45-60.

Al-Krenawi, A., Graham, J. R., & Izzeldin, A. (2001). The psychosocial impact of polygamous marriages on Palestinian women. *Women and Health, 34*(1), 1-16.

Al-Krenawi, A., Graham, J. R., & Maoz, B. (1996). The healing significance of the Negev's Bedouin. *Dervish. Social Science and Medicine, 43*(1), 13-21.

Al-Krenawi, A., & Lightman, E.S. (2000). Learning achievement, social adjustment, and family conflict among Bedouin-Arab children from polygamous and monogamous families. *Social Psychology, 140*(3), 345-355.

Al-Krenawi, A., Maoz. B., & Riecher, B. (1994). Familial and cultural issues in the brief strategic treatment of Israeli Bedouin. *Family Systems Medicine, 12*(4), 415-425.

Al-Krenawi, A., Maoz, B., & Shiber, A. (1995). Integration of modern medical methods with popular methods in treating mental disorders in Bedouins. *Sihot-Dialogue, Israel Journal of psychotherapy, 10*(1), 42-48 (in Hebrew).

Al-Krenawi, A., Slonim-Nevo, V., & Graham, J.R. (2006). Polygyny and its impact on the psychosocial well-being of husbands. *Journal of Comparative Family Studies, 37*(2), 173-89.

Al-Krenawi, A., Slonim-Nevo, V., Maymon, Y., & Al-Krenawi, S. (2001). Psychological responses to blood vengeance among Arab adolescents. *Child Abuse & Neglect, 25*(4), 457-472.

Al-Munjed (1975). *Arabic dictionary*. Beirut, Lebanon: Dar El-Mashreq Publishers (in Arabic).

Al-Nasimi, M. N. (1984). *The prophetic medicine*. Syria: Al-Sharekh Al-Mothedh Lltozih (in Arabic).

Al-Sabaie, A. (1989). Psychiatry in Saudi Arabia: Cultural perspectives. *Transcultural Psychiatric Research Review, 26*(4), 245-262.

Al-Safi, A. (1982). Traditional healing in Sudan. *Bulletin of Sudanese Studies, 1*(7), 27-45 (in Arabic)

Almi, O. (2003). *No man's land: Health in the unrecognized villages of the Negev*. Israel: Physicians for Human Rights.

Almi, O., Dloomy, A., & Sawalha, F. (2006). *The Arab Bedouins of the Naqab-Negev Desert in Israel*. UN Committee for the Elimination of Racial Descrimination.

Amar, A. (1984). *Islamic tradition related to marriage*. Saudi Arabia: Daar Al-Fikir Arabi (in Arabic).

Anderson, B. (1991). *Imagined communities: Reflections on the Origin and spread of Nationalism*. New York: Verso.

Apshtin, E. (1973). *The Bedouin in Israel*. Tel Aviv: Reshafim Press (in Hebrew).

Arad, S. (1984). *Bedouins*. Tel-Aviv: Masada Press.

Archibald, J. (2007). *Indigenous storywork: Educating the heart, mind, body, and soul.* Vancouver: University of British Columbia Press.

Asamoath, Y., Healey, L. M., & Mayadas, N. (1997). Ending the international-domestic dichotomy: New approaches to a global curriculum for the millennium. *Journal of Social Work Education, 33*(2), 389-401.

Ashoor, M. (1989). *The world of the spirits.* Egypt: Maktabat Al-Koran (in Arabic).

———. (1987). *The spiritual medicine.* Cairo: Maktabat Al-Koran (in Arabic).

Atkinson, J. M. (1987), The effectiveness of Shamans in an Indonesian ritual. *American Anthropologist, 89*(2), 342-355.

Azhar, M. Z., Varma, S. L., & Dharap, A. S. (1994). Religious psychotherapy in anxiety disorder patients. *Acta Psychiatrica Scandinavica, 90*(1), 1-3.

Azrin, N. H., Sneed, T. J., & Foxx, R. M. (1974). Dry-bed training: Rapid elimination of childhood enuresis. *Behavior Research and Therapy, 11,* 147-156.

Badawi, S. A. (1992). *Methods for expelling the Jinn from the person's body.* Cairo: Al-Rodah (in Arabic)

Bali, W. A. (1993). *Protection from the Sorcerers and the Spirits.* Jidda: Maktabat Al-Shabah (in Arabic).

Banawi, R., & Stockton, R. (1993) Islamic values relevant to group work, with practical applications for group leaders. *Journal for Specialists in Group Work, 18,* 151-160.

Barakat, H. (1993). *The Arab world, society, culture, and state.* Berkeley: University of California Press.

Barsky, A. (1999). Community involvement through child protection mediation. *Child Welfare, 78*(4), 481-501.

Bar-Zvi, S. (1988). Oral tradition and customs among the Negev Bedouin. In Y. Iani and A. Aorean (Eds.), *The Bedouin* (pp. 358-369). Seda Boger: Ben-Gurion University of the Negev (in Hebrew).

Bassett, A. S., Remick, R. A., Beiser, M., & Miles, J. E. (1986). The art of pharmacotherapy in depressed outpatients. *Canadian Journal of Psychiatry, 31*(9), 852-856.

Bazzoui, W., & Al-Issa, I. (1966). Psychiatry in Iraq. *British Journal of Psychiatry, 112,* 827-832.

Beavers C. (1986). A cross-cultural look at child abuse. *Public Welfare, 44,* 18-22.

Beiser, M., Gill, K., & Edwards, R. G. (1993). Mental health care in Canada: Is it accessible and equal? *Canada's Mental Health, 41*(2), 2-7.

Ben-David, A. & Erickson, C. (1990). Ethnicity and the therapist's use of self. *Family Therapy, 17*(3), 211-216.

Ben-David, Y. (1981). *Jabaliiyya: Bedouin tribe in the shadow of the monastary.* Jerusalem: Kana Press (in Hebrew).

Bending, R. L. (1997). Training child welfare workers to meet the requirements of the Indian child welfare act. *Journal of Multicultural Social Work, 5*(3/4), 151–164.

Ben-Ezer, G. (1992). *Migration and observation of Ethiopian Jews in Israel.* Jerusalem: Mass (in Hebrew).

Berelson, B. (1952). *Content analysis in communication research.* New York: Free Press.

Bhugra, D. (1993). Cross-cultural aspects of jealousy. *International Review of Psychiatry, 5*(2-3), 271-280.

Bilu Y. & Witztum, E. (1995). Between sacred and medical realities: Culturally-sensitive therapy with Jewish ultra-orthodox patients. *Science in Context, 8*(1), 159-173.

———. (1993).Working with Jewish ultra-orthodox patients: Guidelines for a culturally sensitive therapy. *Culture, Medicine and Psychiatry, 17*(2), 197-233.

Bilu, Y., Witztum, E., & Van der Hart, O. (1990). Paradise regained: 'Miraculous healing' in an Israeli psychiatric clinic. *Culture, Medicine and Psychiatry, 14,* 105-127.

Bisnaire, L. M. C., Firestone, P., & Rynard, D. (1990). Factors associated with academic achievement in children following parental separation. *American Journal of Orthopsychiatry, 60*(1), 67-76.

Boddy, J. (1989). *Wombs and Alien Spirits: Women, men, and the Zar Cult in Northern Sudan.* Madison, WI: University of Wisconsin Press.

Bodeker, G., & Kronenberg, F. (2002). A public health agenda for traditional, complementary, and alternative medicine. *American Journal of Public Health 92*(10): 1582-1591.

Bolton, C., & Camp, D. (1989). The post-funeral ritual in bereavement counseling and grief work. *Journal of Gerontological Social Work, 13*(3/4), 49-59.

Bonnafe, P. (1973). An important life and death ceremony: The Miyali, the funeral of a Kukuya lord of the sky (Congo-Brazzaville). *Homme, 13*(1-2), 97-166.

Borgerhoff-Mulder, M. (1992). Women's strategies in polygamous marriage: Kipsigis, Datoga, and other East African cases. *Human Nature, 3*(1), 45-70.

Bott, D., & Hodes, M. (1989). Structural therapy for a West African family. *Journal of Family Therapy, 11*(2), 169-179.

Bradshaw, C., & Graham, J.R. (2007). Localization of social work practice, education and research: A content analysis. *Social Development Issues, 29*(2), 92-111.

Breuer, J., & Freud, S. (1955). Studies on hysteria. In J. Strachey (Ed), *The standard edition of the complete psychological works of Sigmund Freud,* vol. 19 (pp. 19-305). London: Hogarth Press. (Original work published in 1895)

Brhoom, M. (1987). The phenomenon of divorce in Jordan. *Deraast, 13*(12), 189-205 (in Arabic).

Bronson, D. & Lamarche, L. (2001). *A human rights framework for trade in the Americas.* Montréal: Rights and Democracy,

Broude, G. J. (1994). *Marriage, family, and relationship: A cross-cultural encyclopedia.* Denver: ABC-CLIO

Brown, P. C., & Smith, T.W. (1992). Social influence, marriage, and the heart: Cardiovascular consequences of interpersonal control in husbands and wives. *Health Psychology, 11*(2), 88-96.

Brownlee, K. & Graham, J. R. (2005). *Family violence: Readings and research from rural and northern Canada.* Toronto: Canadian Scholars Press.

Budman, C. L., Lipson, J. G. & Meleis, A. I. (1992). The cultural consultant and mental health care: The case of an Arab adolescent. *American Journal of Orthopsychiatry, 62*(3), 359-70.

Burgess, J. W. (1993). The psychotherapy on giving medications: Therapeutic techniques for interpersonal interventions. *American Journal of Psychotherapy, 47*(3), 393-403.

Butler, B. O., Mellon, M. W., Stroh, S. E., & Stern, H. P. (1995). A therapeutic model to enhance children's adjustment to divorce: A case example. *Journal of Divorce and Remarriage, 22*(3/4), 77-90.

Caliph, A. M. (1989). Beliefs and attitudes of Egyptian students related to mental illness. *Egyptian Journal of Psychology, 11*(3), 103-117 (in Arabic).

Cannon, W. B. (1957). Voodoo death. *Psychosomatic Medicine, 19*, 182-190.

Carden, A. D. (1994). Wife abuse and the wife abuser: Review and recommendations. *Counseling Psychologist, 22*, 539-582.

Cassanas, J. (1992). Le cadre et ses origins. *Psychanalystes, 44*, 29-42.

Chaleby, K. (1985). Women of polygamous marriages in an inpatient psychiatric service in Kuwait. *Journal of Nervous and Mental Disease, 173*(1), 56-58.

Challand, B. (2008). A *Nahda* of charitable organizations? Health service provision and the politics of aid in Palestine. *International Journal of Middle East Studies, 40*, 227-247.

Chamie, J. (1986). Polygyny among Arabs. *Population Studies, 40,* 44-66.

Chekir, H. (1996). Women, the law, and the family in Tunisia. *Gender and Development 4*(2), 43-46.

Cheng, L. (1987). *Assessing Asian language performance: Guidelines for evaluating limited-English-proficient students.* Rockville, MD: Aspen Publications

Cherian, V. I. (1990). Academic achievement of children from monogamous and polygynous families. *Journal of Social Psychology, 130*(1), 117-119

Cherry, C., & Sayers, B. M. A. (1956). Experiments upon the total inhibition of stammering by external control and some clinical results. *Journal of Psychosomatic Research, 1*, 233.

Chi, C. (1995). Integrating traditional medicine into modern health care systems: Examining the role of Chinese medicine in Taiwan. *Social Science and Medicine, 39*(3), 307-321.

Child, N. (1996). Rituals in family therapy: Comment. *Journal of Family Therapy, 18*(1), 119-122.

Chirsman, N. J. (1977). The help seeking process: An approach to the natural history of illness. *Culture, Medicine, and Psychiatry, 1*, 351-377.

Christensen, C. P. (1987). The perceived problems and help seeking preferences of Chinese immigrants in Montreal. *Canadian Journal of Counselling, 21*, 189-199.

Chung, R. C. Y., & Lin, K. M. (1994). Help-seeking behavior among Southeast Asian refugees. *Journal of Community Psychology, 22*(2), 109-120.

Cole, D. P. (2003). Where have the Bedouin gone? *Anthropological Quarterly, 76*(2), 235-266.

Collier, J. (1984). Two models of social control in simple societies. In D. Black (Ed.), *Toward a general theory of social control. Volume 2*. (pp. 105-140). New York: Academic Press.

Comaz-Dias, L. & Griffith, E. (Eds.) (1988). *Clinical guidelines in cross-cultural mental health*. Oxford, England: John Wiley & Sons.

Crichlow, W. (2003). Western colonization as disease: Native adoption and cultural genocide. *Canadian Social Work Journal, 5*(1), 88-107.

Crosson-Tower, C. (1998). *Understanding child abuse and neglect*. (4th ed.). Boston, MA: Allyn and Bacon.

Csordas, T. (1983). The rhetoric of transformation in ritual healing. *Culture, Medicine, and Psychiatry, 7*(4), 333-375.

Cummings, E. M., Zahn-Waxler, C., & Radke-Yarrow, M. (1984). Developmental changes in children's reactions to anger in the home. *Journal of Child Psychology and Psychiatry and Allied Disciplines, 25*(1), 63-74.

Cwikel, J., Lev-Wiesel, R., & Al-Krenawi, A. (2003). The physical and psychosocial health of Bedouin-Arab women of the Negev area of Israel: The impact of high fertility and pervasive domestic violence. *Violence Against Women, 9*(2), 240-257.

D'Aquili, E. G. (1985). Human ceremonial ritual and the modulation of aggression. *Zygon Journal of Religion and Science, 20*(1), 21-30.

Davidson, H. A. (1992). *Alfarabi, Avicenna, and Averroes, on Intellect*. New York: Oxford University Press.

Davies, P. T., Myers, R. L., & Cummings, E. M. (1996). Responses of children and adolescents to marital conflict scenarios as a function of the emotionality of conflict endings. *Merrill Palmer Quarterly, 42*(1), 1-21.

Dean, R.G. (1993). Constructivism: An approach to clinical practice. *Smith College Studies in Social Work, 63*(2), 127-146.

Denny, J. P. (1988). Contextualisation and differentiation in cross-cultural cognition. In J. W. Berry and S. H. Irvine (Eds.), *Indigenous cognition: Functioning in cultural context*. (pp. 213-229). Kluwer Academic Publishers.

Derogatis, L. R. & Melisaratos, N. (1983). The brief symptom inventory: An introductory report. *Psychological Medicine, 13*, 595-605.

Derogatis, L. R., & Spencer, P. M. (1982). *Brief symptom inventory: Administration, scoring, and procedure manual*. Baltimore: Clinical Psychometric Research.

De Santis, L., & Ugarriza, D. N. (1995). Potential for intergenerational conflict in Cuban and Haitian immigrant families. *Archives of Psychiatric Nursing, 9*(6), 354-364.

Devore, W., & Schlesinger, E. G. (1994). *Ethnic-sensitive social work practice*. New York: Macmillan.

Dhaouadi, M. (1990). Ibn-Khaldun: The founding father of Eastern sociology. *International Sociology, 5*(3), 319-335.

D'Hondt W., & Vandewiele, M. (1986). Attitudes of Senegalese adolescents towards setting up and educating a future family. *Scientia Paedagogica Experimentalis, 23*(1), 15-28.

———. (1980). Attitudes of Senegalese secondary school students towards traditional African way of life and Western way of life. *Psychological Reports, 47*(1), 235-242.

Dickie-Clark, H. F. (1966). *The marginal situation: A sociological study of colored group*. London: Routledge & Kegan Paul.

Dickson, H. R. P. (1949). *The Arab of the desert, Bedouin life in Kuwait and Saudi Arabia*. London: Allen an Unwin.

Dinero, S. C. (1998). Social adaptation and welfare planning in the post-nomadic urban environment: The case of the Israeli Negev Bedouin. *Journal of Community Practice, 5*(3), 15-36.

Dloomy, A., Almi, O., & Sawalha, F. (Eds.). (2006). *The Arab-Bedouins of the Naqab-Negev desert in Israel*. Omer: Negev Coexistence Forum for Civil Equality.

Dodd, P. C. (1973). Family honor and the forces of change in Arab society. *International Journal of Middle East Studies 4*, 40-54.

Dorjahn, V. R. (1988). Changes in Temne polygyny. *Ethnology, 27*(4), 367-390.

Doyle, C. (1996). Current issues in child protection: An overview of the debates in contemporary journals. *British Journal of Social Work, 26*, 565-576.

Drever, J. (1956). *Dictionary of psychology*. London: Penguin.

Drower, S. J. (2000). Globalisation: An opportunity for dialogue between South African and Asian social work educators. *The Indian Journal of Social Work, 61*(1), 12-31.

Dubowitz, H., Black, M., Starr, R., & Zuravin, S. (1993). A conceptual definition of child neglect. *Criminal Justice and Behavior, 20*, 8-26.

Durkheim, E. (1965). *Suicide*. New York: Doubleday.

Eapen, V., Al Gazali, L. B., Othman, S., & Abou Saleh, M. (1998). Mental health problems among schoolchildren in United Arab Emirates: Prevalence and risk factors. *Journal of the American Academy of Child and Adolescent Psychiatry, 37*(8), 880-886.

Early, E. A. (1993). *Women of Cairo: Playing with an egg and a stone*. Boulder, CO: Lynne Rienner Publishing.

Edwards, S. D. (1986) Traditional and modern medicine in South Africa: A research study. *Social Science and Medicine, 22*(11), 1273-1276.

Efoghe, G. B. (1990). Nature and type of marriage as predictors of aggressiveness among married men and women in Ekpoma, Bendel State of Nigeria. *International Journal of Sociology of the Family, 20*(1), 67-78.

Eikelman, D. (1968). The Islamic attitude towards possession states. In R. Prince (Ed.), *Trance and possession states* (pp. 189-192). Montreal: Proceeding of the Second Annual Conference, R.M. Bucke Memorial Society.

Eisenbruch, M., & Handelman, L. (1990). Cultural consultation for cancer: Astrocytoma in a Cambodian adolescent. *Social Science and Medicine, 31*(12), 1295-1299.

Elbedour, S., Onwuegbuzie, A. J., Caridine, C., & Abu Saad, H. (2002). The effect of polygamous marital structure on behavioral, emotional, and academic adjustment in children: A comprehensive review of the literature. *Clinical Child and Family Psychology Review, 5*(4), 255-271.

Eliade, M. (Ed.) (1987). *Encyclopedia of religion* Volume 13. New York: Macmillan.

―――. (1957). *The sacred and the profane*, Translated by Willard Trask. New York: Harcourt, Brace and World.

El-Islam, M. F. (1994). Cultural aspects of morbid fears in Qatari women. *Social Psychiatry and Psychiatric Epidemiology, 29*(3), 137-140.

―――. (1982). Arabic cultural psychiatry. *Transcultural Psychiatric Research Review, 19*(1), 5-24.

―――. (1978). Transcultural aspects of psychiatry in Qatar. *Comparative Medicine East and West, 4*(1), 33-36.

———. (1975). Clinical bound neurosis in Qatari women. *Social Psychiatry, 10*(1), 25-29.

———. (1967). The psychotherapeutic basis of some Arab rituals. *International Journal of Social Psychiatry, 13,* 265-68.

El-Islam, M. F., & Abu-Dagga, S. (1992). Lay explanation of symptoms of mental health in Kuwait. *International Journal of Social Psychiatry, 38*(2), 150-156.

El-Shamy, H. (1977). *The supernatural belief-practice system in the contemporary folk culture of Egypt,* Mimeographed. Bloomington, Indiana: Folklore publication group monograph series.

El-Sheikh, M. (1994). Children's emotional and physiological responses to interadult angry behavior: The role of history of interparental hostility. *Journal of Abnormal Child Psychology, 22,* 661-678.

Emery, R. E., & O'Leary, K. D. (1982). Children's perceptions of marital discord and behavior problems of boys and girls. *Journal of Abnormal Child Psychology, 10,* 11-24.

Engfer, A. (1988). The interrelatedness of marriage and the mother-child relationship. In R. A. Hinde and J. Stevenson-Hinde (Eds.), *Relationships within families: Mutual influences* (pp. 105-118). Oxford, UK: Clarendon.

Epstein, N. B., Baldwin, L., & Bishop, D. S. (1983). The McMaster Family Assessment Device. *Journal of Marital and Family Therapy, 9,* 171-180.

Erickson, M. F., Egeland, B., & Pianta, R. (1989). Effects of on the development of young children. In Cicchetti, N., and Carlson, V. (Eds.), *Child maltreatment: Theory & research on the causes & consequences of child abuse and neglect* (pp. 647-684). Cambridge: Cambridge University Press.

Fabrega, H. (1991). Psychiatric stigma in non-Western societies. *Comprehensive Psychiatry, 32*(6), 534-551.

Fabrega, H., Ulrich, R., & Mezzich, J. E. (1993). Do caucasians and black adolescents differ at psychiatric intake? *Journal of the American Academy of Child and Adolescent Psychiatry, 32*(2), 407-413.

Falah, G. (1989). Israeli state policy toward Bedouin sedentarization in the Negev. *Journal of Palestine Studies, 18*(2), 71-91.

Fandetti, D. V., & Goldmeier, J. (1988). Social workers as culture mediators in health care settings. *Health and Social Work, 13*(3), 171-179.

Faour, M. (1997). Conflict management within the Muslim Arab family. In P. Salem (Ed.), *Conflict resolution in the Arab world: Selected essays* (pp. 175-196). Beirut: American University of Beirut Press.

Farrag, A. (1977). The Wasta in Jordanian villages. In E. Gellner and J. Waterbury (Eds.), *Patron and clients* (pp. 225-238). London: Duckworth.

Farsy, S. M. (1964). *Islam and hygiene.* Leiden, Netherlands: Brill.

Feinson, M., Popper, M., & Handelsman, M. (1992). *Utilization of public ambulatory mental health services in Israel: A focus on age and gender patterns.* Jerusalem: State of Israel, Ministry of Health.

Ferraro, G. P. (1991). Marriage and conjugal roles in Swaziland: Persistence and change. *International Journal of Sociology of the Family, 21*(2), 89-128.

Frank, J. D. (1973). *Persuasion and healing.* New York: Schocken.

Frank, J. D., & Frank, J. B. (1991). *Persuasion and healing: A comparative study of psychotherapy.* Baltimore: Johns Hopkins University Press.

Frank, R. M. (1994). *Al-Ghazali and the Ash'arite School.* Durham, NC: Duke University Press.

Freeman, J. (1981). A firewalking ceremony that failed. In Gira Raj Gupta (Ed.), *The social and cultural context of medicine in India* (pp. 308-336). New Delhi: Vikas.

Freire, P. (1971). *Pedagogy of the oppressed.* New York: Seabury.

Freud, S. 1905/1953. Fragment of an analysis of a case of hysteria. In J. Stachey (Ed.) *The standard edition of the complete works of Sigmund Freud, volume 7* (pp. 3–122). London, UK: Hogarth Press.

Frey, L. A., & Edinburg, G. M. (1978). Helping, manipulation, and magic. *Social Work, 23*(2), 89-93.

Friedman, S., & Pettus, S. (1985). Brief strategic interventions with families of adolescents. *Family Therapy, 12*(3), 197-210.

Fry, D. P., & Fry, C. B. (1997). Culture and conflict resolution models: Exploring alternatives to violence. In D.P. Fry and K. Björkqvist (Eds.), *Cultural variation in conflict resolution* (pp. 9-23). Mahwah, NJ: Lawrence Erlbaum Associates.

Furman, F. (1981). Ritual as social mirror and agent of cultural change: A case study in synagogue life. *Journal for the Scientific Study of Religion, 20*(3), 228-241.

Gabriel, M. A., & Monaco, G. M. (1994). 'Getting even': Clinical considerations of adaptive and maladaptive vengeance. *Clinical Social Work Journal, 22*(2), 165-178.

Gaines, A.D. (1992). From DSM-I to III--R; voices of self, mastery and the other: A cultural constructivist reading of U.S. psychiatric classification. *Social Science and Medicine, 35*(1), 3-24.

Galaway, B. (1988). Crime victim and offender mediation as a social work strategy. *Social Service Review, 62*(4), 668-83.

Gardner, A., & Marx, E. (2000). Employment and unemployment among Bedouin. *Nomadic Peoples, 4*(2), 21-27.

Garrison, V. (1977) Doctor, espiritista or psychiatrist? Health seeking behavior in a Puerto Rican neighborhood of New York City. *Medical Anthropology 1*, 65-191.

Geertz, C. (1973). *The interpretation of culture: Selected essays.* New York: Basic Books.

———. (1968). *Islam observed: Religious development in Morocco and Indonesia.* New Haven: Yale University Press.

Gergen, K. (1985). The social constructionist movement in modern psychology. *American Psychologist, 40*(3), 266-275.

Germain, C. & Gitterman, A. (1980). *The life model of social work practice.* New York: Columbia University Press.

Ginat, J. (1987). *Blood disputes among Bedouin and rural Arabs in Israel. Revenge, mediation, outcasting and family honor.* Pittsburgh, PA: University of Pittsburgh Press.

———. (1984). Blood revenge in Bedouin society. In E. Marx and A. Shmueli (Eds.), *The changing Bedouin* (pp. 59-82). London: Transaction.

Ginguld, M., Perevolostky, A., & Ungar, E. D. (1997). Living on the margins: Livelihood strategies of Bedouin herd-owners in the northern Negev, Israel. *Human Ecology, 25*(4), 567-591.

Glasser, I. (1983). Guidelines for using an interpreter in social work. *Child Welfare, 57*, 468-470.

Gluckman, M. (1963). *Order and rebellion in tribal Africa.* New York: Free Press.

———. (1954). *Rituals of rebellion in South-East Africa.* Manchester: University of Manchester Press.

Godoy, R., Reyes-Garcia, V., Byron, E., Leonard, W. R., & Vadez, V. (2005). The effect of market economies on the well-being of indigenous peoples and their use of renewable natural resources. *Annual Review of Anthropology, 34*, 121-138.

Goldstein, H. (1973). *Social work practice: A unitary approach.* Columbia, South Carolina: University of South Carolina Press.

Good, B. (1977). The heart of what's matter: The semantics of illness in Iran. *Culture, Medicine, and Psychiatry, 1*, 25-58.

Gorkin, M. (1986). Countertransference in cross-cultural psychotherapy: The example of Jewish therapist and Arab patient. *Psychiatry, 49*(1), 69-79.

Gorkin, M., & Othman, R. (1994). Traditional psychotherapeutic healing and healers in the Palestinian community. *Israel Journal of Psychiatry and Related Sciences, 31*(3), 221-231.

Gottman, J. M. (1994). An agenda for marital therapy. In L. S. Greenberg and S.M. Johnson (Eds.), *The heart of the matter: Perspectives on emotion in marital therapy* (256-293). Philadelphia, PA, US: Brunner/Mazel.

Gottman, J. M., & Notarius, C. I. (2000). Decade review: Observing marital interaction. *Journal of Marriage and the Family, 62*(4), 927-947.

Gove, W. R., Hughes, M., & Galle, O. R. (1983). *Overcrowding in the household*. New York: Academic press.

Graham, J.R. (2006). Spirituality and social work: A call for an international focus of research. *Arete: A Professional Journal Devoted to Excellence in Social Work, 30*(1): 63-77

Graham J. R., & Al-Krenawi, A. (1996). A comparison study of traditional helpers in a late nineteenth century Canadian (Christian) society and a late twentieth century Bedouin (Muslim) society in the Negev, Israel. *Journal of Multicultural Social Work, 4*(2), 31-45.

Graham, J. R., Swift, K., & Delaney, R. (2003). *Canadian social policy: An introduction.* (2nd ed.). Toronto: Prentice Hall.

Gray, M. (2005). Dilemmas of international social work: Paradoxical processes in indigenisation, universalism, and imperialism. *International Journal of Social Welfare, 14*, 231-238.

Grotberg, E. H. (1990). Mental health aspects of the Zar for women in Sudan. *Women and Therapy, 10*(2), 15-24.

Gutheil, I. A. (1993). Rituals and termination procedures. *Smith College Studies in Social Work, 63*(2), 163-176.

Haj, S. (1992). Palestinian women and patriarchal relations. *Signs: Journal of Women in Culture and Society, 17*(4), 761-778.

Hall, T. D., & Nagel, J. (2000). Indigenous Peoples. In E.F. Borgetta and R.J.V. Montgomery (Eds.), *The encyclopedia of sociology, Vol. 2, revised edition* (pp. 1295-1301). New York: Macmillan.

Halifax, J. (1982). *Shaman, The wounded healer*. New York: Crossroad Publishing Company.

Hamilton, G. (1951). *Theory and practice of social work*. New York: Columbia University Press.

Hartman, A. (1978). Diagrammatic assessment of family relationships. *Social Casework, 59*(8), 465-476.

———. (1979). *Finding families: An ecological approach to a project craft publication*. Beverly Hills, California: Sage.

Har-Zion, N. (1988). The traditional music among the Bedouin: Its characteristics, constructions and function in Bedouin life. In Y. Aini and A. Aorean (Eds.), *The Bedouin* (pp. 398-404). Seda Boqer, Ben-Gurion University of the Negev (in Hebrew).

Hasson, Y.M & Swirski, S. (2006). *Invisible citizens: Israel government policy toward the Negev Bedouin*. Tel Aviv: Adva Center.

Hassouneh-Phillips, D. S. (2001). Polygamy and wife abuse: A qualitative study of Muslim women in America. *Health Care for Women International, 22*(8), 735-748.

Heilman, S. C., & Witztum, E. (1994). Patients, chaperons and healers: Enlarging the therapeutic encounter. *Social Science and Medicine, 39*(1), 133-143.

Herman, J. (1992). *Trauma and recovery: The aftermath of violence – from domestic abuse to political terror*. New York: BasicBooks.

Herzog, J. D. (1972). The anthropologist as broker in community education: A case study and some general propositions. *Council on Anthropology and Education Newsletter, 3*, 9-14.

Hiltermann, J. R. (1991). The women's movement during the uprising. *Journal of Palestine Studies, 20*(3), 48-57.

Hirayama, H., & Cestingok, M. (1988). Empowerment: A social work approach for Asian immigrants. *Social Casework, 69*(1), 41-47.

Ho, Y. F. (1998). Indigenous psychologies: Asian perspectives. *Journal of Cross-Cultural Psychology, 29*, 88-103.

Ho, Y. F., Ping, S., Lai, A. C., & Chan, S. F. (2001). Indigenization and beyond: Methodological relationism in the study of personality across cultural traditions. *Journal of Personality, 69*(6), 925-953.

Hoch-Smith, J., & Spring, A. (1978). Introduction. In J. Hoch-Smith and A. Spring (Eds.), *Women in ritual and symbolic roles* (1-23). New York: Plenum Press.

Hogan, P. T., & Siu S. F. (1988). Minority children and the child welfare system: An historical perspective. *Social Work, 33*, 493-98.

Holmes-Eber, P. (1997). Migration, urbanization, and women's kin. *Journal of Comparative Family Studies, 28*(2), 54-73.

Hwang, K. K. (2005). A philosophical reflection on the epistemology and methodology of indigenous psychologies. *Asian Journal of Social Psychology, 8*(1), 5-17.

Ibn-Taymeh, A. (1957). *The task of the Jinn*. Egypt: Matbaat Al-Sunna Al-Muhammadeh (in Arabic).

Ibrahim, F. A. (1985). Effective cross-cultural counseling and psychotherapy: A framework. *Counseling Psychologist, 13*(4), 625-638.

Inhorn, M. (1994). Kabsa and threatened fertility in Egypt. *Social Science and Medicine, 39*(4), 487-505.

Irani, G. E. (1999). Islamic mediation techniques for Middle East conflicts. *Middle East Review of International Affairs, 3*(2), 1-18.

Irving, H., & Benjamin, M. (1987). *Family mediation: Theory and practice of dispute resolution.* Toronto, Carswell.

Ismael, T.Y. (2001). *Middle East Politics today: Government and civil society.* Talahasee: University Press of Florida.

Ismael, T.Y, & Ismael, J.S. (2004). *The Iraqi predicament: People in the quagmire of power politics.* London: Pluto Press.

Jabbur, J. S. (1995). *The Bedouins and the desert: Aspects of nomadic Life in the Arab East.* New York: State University of New York Press.

Jackson, P. R. (2005). Indigenous theorizing in a complex world. *Asian Journal of Social Psychology, 8*(1), 51-64.

Jakubowska, L. (1992). Resisting 'ethnicity': The Israeli state and Bedouin identity. In C. Nordstrom and J.A. Martin (Eds.), *The paths to domination, resistance, and terror* (pp. 85-105). Berkeley: University of California Press.

Jamal, M. (1974). *Basic principles of Islamic society.* Cairo: Iheah Al-Torath Al-Islami (in Arabic).

Joseph, S. (1996). Patriarchy and development in the Arab world. *Gender and Development, 4*(2), 14-19.

Joseph, M. V. (1988). Religion and social work practice. *Social Casework, 69,* 443-452.

Kadiyoti, D. (1988). Bargaining with patriarchy. *Gender and Society, 2*(3), 274-290.

Kashima, Y. (2005) Is culture a problem for social psychology? *Asian Journal of Social Psychology, 8*(1), 19-38.

Katz, E. (1998). *Leisure culture in Israel.* Jerusalem: Guttman Institute.

Katz, L. F., & Gottman, J. M. (1993). Patterns of marital conflict predict children's internalizing and externalizing behaviors. *Developmental Psychology, 29*(6), 940-950.

Kay, S. (1978) *The Bedouin.* New York: Crane Rvssak.

Kazaz, N. (1989). *The practice of the Bisha ritual Among the Bedouin of the Negev.* Beer-Sheva: Ben Gurion University of the Negev (in Hebrew).

Kelley, P., & Kelley, V. (1985). Supporting natural helpers: A cross-cultural study. *Social Casework, 66,* 358-66.

Kennedy, J. G. (1967). Nubian Zar ceremonies as psychotherapy. *Human Organization, 26*(4), 185-194.

Khadduri, M. (1997). Sulh. In C.E. Boswroth, E. van Donzel, W.P. Heinrichs, & G. Lecomte (Eds.), *The encyclopedia of Islam, Vol. 9* (pp. 845-846). Leiden, Holland: Brill.

Kiev, A. (1964). Magic, faith, and healing. *Studies in primitive psychiatry today.* New York: Free Press.

Kiecolt-Glaser, J. K., Fisher, L. D., Ogrocki, P., & Stout, J. C. (1987). Marital quality, marital disruption, and immune function. *Psychosomatic Medicine, 49*(1), 13-34.

Kilbride, P. (1994). *Plural marriage for our times: A reinvented option?* Eastport, CT: Bergin & Garvey.

Kilgus, M. D., Pumariega, A. J. & Cuff, S. P. (1995). Race and diagnosis in adolescent psychiatric inpatients. *Journal of the American Academy of Child and Adolescent Psychiatry, 34*(1), 67-72.

Kim, Y. O. (1995). Culture, pluralism, and Asian-Americans: Culturally-sensitive social work practice. *International Social Work, 38*(1), 69-78.

Kirman, W. J. (1989). Revenge and accommodation in the family. *Modern Psychoanalysis, 14*(1), 89-95.

Kirmayer, L. (1986). Somatization and the social construction of illness experience. In T.M. Vallis and S. McHugh (Eds.), *Illness behavior: A multidisciplinary model* (pp.111-133). New York: Plenum Press.

Kissman, K. (1990). The role of fortune telling as a supportive function among Icelandic women. *International Social Work, 33*, 137-144.

———. (1986). *Social origins of distress and disease.* New Haven: Yale University Press.

———. (1982). Neurasthenia and depression: A study of somatization and culture in China. *Culture, Medicine and Psychiatry, 6,* 170-190.

Kleinman, A. & Kleinman, J. (1994). How bodies remember: Social memory and bodily experience of criticism, resistance, and delegitimation following China's cultural revolution. *New Literary History, 25*(3), 707-723.

Kline, N., S. (1963). Psychiatry in Kuwait. *British Journal of Psychiatry, 109,* 766-774.

Kobak, R. G., & Waters, D. B. (1984). Family therapy as a rite of passage: Play's the thing. *Family Process, 23*(1), 89-100.

Kondas, O. (1967). The treatment of stammering in children by the shadowing method. *Behavior Research and Therapy, 5,* 325-329.

Koran. Suruh Al-Isra, v. 22-23.

———. Surah Al-Hijr, v. 28-40.

———. Surah 49, v. 19.

———. Surah 4, v. 3.

Korbin, J. E. (Ed.) (1981). *Child abuse and neglect: Cross-cultural perspectives.* Berkeley: University of California Press.

———. (1980). The cultural context of child abuse and neglect. *Child Abuse and Neglect, 4,* 3-13.

Korr, W. S. (1986). Exploring differences among women in social work. *Social Service Review, 60,* 555-567.

Krajewski-Jaime, E. R. (1991). Folk healing among Mexican-American families as a consideration in the delivery of child welfare and child health care services. *Child Welfare, 70,* 157-167.

Krippendorff, K. (1980). *Content analysis: An introduction to its methodology.* Beverly Hills: Sage Publications.

Krishnakumar, A., & Buehler, C. (2000). Interparental conflict and parenting behaviors: A meta-analytic review. *Family Relations: Interdisciplinary Journal of Applied Family Studies, 49*(1), 5-44.

Kruk, E. (Ed.) (1997). *Mediation and conflict resolution in social work and the human services.* Chicago: Nelson-Hall Inc.

Kunitz, S. J. (2000). Globalization, states, and the health of indigenous peoples. *American Journal of Public Health, 90*(10), 1531-1539.

Kuokkanen, R. (2007). *Reshaping the university: Reseponsibility, indigenous episemes, and the logic of the gift.* Vancouver: University of British Columbia Press.

Kurtz, L. (1995). The relationship between parental coping strategies and children's adaptive processes in divorced and intact families. *Journal of Divorce and Remarriage, 24*(3/4), 89-110.

Lambo, T. A. (1978). Psychotherapy in Africa. *Human Nature, 1,* 32-40.

Landsman, M. (1988). Cultural techniques in psychotherapy: A case in point. *American Psychologist, 43,* 597-598.

Lavee, Y. (1987) Partner understanding and marital happiness: Reestimation of Honeycutt's model. *Journal of Marriage & the Family, 49*(4), 939-944.

Lederach, N. K., & Lederach, J. P. (1987). Religion and psychiatry: Cognitive dissonance in nursing students. *Journal of Psychosocial Nursing and Mental Health Services, 25*(3), 32-36.

LeResche, D. (1992). Comparison of the American mediation process with a Korean-American harmony restoration process. *Mediation Quarterly, 9*(4), 323-339.

Leung, A. K. D., & Robson, W. L. M. (1991). Sibling rivalry. *Clinical Pediatrics, 30*(5), 314-317.

Lewando-Hundt, G. (1984). The experience of power by Bedouin women in the Negev. In E. Marks and A. Shmueli (Eds.), *The changing Bedouin* (83-124) New Brunswick, NJ: Transation.

Lewis, J. & Dowsey-Magog, P. (1993). The Maleny 'fire event': Rehearsals toward neo-liminality. *The Australian Journal of Anthropology, 4*(3), 198-219.

Lieberman, A. F. (1990). Culturally sensitive intervention with children and families. *Child and Adolescent Social Work Journal, 7*(2), 101-120.

Lincoln, B. (1989). *Discourse and the construction of society*. New York: Oxford University Press.

Lipton A., & Simon, F. (1985). Psychiatric diagnosis in a state hospital, Manhattan State revised. *Hospital and Community Psychiatry, 36*, 368-373.

Low, B. S. (1988). Measures of polygyny in humans. *Current Anthropology, 29*(1), 189-194.

Lum, D. (1995). Cultural values and minority people of color. *Journal of Sociology and Social Welfare, 22*, 59-74.

———. (1992). *Social work practice and people of color*. Monterey, CA: Brooks/Cole Publishing Company.

———. (1982). Toward a framework for social work practice with minorities. *Social Work, 27*(3), 244-249.

Macmillan Dictionary of Anthropology (1986). London: Macmillan.

Mahjoob, M. A. (1973). *Social control in Bedouin societies: A study in political anthropology*, Alexandria: Public Egyptian Institution for Books.

———. (1977). *Anthropology of Bedouin societies*, Alexandria: Public Egyptian Institution for Books.

Makhlouf-Obermeyer, C. (1979). *Changing veils: A study of women in South Arabia*. Austin: University of Texas Press.

Marica, J. E., Rubin, B. M., & Efran, J. S. (1969). Systematic desensitization: Expectancy change or counterconditioning? *Journal of Abnormal Psychology, 74*, 382-387.

Marks, E. (1974). *The Bedouin society of the Negev*. Tel-Aviv: Reshafim Press. (in Hebrew)

Marks, E., & Shmueli, A. (1984). *The changing Bedouin*. London: Transaction Books.

Martin, R. (2000) Institutional approaches in economic geography. In E. Sheppard and T. J. Barnes (Eds.), *A companion to economic geography* (pp. 77-94). Blackwell: Oxford.

Martin, M. J., & Walters, J. (1982). Familial correlates of selected types of child abuse and neglect. *Journal of Marriage and Family, 44*, 267-276.

Mass, M., & Al-Krenawi, A. (1994). When a man encounters a woman, Satan is also present: Clinical relationships in Bedouin society. *American Journal of Orthopsychiatry, 64*(3), 357-367.

McNaughton, C. & Rock, D. (2002). *Opportunities in Aboriginal research: Results of SSHRC's dialogue on research and Aboriginal peoples*. Ottawa, ON: Social Sciences and Humanities Research Council of Canada.

Meketon, M. J. (1982). The integration of scientific and traditional healing in the Indian Health Service. *American Psychologist, 37*(6), 714-715.

Merry, S. E. (1989). Mediation in nonindustrial societies. In K. Kressel and D. Pruitt (Eds.), *Mediation research* (pp. 68-90). London: Jossey-Bass.

Meyer, V., & Mair, J. M. M. (1963). A new technique to control stammering: A preliminary report. *Behavior Research Therapy, 1*, 251-254.

Midgley, G. (2000). *Systemic intervention: Philosophy, methodology and practice.* New York: Kluwer Academic/Plenum.

Midgley, J. (2001). Globalization, capitalism and social welfare: A social development perspective. *Canadian Journal of Social Work* (Special Issue on Social Work and Globalization), *2*(1), 13-28.

———. (1981). *Professional imperialism: Social work in the Third World.* London: Heinemann.

Miller, I. W., Epstein, N. B., Bishop, D. S., & Keitner, G. I. (1985). The McMaster family assessment device: Reliability and validity. *Journal of Marital and Family Therapy, 11*, 345-356.

Mills, C. W. (1963). *Power, politics, and people.* New York: Balantine.

Ministry of Education and Culture (2004). *Matriculation examination data for 2003.* Jerusalem, Israel: Ministry of Education and Culture,

Morrissette, V., McKenzie, B., & Morrissette, L. (1993). Towards an Aboriginal model of social work practice: Cultural knowledge and traditional practices. *Canadian Social Work, 10*(1), 91-108.

Morsy, S. A. (1993). *Gender, sickness, and healing in rural Egypt: Ethnography in historical context.* San Francisco: Westview Press.

Moussalli, A. S. (1997). *An Islamic model for political conflict resolution: Tahkim (arbitration).* In P. Salem (Ed.), *Conflict resolution in the Arab world: Selected essays* (pp. 44-71). Beirut: American University of Beirut Press.

Mulder, M. B. (1992). Women's strategies in polygynous marriage: Kipsigis, Datoga, and other East African cases. *Human Nature, 3*(1), 45-70.

Mullaly, B. (2002). *Challenging oppression: A critical social work approach.* Don Mills, Ont.: Oxford University Press.

Murphy, H. B. M. (1973). Current trends in transcultural psychiatry. *Proceedings of the Royal Society of Medicine, 66*: 711-716.

Nagel, J. (1996). *American Indian ethnic renewal: Red power and the resurgence of identity and culture.* New York: Oxford University Press.

Nagpaul, H. (1993). Analysis of social work teaching material in India: The need for indigenous foundations. *International Social Work, 36*(3), 207-220.

———. (1996a). *Modernization and urbanization in India: Problems and issues.* Jaipur & New Delhi: Rawat.

———. (1996b). *Social work in urban India.* Jaipur & New Delhi: Rawat.

Najati, M. U. (1993). *Al-dirasat al-nafsaniyyah 'inda al-'ulama' al-Muslimin.* Beirut: Dar al-Shuruq.

Najib, A. (1982). *The Islamic medicine and its cure.* Cairo: Wahab Press (in Arabic).

Navdi, S. H. H. (1983). *Medical philosophy in Islam and the contribution of Muslims in the advancement of Medical Science, Academia.* Durham: University of Durham.

Nelson, C. (Ed.) (1974). *The desert and sown, nomads in the wider society.* Berkeley: University of California Press.

———. (1997). Public and private politics: Women in the Middle Eastern world. In C. B Brettell, and C. F. Sargent (Eds.), *Gender in cross-cultural perspective* (pp. 111-128). New York: Allyn Bacon.

Neuendorf, K. A. (2001). *The content analysis guidebook.* Thousand Oaks, CA: Sage.

Neutze, M. (2000). Housing for indigenous Australians. *Housing Studies, 15*(4), 485–504.

Norell, D., & Walz, T. (1994). Reflections from the field: Toward a theory and practice of reconciliation in ethnic conflict resolution. *Social Development Issues, 16*(2), 99-111.

Obenchain, J., & Silver, S. (1992). Symbolic recognition: Ceremony in a treatment of post-traumatic stress disorder. *Journal of Traumatic Stress, 5*(1), 37-43.

O'Dea, T. (1966). *The sociology of religion.* Englewood Cliffs, NJ: Prentice Hall.

Okasha, A. (1966). A cultural psychiatric study of El-Zar in UAR. *British Journal of Psychiatry, 112*, 1217.

Okasha, A., & Lotailf, F. (1979). Attempted suicide: An Egyptian investigation. *Acta Psychiatrica Scandinavica, 60*(1), 69-75.

Osei, H. K. (1996). The indigenisation of social work practice and education in Africa: The dilemma of theory and method. *Maatskaplike-Werk / Social-Work, 32*(3), 215-225.

Osmond, M. W. (1988). Theorizing on the interrelationship of race, class, and gender. *American Sociological Association Papers.*

Owuamanam, D. O. (1984). Adolescents' perception of the polygamous family and its relationship to self-concept. *International Journal of Psychology, 19*(6), 593-598.

Oyefeso, A. O., & Adegoke, A. R. (1981). Psychological adjustment of Yoruba adolescents as influenced by family type: A research note. *Child Psychology and Psychiatry, 33*(4), 785-788.

Paine, R. (1971). *Patrons and brokers in the East Arctic*. Toronto: University of Toronto Press.

Palazzoli, M.S.L., Boscolo, G., Cecchin, G., & Parata, G. (1978). *Paradox and counterparadox: A new model in the therapy of the family in Schizophrenic transaction*. New York: Jason Aronson.

Park, K. S. (1999). Internationalization: Direction of social welfare policy education in the future. *Arete, 23*(2), 33-45.

Payton, J. W., & Tedesco, J. (1982). Mediation solves neighbourhood disputes. *Practice Digest, 4*(4), 18-22.

Peristiany, J. G. (Ed.). (1974). *Honor and shame: The values of Mediterranean society*. Chicago: University of Chicago Press.

Perlman, H. H. (1979). *Relationship: The heart of helping people*. Chicago: University of Chicago Press.

Pederson, F., Anderson, B., & Cain, R. (1977). *An approach to understanding linkages between parent-infant and spouse relationships*. Paper presented at the biennial meeting of the Society for Research in Child Development, New Orleans, LA.

Pilgrim, R. (1978). Ritual. In T. William Hall (Ed.), *Introduction to the study of religion* (pp. 64-84). New York: Harper and Row.

Pincus, A., & Minahan, A. (1973). *Social work practice: Model and method*. Itasca, Illinois: Peacock.

Pliskin, K. (1987). *Silent boundaries: Cultural constraints on sickness and diagnosis of Iranians of Israel*. New Haven: Yale University Press.

Pool, J. E. (1972). A cross-comparative study of aspects of conjugal behaviour among women of three West African countries. *Canadian Journal of African Studies, 6*(2), 233-259.

Popper, M. (1993). *Trends in psychiatric hospitalization*. Jerusalem: Department of Information and Assessment, Mental Health Services, Ministry of Health (in Hebrew).

Popper M., & Horwitz R. (1996). *First admission to mental health hospitals in Israel*. Jerusalem: Department of Information and Assessment, Mental Health Services, Ministry of Health (in Hebrew).

Potocky-Tripodi, M. (2002). *Best practices for social work with refugees and immigrants*. New York: Columbia University Press.

Pottinger, A., Perivolaris, A., & Howes, D. (2007). The End of Life. In R. Srivastava (Eds.), *The healthcare professional's guide to clinical cultural competence* (pp. 227-246). Toronto: Mosby Elsevier

Prince, R. (1976). Psychotherapy as the manipulation of indigenous healing mechanisms: A transcultural survey. *Transcultural Psychiatric Research Review, 13*, 115-133.

Pringle, R. (1997). Feminist theory and the world of the social. *Current Sociology*, *45*(2), 75-89.

Qutib, S. (1967). *In the shadow of the Koran*. Lebanon: Daar Iheah Al-Torath Al-Arabi (in Arabic).

Rabinowitz, D., Abu Baker, K. (2002). *The stand tall generation: The Palestinian citizens of Israel today*. Jerusalem: Keter. (in Hebrew).

Racker, H. (1968). *Transference and countertransference*. New York: International Universities Press.

Racy, J. (1985). Commentary on "psychotherapy of Arab-Israeli patients." *Journal of Psychoanalytic Anthropology*, *8*(4), 231-233.

———. (1980). Somatization in Saudi women: A therapeutic challenge. *British Journal of Psychiatry*, *137*, 212-216.

Ragab, I. A. (1990). How social work can take root in developing countries. *Social Development Issues*, *12*(3), 38-51.

Rahat City Annual Report 1998 (in Arabic).

Rahat City Annual Report 1997 (in Arabic).

Rando, T. (1985). Creating therapeutic rituals in the psychotherapy of the bereaved. *Psychotherapy*, *22*(2), 236-240.

Rao, A. (1996). Home-word bound: Women's place in the family of international human rights. *Global Governance*, *2*(2), 241-260.

Rappaport, H. (1972). Modification of avoidance behaviour: Expectancy, autonomic reactivity, and verbal report. *Journal of Consulting and Clinical Psychology*, *39*, 404-414.

Rappaport H., & Rappaport, M. (1981). The integration of scientific and traditional healing: A proposed model. *American Psychologist*, *36*(7), 774-781.

Rappaport, J., & Simkins, R. (1991). Healing and empowering through community narrative. *Prevention in Human Services*, *10*(1), 29-50.

Regional Council for the Unrecognized Villages in the Negev. (2008). *Villages Map* [map]. Scale undetermined. "Regional Council for the Unrecognized Villages in the Negev". Retrieved July 31, 2008, from http://www.rcuv.net

Reisher, A. D., & Lawson, P. (1992). Psychotherapy, sin, and mental health. *Pastoral and Psychology*, *40*(5), 303-311.

Rieder, J. (1984). The social organization of vengeance. In B. Donald (Ed.), *Toward a general theory of social control: Fundamentals, volume one* (pp. 131-162). Toronto: Academic Press.

Rivett, M., & Street, E. (1993). Informal polygamy: A suitable case for treatment? *Journal of Family Therapy*, *15*(1), 71-79.

Rizvi, S. (1989). *Muslim tradition in psychotherapy and modern trends*. Lahor: Institute of Islamic Culture.

Robertson, P. J., Futterman-Collier, A., Sellman, J. D., Adamson, S. J., Todd, F. C., Deering, D. E., and Huriwai, T. (2001). Clinician beliefs and practices related to increasing responsivity to the needs of Maori with alcohol and drug problems. *Substance Use and Misuse, 36*(8), 1015-1032.

Robin, R. W., Rasmussen, J. K., & Gonzalez-Santin, E. (1999). Impact of childhood out-of-home placement on a southwestern American Indian tribe. *Journal of Human Behavior in the Social Environment, 2*(1), 69-89.

Rockwell, S. (1985). Palestinian women workers in the Israeli occupied Gaza strip. *Journal of Palestine Studies, 14*(2), 115-136.

Rogler, L. H., & Cortes, D. E. (1993). Help-seeking pathways: A unifying concept in mental health care. *American Journal of Psychiatry, 150*(4), 554-561.

Rothenberger, J. E. (1978). The social dynamics of dispute settlement in a Sunni Muslim village in Lebanon. In L. Nader & H. F.Todd (Eds.), *The disputing process—Law in ten societies* (pp. 152-180). New York: Columbia University Press.

Rubin, J. (1997). Introduction. In P. Salem (Ed.), *Conflict resolution in the Arab world: Selected essays* (pp. 3-9). Beirut: American University of Beirut Press.

Ruiz, P., & Griffith, E. H. (1977). Hex and possession: Two problematic areas in the psychiatrist's approach to religion. In E. Foulkes, R. Wintrob, J. Westrermeyer, and A. Favazza. (Eds.), *Current perspectives in cultural psychiatry* (pp. 93-102). New York: Spectrum.

Ruiz, P., & Langrod, J. (1976). The role of folk healers in community mental health services. *Community Mental Health Journal, 12*(4), 392-398.

Rutter, M. (1975). *Helping troubled children*. Oxford, England: Plenum.

Saber, M. A. D. (1989). *Some development issues in the Arab society*. Aman: Modern Bookstore.

Said, E. (1978). *Orientalism*. London: Routledge & Kegan Paul.

Salem, P. E. (1997). A critique of Western conflict resolution from a non-Western perspective. In Salem, P. E. (Ed.), *Conflict resolution in the Arab world: Selected essays* (pp. 11-24). Beirut: American University of Beirut Press.

Salim, M. A. (1986). *The treatment according to the Koran*. Cairo: Alkoran Press (in Arabic).

Sandgrund, A., & Gaines, R. W. (1974). Child abuse and mental retardation. *Journal of Mental Deficiency, 79*, 327-330.

Sandler, J., Dare, C., & Holder, A. (1979). *The Patient and the analyst*. London: Maresfield.

Sanua, V. D. (1979). Psychological intervention in the Arab world: A review of folk treatment. *Transcultural Psychiatric Research Review 1*, 205-208.

Sarwer-Foner, G. J. (1993). The relationship between psychotherapy and pharmacotherapy: An introduction. *American Journal of Psychotherapy, 47*(3), 387-392.

Saunders, E., Nelson, K., & Landsman, M. (1993). Racial inequality and child neglect: Findings in a metropolitan area. *Child Welfare, 72*, 341-354.

Savaya, R. (1995). Attitudes towards family and marital counseling among Israeli Arab Women. *Journal of Social Service Research, 21*(1), 35-51.

———. (1998). The under-use of psychological services by Israeli Arabs: An examination of the roles of negative attitudes and the use of alternative sources of help. *International Social Work, 41*(2), 195-209.

Savaya, R., & Malkinson, R. (1997). When clients stay away. *Social Service Review, 71*(2), 214-230.

Scheff, T. (1977). *Catharsis in healing, ritual and drama.* Berkeley: University of California Press.

Schellenberg, J. A. (1996). *Conflict resolution: Theory, research and practice.* New York: State University of New York Press.

Schiele, J. H. (1996). Afrocentricity: An emerging paradigm in social work. *Social Work, 41*(3), 284-294.

———. (1997). The contour and meaning of Afrocentric social work. *Journal of Black Studies, 27*(6), 800-819.

Schimmel A. (1975). *Mystical dimensions of Islam.* Chapel Hill: University of North Carolina Press.

Schindler, R. (1993). Emigration and the black Jews of Ethiopia: dealing with bereavement and loss. *International Social Work, 36*(1), 7-19.

Schwartz, D. (1985). Caribbean folk beliefs and Western psychiatry. *Journal of Psychosocial Nursing and Mental Health Services, 23*(11), 26-30.

Shalhoub-Kevorkian, N. (1997). Wife abuse: A method of social control. *Israel Social Science Research, 12*(1), 59-72.

Shamir, R. (1996). Suspended in space: Bedouins under the law of Israel. *Law and Society Review, 30*(2), 231-257.

Sharabi, H. (1975). *Introduction to the study of Arab society.* Jerusalem: Salah Eldin Publisher.

Sharafeldin, E. A. (1983). *A study of contemporary Sudanese Muslims Saints' legends in sociocultural context.* Unpublished doctoral dissertation, Indiana University, Indiana.

Sharp, L. A. (1994). Exorcists, psychiatrists, and the problems of possession in Northwest Madagascar. *Social Science and Medicine, 38*(4), 525-542.

Shemer, A., & Bar-Gay, E. (2001). Cultural mediating among the community. *Mifgash: Journal for Social-Educational Work, 14*, 161-175. (In Hebrew).

Sherif, Y. A. (1972). *The history of the Arab medicine.* Cairo: Matbaat Sjeed Al-Arab (in Arabic).

Shilon, A. (1981). *Faith healing: The religious experience as a therapeutic process.* Chicago, IL: Charles C. Thomas Publisher.

Shulman, L. (1984). *The skills of helping individuals and groups, 2nd ed.* Itasca, IL: Peacock.

Shuval, J. T. (1985). Social functions of medical licensing: A case study of Soviet immigrant physicians in Israel. *Social Science and Medicine, 20*(9), 901-909.

———. (1990). Health in Israel: Patterns of equality and inequality. *Social Science and Medicine, 31*, 291-303.

Siegel, L. (1994). Cultural differences and their impact on practice in child welfare. *Journal of Multicultural Social Work, 3*, 87-96.

Singh, N. N., McKay, J. D., & Singh, A. N. (1999). The need for cultural brokers in mental health services. *Journal of Child and Family Studies, 8*(1), 1-10.

———. (1998). Culture and mental health: Nonverbal communication. *Journal of Child and Family Studies, 7*, 403-409.

Siporin, M. (1985). Current social work perspectives on clinical practice. *Clinical Social Work Journal, 13*, 198-217.

Slattery, G. (1987). Transcultural therapy with aboriginal families: Working with the belief system. *Australian and New Zealand Journal of Family Therapy, 8*(2), 61-71.

Southwick S. T., & Yehoda, R. (1993). The interaction between and pharmacotherapy and psychotherapy in the treatment of posttraumatic stress disorder. *American Journal of Psychotherapy, 47*(3), 404-410.

Speck, R. V., & Attneave, C. L. (1973). *Family networks.* London: Pantheon Books.

Statistical Yearbook of the Negev Bedouin (2004). Beer-Sheva: The Center for Bedouin Studies and Development, Ben-Gurion University of the Negev.

Sterba, R. (1948). *Transference in casework.* New York: Family Service Association of America.

Stuckless, N., & Goranson, R. (1994). A selected bibliography of literature on revenge. *Psychological Reports, 75*, 803-811.

Sue, D. W. (1990). *Counselling the culturally different: Theory and practice.* New York: John Wiley and Sons.

Sue, S., & Zane, N. (1987). The role of culture and cultural techniques in psychotherapy: A critique and reformulation. *American Psychologist, 42*, 34-45.

Swigonski, M. (1996). Challenging privilege through Afrocentric social work practice. *Social Work, 41*(2), 153-161.

Tabarah, A. A. (1977). *The spirit of the Islamic religion*. Lebanon: Daar Al-aalam Llmalaeen (in Arabic).

Torrey, E. F. (1972). What Western psychotherapists can learn from witchdoctors. *American Journal of Orthopsychiatry, 42*(1), 69-76.

———. (1986). *Witchdoctors and psychiatrists*. Northvale, NJ: Jason Aronson.

Trimingham, J. S. (1949). *Islam in the Sudan*. London: Oxford University Press.

Trocme, N. (1996). Development and preliminary evaluation of the Ontario Child Neglect Index. *Child Maltreatment, 1*, 145-155.

Turner, V. (1969). *The ritual process*. Ithaca: Cornell University Press.

———. (1967). *The forest of symbols*. Ithaca: Cornell University Press.

Umoren, U. E. (1990). Religion and traditional medicine: An anthropological case study of a Nigerian treatment of mental illness. *Medical Anthropology, 12*(4), 289-400.

Valsiner, J. (1989). Organization of children's social development in polygamic families. In J. Valsiner (Ed.), *Child development in cultural context* (pp. 67-86). Toronto: Hogrefe and Huber Publishers.

Van der Hart, O., Witztum, E., & de-Voogt, A. (1988). Myth and rituals: Anthropological views and their application in strategic family therapy. *Journal of Psychotherapy and the Family, 4*(3/4), 57-79.

Van Gennep, A. (1960). *The rites of passage*. Chicago: University of Chicago Press.

Versper, J. (1991). The use of healing ceremonies in the treatment of multiple personality disorder. *Dissociation Progress in the Dissociative Disorders, 4*(2), 109-114.

von Bertalanffy, L. (1971). *General system theory: Foundations, development, application*. London: Allen Lane.

Waldman, J. B. (1990). Access to traditional medicine in a Western Canadian city. *Medical Anthropology, 12*(3), 325-348.

Waltman, G. H. (1986). Main street revisited: Social work practice in rural areas. *Social Casework, 67*(8), 466-474.

Walton, R. G., & Abo-El-Nasr, M. M. (1988). Indigenization and authentization in terms of social work in Egypt. *International Social Work, 31*(2), 135-144.

Ward, C. (1984). Thaipusam in Malaysia: A psycho-anthropological analysis of ritual trance, ceremonial possession and self-mortification practices. *Ethos, 12(4)*, 307-334.

Ware, H. (1979). Polygyny: Women's views in a transitional society, Nigeria, 1975. *Journal of Marriage and the Family, 41*(1), 185-195.

Waters, M. (2001). *Globalization*. (2nd ed.). London: Routledge.

Waxler, N. E. (1977). Is mental illness cured in traditional societies? A theoretical analysis. *Culture, Medicine and Psychiatry, 1*(3), 233-253.

Weaver, H. (2001). Indigenous identity: What is it, and who really has it? *American Indian Quarterly, 25*(2): 240-255.

Weber, R. P. (1990). *Basic content analysis* (2nd ed.). Newbury Park, CA: Sage Publications.

Weidman, H. H. (1982). Research strategies, structural alterations and clinically applied anthropology. In N. Chrisman and T. Maretzki (Eds.), *Clinically applied anthropology: Anthropologists in health science settings* (pp. 201-241). Boston: D. Reidel Publishers.

———. (1975). Concepts as strategies for change. *Psychiatric Annals, 5*, 312-314.

Wessels, W. H. (1985). The traditional healer and psychiatry. *Australian and New Zealand Journal of Psychiatry, 19*(3), 283-286.

West, J. (1987). Psychotherapy in the Eastern province of Saudi Arabia. *Psychotherapy, 24*(1), 105-107.

Westermeyer, J. (1993). Cross-cultural psychiatric assessment. In G. Gaw (Ed.), *Culture, Ethnicity and Mental Illness* (pp. 125-144). Washington: American Psychiatric Press.

Whitaker, L.C. (1985). Visiting the parental grave in psychotherapy. *Psychotherapy, 22*(2), 241-247.

White, D. R. (1988a). Causes of polygyny: Ecology, economy, kinship, and warfare. *American Anthropologist, 90*(4), 871-887.

———. (1988b). Rethinking polygyny: Co-wives, codes and cultural systems. *Current Anthropology, 29*(4), 529-572.

Wiehe, V. R. (1984). Self-esteem, attitude towards parents, and locus of control in children of divorced and non-divorced families. *Journal of Social Service Research, 8*(1), 17-28.

Wikan, U. (1988). Bereavement and loss in two Muslim communities: Egypt and Bali compared. *Social Science and Medicine, 27*, 451-460.

Wilkerson, R. B. (1987). The influence of religion on the subjective well-being of the widowed. In H. Z. Lopata (Ed.), *Widows, vol. 2: North America* (pp. 95-108). Durham, NC: Duke University Press.

Williams, D. R., Yu, Y., Jackson, J. S., & Anderson, N. B. (1997). Racial differences in physical and mental health: Socio-economic status, stress and discrimination. *Journal of Health Psychology, 2*(3), 335-351.

Wilmer, F. (1993). *Indigenous voice in world politics*. Sage Publications: London.

Winick, C. (1956). *Dictionary of anthropology*. New York: Philosophical Library.

Winslow, S. (1990). The use of ritual in incest healing. *Smith College Studies in Social Work, 61*(1), 27-41.

Witty, C. J. (1980). *Mediation and society. Conflict management in Lebanon*, New York, Academic Press.

———. (1978). Disputing issues in Shechaam, A multireligious village in Lebanon. In L. Nader and H.F. Todd (Eds.), *The disputing process—Law in ten societies* (pp. 281-315). New York: Columbia University Press.

Witztum, E., Buchbinder, J. T., & Van der Hart, O. (1990). Summoning a punishing angel: Treatment of a depressed patient with dissociative features. *Bulletin of the Menninger Clinic, 54*(4), 524-537.

Wyrostok, N. (1995). The ritual as a psychotherapeutic intervention. *Psychotherapy 32*(3), 397-404.

Yeoman, S. (1998). Occupation and disability: A role for occupational therapists in developing countries. *British Journal of Occupational Therapy, 61*(11), 523-527.

Yiftachel, O. (2004). *The making of an urban ethnocracy: Jews and Arabs in the Beer-Sheva Region, Israel.* Revised version of a paper co-written with Haim Yacobi, presented at the conference "Urban informality in the age of liberalization," Berkeley, April 2003.

———. (2003). Bedouin Arabs and the Israeli settler state: Land policies and indigenous resistance. In D. Champagne and A. Saad (Eds.), *The future of indigenous peoples: Strategies for survival and development* (pp. 21-47). Los Angeles: UCLA American Indian Studies Center.

Yngvesson, B. (1984). What is a dispute about? The political interpretation of social control. In D. Black (Ed.), *Toward a general theory of social control, Volume 2* (pp. 235-260). New York: Academic Press.

Young, A. (1976). Internalizing and externalizing medical belief systems: An Ethiopian example, *Social Science and Medicine 10,* 147-156.

Zola, I. K. (1973). Pathways to the doctor: From person to patient. *Social Science and Medicine, 7*(7), 677-689.

INDEX

Arad – 28, 29
Arara – 29-30
Asabiyya (Tribal Cohesion) – 23
Bedouin – 2-4, 8-9, 21-27, 29-43, 45-48, 50, 53-73, 75-76, 80-81, 88-90, 92-99, 101-107, 109-110, 112-116, 120-121, 123-125, 130-134, 136-140, 143, 145-151, 153-156, 158-160, 165, 167-173, 175
Beer-Sheva – 1-2, 26, 29-30, 33, 108, 175
Bisha Ritual – 116, 131-137
Blood Vengeance – 8, 18, 87, 99, 101-114, 124, 169
Boys – 24, 33-34, 38, 41, 61-62, 84, 87- 88, 90, 93, 109-110
Children – 8, 13, 23-24, 28, 30, 33-38, 41, 46, 55, 65-68, 70-71, 73, 75-77, 79, 81-91, 93-98, 101, 105-114, 123, 125-127, 129, 131, 137-138, 143, 160
Collective versus Individual Decision Making – 34, 38-39, 50, 52, 55, 117, 149, 152-153
Common Patterns and Perceptions of Mental Health Care Utilization – 40, 148-149, 151-154
Community Development – 15, 114

Coping Strategies – 69-71, 90-92, 96, 107, 109-110, 144, 147, 154
Courts – 41, 126
Co-wives – 75, 81, 96. 98
Cultural Broker – 16, 54, 113-114, 117-119, 137
Cultural Consultant – 112, 118-119, 137
Cultural Mediators (CMs) – 7, 36, 61-63, 97, 104-105, 114, 116, 119-124, 126-131, 134, 137-138, 169
Dervish – 46, 49-53, 62, 137, 146-148, 155
Dhikr (Invoking God's Name) – 140, 143, 146
Diagnosis/Analysis – 48, 52, 149-155, 159, 162-163, 168
Divorce – 34, 55, 61, 82, 84, 91, 96, 122-125, 127, 137-138, 152
Dreams – 65, 69-70, 156-157, 163
Economy – 22, 24-25, 28, 31-32
Egypt – 1, 22, 25, 103, 133-134, 146, 160
Family – 2, 7, 11-15, 23-24, 32-39, 45-47, 49, 52-53, 55, 61-62, 64, 67-68, 70, 72-80, 84-85, 87, 89-94, 96-98, 101-114, 116-117, 119-128, 130-131, 133,

135-138, 143-145, 151-153, 155-156, 158, 164, 166, 168
Gaza – 84, 87, 89, 160
Gender Differences – 32-33, 38, 45, 80, 93, 95, 110, 121, 123, 129-130, 152-159, 165
Ghura – 104, 113
Girls – 24, 35, 37-38, 47, 52, 61-62, 82, 84, 88, 93, 109-110
Globalization – 9, 11, 138, 170-172
Group Therapy – 67, 70-71, 96
Hamula (Extended Family) – 23-24, 37, 90, 121-123, 128, 137
Helping Relationship/Alliance –54, 56, 64-65, 71, 107-108, 111, 140, 171
Hura – 29
Indigenization – 5, 6, 10, 15
Integration of Traditional Healing with Modern Methods of Helping Professional Practice – 148-151
Intervention (Clinical/Direct/Social Work) – 7-8, 14, 18, 45, 49, 59, 65, 71, 73-74, 96-99, 101-102, 107-108, 111, 113, 115, 120-126, 128-131, 137-140, 145, 151, 159-160, 169, 171-172, 180
Islam – 2, 5, 22, 35, 51, 53, 73, 82, 84, 90, 98, 102, 120-121, 125, 130, 137, 140-148, 159-165, 170
Israel – 1-3, 18, 22, 25-29, 31-33, 39-41, 43, 46, 65-66, 77, 82-83, 89, 93, 103, 106, 119-125, 130, 134, 126, 138, 143, 148-150, 160, 166, 171
Jordan, Trans-Jordan – 1, 22, 26, 103, 133

Koran – 53, 98, 102, 137, 140-141, 143-146, 148, 157, 159-165
Koranic Healing/Healers – 137, 140-141, 146, 148, 157, 159-165, 178
Ksaifa – 29-30
Laqia – 29
Law – 25-28, 41, 75, 82, 102, 106, 120, 125, 137
Localization – 1-19, 138, 171-173
Marriage – 24, 33-37, 46-47, 52-53, 55-57, 59, 61-63, 66, 68-69, 73-79, 82-89, 89-91, 93, 95, 98, 104, 124-125, 127, 130, 152, 154, 160-162, 166
Mediation – 41, 61-62, 101-102, 106, 115, 119-130, 134-138, 169
Men – 29, 32-35, 37, 41-42, 45, 50, 53-58, 62-64, 66, 68, 74-75, 82-85, 87, 89-90, 95, 103, 105-107, 121-122, 125-127, 130, 133-134, 146-147, 149, 152-154, 158, 160-162
Mental Health – 13, 31, 39-40, 45-46, 49, 52, 55, 58, 64-65, 73, 76, 91, 105-106, 108, 115-119, 132, 136-137, 139, 143-146, 148-149, 151, 155, 164-165
Mosque – 160, 164
Mukhtar – 24
Muslim – 1-2, 17, 22, 36, 49, 53, 110, 120, 140-141, 143, 145, 147, 150, 160-161, 163-166
Nasab (Kinship Ties) – 23
Palestinian – 18, 89, 121, 127
Polygamy, Polygamous Families – 7-8, 18, 37, 72, 73-99, 124, 127, 154, 169

Index

Poverty – 13, 32, 67, 86, 89, 105-106, 108, 113, 130, 170
Prayer – 49-51, 109-110, 143-145, 147, 160, 164
Primary Care – 118
Psychosis – 79, 149
Rahamah (Memorial Ritual for the Dead) – 70, 140, 143, 145
Rahat – 2, 29-30, 33, 65, 67, 93-94, 120-123, 125, 131, 138
Religion – 2-3, 12, 18, 69, 89, 110, 128, 140-141, 145-148, 156, 160, 163
Remarriage – 70, 97, 152
Rituals – 14-15, 51, 69-70, 104, 115-117, 120, 127, 131-137, 140, 142-148, 156-157, 164, 167
Segev Shalom – 29, 83
Self (concept) – 11-12, 38-39, 56, 71, 93, 95-96, 106, 140, 144, 146, 159
Shariah – 82, 102
Sheikh – 24, 29, 41, 62, 104-105, 122, 125, 127, 135, 160
Sibling – 23, 38, 76, 91, 93-94, 97-98, 112
Social Work Education – 10, 16-17
Stages of Mental Illness Treated by a Koranic Healer – 159, 162-165
Tel-Sheva – 29-30
Therapeutic Relationship – 59-63

Therapy – 49, 53-54, 56, 58-60, 62-67, 70, 74, 96, 111, 136, 139, 142, 144, 152, 155-156, 165, 168, 172
Traditional Healing – 7-8, 18, 45-46, 51, 62, 122, 132, 136-138, 140, 142, 146-149, 151-157, 160, 162, 166-169
Transference – 54, 58-64, 66, 144
Tribal Elders – 16, 22, 24, 30, 34, 48, 62, 126
Tribe – 2, 21-24, 26, 28-29, 32-33, 35, 37, 47-48, 52-55, 61-62, 65, 68, 80-81, 83, 85, 87, 97, 101, 103-104, 106-107, 110, 121-122, 125-128, 132-136, 143-144, 153, 158
Unrecognized Villages – 2, 28-32, 39-40, 43, 79, 170
Wasit (Mediator) – 121-122
West Bank – 89, 160
Women – 8, 13, 29, 32-37, 39-40, 42, 45, 47, 52, 54-71, 73-76, 79-81, 83-86, 88-91, 93, 97-98, 107, 110, 122, 125-127, 129-130, 145, 147, 149, 152-158, 160-162
Zurah (Visiting Saints' tombs) – 140, 143-144

AUTHOR BIOS

Alean Al-Krenawi, PhD is Chair and Associate Professor, Spitzer Department of Social Work, Ben Gurion University of the Negev. Professor Al-Krenawi's research interests include multicultural mental-health and social work with indigenous populations. He conducts studies in Israel, Canada, Palestine and other Arab countries.

John R. Graham, PhD RSW is Murray Fraser Professor of Community Economic Development at the Faculty of Social Work, University of Calgary, Canada.

Together, Al-Krenawi and Graham have published over 40 journal articles and have worked together for 15 years.